Diverse Populations of Gifted Children

Meeting Their Needs in the Regular Classroom and Beyond

STARR CLINE

Adelphi University and Teacher/Coordinator Gifted Elementary Program, Herricks Public Schools, New Hyde Park, New York

DIANE SCHWARTZ

Hofstra University

Merrill
an imprint of Prentice Hall
Upper Saddle River, New Jersey   *Columbus, Ohio*

Library of Congress Cataloging-in-Publication Data

Cline, Starr.
  Diverse populations of gifted children : meeting their needs in the regular classroom and beyond/Starr Cline, Diane Schwartz.
      p. cm.
  Includes bibliographical references and index.
  ISBN 0-13-399908-4 (pbk.)
  1. Gifted children—Education—United States. 2. Handicapped children—Education—United States. 3. Minorities—Education—United States. 4. Special education—United States. I. Schwartz, Diane, 1944– .II. Title.
  LC3993.9.C55 1999
  371.95'0973—dc21

                                                                          98-37392
                                                                              CIP

Cover art: © The cover watercolor is by thirteen-year-old artist, David Dow, using his non-dominant left hand. At the age of ten, this gifted student suffered a massive stroke causing partial paralysis and aphasia. David's art is an inspiration, as he continues to focus on his abilities and giftedness, in spite of his new disabilities.

Editor: Ann Castel Davis
Production Editor: Sheryl Glicker Langner
Design Coordinator: Diane C. Lorenzo
Text Designer: STELLARViSIONs
Cover Designer: Ceri Fitzgerald
Production Manager: Laura Messerly
Electronic Text Management: Marilyn Wilson Phelps, Karen L. Bretz, Tracey B. Ward
Director of Marketing: Kevin Flanagan
Marketing Manager: Suzanne Stanton
Marketing Coordinator: Krista Groshong

This book was set in Baskerville by Prentice Hall and was printed and bound by R. R. Donnelley & Sons Co. The cover was printed by Phoenix Color Corp.

©1998 by Prentice-Hall, Inc.
A Pearson Education Company
Upper Saddle River, NJ 07458

Photo credits: pp. 2, 14, 52, 70, 96, 110, 136, 154 by Anthony Magnacca/Merrill; pp. 42, 168 by Scott Cunningham/Merrill; p. 124 courtesy of Carol Myers.

Printed in the United States of America

10 9 8 7 6 5 4 3 2 1

ISBN: 0-13-399908-4

Prentice-Hall International (UK) Limited,London
Prentice-Hall of Australia Pty. Limited, Sydney
Prentice-Hall Canada Inc., Toronto
Prentice-Hall Hispanoamericana, S.A., Mexico
Prentice-Hall of India Private Limited, New Delhi
Prentice-Hall of Japan, Inc., Tokyo
Pearson Education Asia Pte. Ltd., Singapore
Editora Prentice-Hall do Brasil, Ltda., Rio de Janeiro

To my husband and friend, Jerry,
whose encouragement and support have been unending.

Starr

To Mama Berr', my very first teacher,
and to GT, thank you for always being there.

Diane

Preface

Reports through the years have informed us of our failed attempts to meet the needs of gifted students. As we have claimed to recognize the needs of gifted students, we have historically vacillated in our quest for excellence between providing opportunities for the gifted and providing a "democratic education" for all students. However, even as we have attempted to recognize the needs of the gifted, a segment of the population has still been omitted. This underserved population suffers from neglect because of insufficient conditions and opportunities to nurture, stimulate, and guide the full potential of their individual abilities. This underserved segment of gifted children includes children with disabilities, ethnic/minorities, children with learning disabilities, preschoolers, exceptionally gifted children, gifted females, and underachievers.

We have not succeeded in establishing appropriate identification procedures for the gifted. Our inability to identify gifted individuals properly is compounded when it concerns identifying the gifted in special populations. Lack of appropriate identification has led to underrepresentation of special populations in programs for the gifted. We need to address ways in which gifted students might be identified in all domains of intelligence: verbal-linguistic, logical-mathematical, spatial, bodily kinesthetic, musical, interpersonal, and intrapersonal. There is a great need to find alternative authentic assessments to recognize gifted children with special needs. Settings need to be reevaluated so that gifted children from all segments of the population have the opportunity to be educated with their intellectual peers.

PURPOSE

We wrote this volume to help classroom teachers identify and plan for gifted children from special populations. It examines ways in which teachers can help these students reach their potential. Teachers today are faced with the challenge of meeting the needs of all children in diverse classrooms. The chapters on special populations (1) describe each special population; (2) discuss challenges involved in identifying giftedness in each population; and (3) based on current theories of intelligence, tell how to identify gifts, differentiate the curriculum according to areas of giftedness or ability, and break down existing barriers so that children's individual gifts can be valued and nurtured in the classroom and beyond. We also suggest ways in which to weave gifted education into every aspect of the curriculum for every child.

Gifted children exist in all segments of our population. If we are to succeed in identifying them and meeting their needs, dramatic changes are necessary.

ORGANIZATION OF THE BOOK

The first section, Background for Changing the Present Educational Paradigm, includes Chapters 1 and 2. Chapter 1 discusses reasons for our failure to integrate gifted education into the fabric of the school. The background that sets the stage for inclusive classrooms is established.

Chapter 2 establishes a relationship between multiple intelligence philosophy and the curriculum. Principles and strategies for differentiating the curriculum are presented.

Chapters 3, 4, and 5 make up Section 2, Twice Exceptional: Gifted Children with Disabilities. Chapter 3 discusses the need to include gifted children with physical disabilities in the regular classroom, when the appropriate supports are provided. Physical disabilities do not affect intellectual ability. With the appropriate physical and emotional support, gifted children who are disabled should have the same opportunities as other gifted children.

Chapter 4 discusses how to identify and support gifted children with sensory difficulties. Gifted children who are hearing impaired should have special supports, depending on the degree of impairment. They may be deprived of early metacognitive interaction with parents that fosters intellectual development. American Sign Language, separate and distinct from the English language, presents additional challenges for these students.

We also discuss in Chapter 4 the challenges involved in educating gifted children with visual impairments. Conventional IQ tests will not reveal intellectual abilities of gifted children with sensory impairments. Some of the obstacles to identification include developmental delays and incomplete information about the child. Gifted children with visual impairments require a dual curriculum to compensate for challenges presented by the impairment.

Challenges involved in educating children with learning disabilities are discussed in Chapter 5. IQ profiles of intellectually gifted children with learning disabilities will reveal discrepancies in verbal and performance scores. These discrepancies can serve to identify gifted children with learning disabilities. When strengths are noted and accommodations made, these children are capable of achieving at high levels.

Chapter 5 also includes a discussion of gifted students who have been diagnosed with attention deficit hyperactivity disorder (AD/HD). Gifted children with AD/HD are cognitively able as opposed to children with learning disabilities whose specific disabilities interfere with performance. Qualified professionals need to be consulted inasmuch as there is no test to diagnose AD/HD. Once identified, special accommodations should be made

Section 3, Special Populations of Gifted Children, includes discussions of gifted children from diverse backgrounds, exceptionally gifted children, young gifted children, and gifted females.

The special challenges are presented in nurturing and identifying children from culturally diverse backgrounds in Chapter 6. The classroom is an important place to begin to acknowledge differences and provide for environmental deficits. In Chapter 7 we address the concerns involved in identifying and planning for exceptionally gifted children. The exceptionally gifted child should be identified and nurtured early on. When children's intellectual abilities far surpass their peers, accommodations should be made so that they do not act out, withdraw, become bored, or underachieve.

Challenges involved in the identification and nurturance of young gifted children are discussed in Chapter 8. Uneven development between social, emotional, intellectual, and gross- or fine-motor skills can cause frustration for young gifted children. Recognition of the dyssynchrony that occurs assists in providing appropriate opportunities for them.

Chapter 9 includes a discussion of how to nurture and support gifted females in order to cultivate their gifts. Gifted females present unique challenges because of the nature of their differences. They need support and encouragement to develop areas of strength.

Section 4 concludes with two chapters that address issues and concerns surrounding the education of students with exceptional abilities. Chapter 10 presents different views regarding the social and emotional development of the gifted. Different factors impacting the social and emotional development of gifted children are discussed. Piechowski's theories of overexcitability are reviewed. Moral development is presented as are special concerns regarding gifted children at risk and underachievers. Suggestions are made as to how to address these concerns.

Chapter 11 stresses the need to change the focus of our educational paradigm from a deficit model to a strength model. Teacher preparation is stressed.

ACKNOWLEDGMENTS

This book is the result of our combined 40 years of reflective practice working with exceptional children. Coming from different perspectives, namely gifted education and special education, it is our shared belief that educators need to move from a deficit-driven paradigm to one that seeks to develop the gifts and talents in children. This is the foundation of our text. Many individuals have encouraged and supported us in this endeavor. Special appreciation goes to Dr. Susan Semel and Dr. Alan Sadovnik for having the vision to initiate this collaboration. Special appreciation goes to Dr. Abraham Tannenbaum, Dr. Harry Passow, Dr. Ann Corn, Dr. Kathryn Hegeman, Dr. Michael Piechowski, Dr. Michael Pyryt, and Dr. Rena Subotnik.

We also wish to extend our sincere gratitude to the many students, teachers, and parents who have worked with us along the way and generously shared their stories. Thanks to our colleagues, families, and children at the Herricks School District and the Special Education Program at Hofstra University.

We would also like to thank our editor, Ann Davis, and our production editor, Sheryl Langner.

We would like to thank all of our reviewers for their valuable input and suggestions: Dorothy C. Armstrong, Grand Valley State University; Ellen D. Fiedler, Northeastern Illinois University; Synnove J. Heggoy, Georgia Southern University; Scott L. Hunsaker, Utah State University; Maurice Miller, Indiana State University; Micheal Sayler, University of North Texas; George Sheperd, University of Oregon; Sally M. Todd, Brigham Young University; and Jerry J. Wellik, St. Cloud State University.

Contents

Section 1
Background for Changing the Present Educational Paradigm   *1*

Section 2
Twice Exceptional: Gifted Children with Disabilities   **37**

Section **4**

Issues and Concerns: Addressing the Needs of Students with Exceptional Abilities in the Twenty-First Century   153

Section 1

Background for Changing the Present Educational Paradigm

Chapter 1 discusses reasons for our failure to integrate gifted education into the fabric of the school. A background is established that argues for the instruction of gifted students to begin in inclusive classrooms.

In Chapter 2, the relationship between multiple intelligence philosophy and the curriculum is established. Principles and strategies for differentiating the curriculum are presented.

Failure to Meet the Needs of Gifted Children

Typical questions a classroom teacher might ask include these:

Why have we been unable to meet the needs of gifted children in regular classrooms?

How do we identify gifted children?

Should gifted children be included in regular classrooms?

How many types of giftedness can one classroom accommodate?

How might I meet the needs of special populations in my room?

To answer these questions, this chapter does the following:

Presents an overview of the history of education for the gifted.

Discusses obstacles that have prevented education for the gifted from being integrated into classroom practice.

Outlines issues of inclusion as they relate to the needs of gifted students with disabilities.

DEFINING GIFTEDNESS

Potential giftedness exists in every segment of our population. A review of the history of our initiatives to integrate opportunities for able students into the fabric of the school indicates that attempts made through the years have not succeeded (Tannenbaum, 1979, 1983, 1986, 1993). As of the late 1990s, there is no federal mandate entitling these students to an education that is commensurate with their abilities. Wide discrepancies exist in types of services provided across the country (Council of State Directors, 1991, 1994, 1996). Two major reasons for our failure include our inability to identify which students are gifted and our lack of attention to special populations of gifted that have been underserved, such as children with physical/sensory impairments or learning disabilities, ethnic minorities, young gifted children, gifted females, exceptionally gifted and underachieving gifted children (Passow, 1982; Frasier, Garcia, & Passow, 1995). Underserved populations suffer from neglect because the conditions and opportunities they are exposed to are insufficient to nurture, stimulate, and guide the full potential of their individual abilities. Public policy set by the Individuals with Disabilities Education Act of 1990 dictates that, to the extent possible, we include students of all abilities and disabilities in regular classrooms. We now need to reassess the way we view giftedness and provide teachers with insights and strategies that reveal the many faces of giftedness in their students, including those from populations that have previously been neglected.

Recent theories of intelligence and giftedness call into question traditional models favoring general intelligence as measured by intelligence tests. The IQ or intelligence type test that has been used as the primary identifier of giftedness is now being seen "as a gate" that prevents children from reaching their potential. The limiting nature of IQ tests with regard to identification of the gifted has served as an obstacle to development of appropriate educational opportunities for them. Current theories of intelligence indicate that intelligence is pluralistic in nature. Pluralistic models broaden the lens through which giftedness is viewed, look at the different ways in which children can be gifted, and question the extent to which tests can capture these diverse gifts. In essence, recent theories ask educators to rethink the identification and instruction of gifted students.

The two theorists currently influencing our thinking with regard to the way we view intelligence and intelligence tests are Dr. Howard Gardner and Dr. Robert Sternberg. Both have called into question the validity of using IQ or "g" type tests as the predominant way of measuring intelligence. Sternberg (1988) saw intelligence as having three major aspects: analytical, creative, and practical. Conventional good test-takers tend to excel in analytical intelligence but not necessarily in creative or practical tasks. He believed that practical and creative skills are oftentimes discouraged in schools. Gardner (1983) published his theory of multiple intelligences in which he describes intelligence as being of a pluralistic nature. In this book, we use Gardner's theory of multiple intelligences as a framework that provides a lens to assist teachers in viewing students in a positive light in areas of potential.

In his research with individuals who had suffered brain damage, Gardner observed that the human mind might be modular in design with separate processes involved in different symbol systems, such as numerical, linguistic, pictorial, and gestural. Individual profiles vary. "Moreover, there is no necessary correlation between any two intelligences, and they may indeed entail quite distinct forms of perception, memory, and other psychological processes" (Gardner & Hatch, 1989, p. 5). One system might become damaged without compromising another. Gardner's observations led him to become distressed with the almost exclusive use of only two types of symbol systems in schools: verbal-linguistic and logical-mathematical. These same two systems also dominate test construction.

As we view the educational landscape, Gardner's work brings us to a new frontier. It dictates that education needs to provide for the diverse nature of students we teach. The use of multiple intelligence (MI) theory in classrooms promises to increase self-esteem (Callahan, 1997) and promote greater tolerance in a democratic environment that recognizes a variety of potentials in all students.

MI theory is not a curriculum, but a philosophy that can guide teachers in the identification and nurturance of giftedness. MI theory addresses abilities in specific domains of intelligence that include logical-mathematical, verbal-linguistic, spatial, bodily kinesthetic, musical, intrapersonal, and interpersonal. In this book, the curriculum becomes the vehicle used to include opportunities for giftedness to be expressed and recognized. Identification of potential is linked to a differentiated curriculum that nurtures these gifts.

OVERVIEW OF ATTEMPTS TO MEASURE INTELLIGENCE

Interest in intelligence and intelligence testing dates back to 200 B.C. (Sattler, 1992). Development of quantitative data to test for intelligence began with Alfred Binet, who undertook the task of constructing mental tests that would discriminate between normal and mentally deficient children. Binet's ideas led to the development of the Stanford–Binet Intelligence Scale, which yielded one composite score known as an "intelligence quotient" or "g." Lewis Terman (1926) in his longitudinal studies of giftedness used high IQ as the measure of intelligence. As a result, tests have been created that tap into abilities that are primarily of a logical-mathematical and verbal-linguistic nature, and they are usually taken under stressful conditions. The score reflects a snapshot of a moment in time of a limited set of abilities. These same tests have been used as the basis for entry into special programs for gifted children that provide special opportunities for some, while neglecting others.

Research Supporting the Existence of Specific Abilities

Through the years, other researchers have observed the existence of multiple factors that influence intelligence. Thurstone (1947), when examining factors involved in measuring intelligence, identified those involved in verbal, numerical, spatial, memory, fluency, and reasoning abilities, along with a factor for perceptual or judgment speed and a second-order factor dominated by inductive reasoning. Burt (1949) identified two main groups of abilities, one of which included a higher order factor for reasoning, judgment, or evaluation and a second group composed of artistic or aesthetic understanding. Vernon (1950, 1979) suggested that intelligence consisted of more than one facet and that verbal abilities should be separated from spatial and mechanical skills. Cattell (1971, 1987) identified two types of mental capacity: fluid and crystallized. Fluid capacity refers to the ability to be directed to almost any problem requiring adaptation, and crystallized capacity is the result of learning experiences acquired through education and daily life experiences. Guilford (1967) designed a "structure of the intellect" model in which he observed variations in information processing that included operations, products, and content. Each dimension was divided into categories: operations (evaluation, convergent production, divergent production, memory, cognition), product (units, classes, relations, systems, transformations, implications), and content (figural, symbolic, semantic, behavioral). Using multiple factor analysis, he attempted to identify or isolate each of the abilities that is a part of human intelligence. He maintained that every human ability has three dimensions and can be classified according to the subcategories within each dimension. These abilities are related, but are identifiable as more than 120 separate entities.

Different Conceptions of Giftedness

As we have struggled to understand the nature of giftedness, some have attempted to quantify it and break it down into its components, some have considered the nature of giftedness and intelligence in global terms, others have considered it in terms of development or behaviors, and yet others in terms of potential future contributions. Some of the interpretations include the following.

The Marland report (Marland, 1972) recognized various dimensions of giftedness and defined giftedness as those identified by professionally qualified persons who were, by virtue of outstanding abilities, capable of high performance in areas of general intellectual ability, specific academic aptitude, creative or productive thinking, leadership ability, visual and performing arts, or psychomotor ability (psychomotor was subsequently eliminated). The report recognized that differentiated educational programs and services beyond those normally provided by the regular school program were necessary in order for these students to realize their contribution to self and society. Children capable of high performance included those with demonstrated achievement or potential ability in any of the areas, singly or in combination.

Renzulli (1977) defined giftedness as having three components: above average ability, task commitment, and creativity. He graphically demonstrated these as a Venn diagram, with giftedness viewed as the intersection of the three.

Tannenbaum (1986) believed that giftedness denotes a potential "for becoming critically acclaimed performers or exemplary producers of ideas in spheres of activity that enhance the moral, physical, emotional, social, intellectual, or aesthetic life of humanity" (p. 3). "Identification is, therefore, a matter of locating children who possess high potential in comparison to other children, with no guarantees that they will eventually excel by universal standards as adults, even with proper nurturance" (Tannenbaum & Baldwin, 1983, p. 11).

The Jacob K. Javits Gifted and Talented Students Education Program (Ross, 1994) echoed what had been stated in the Marland report; that is, that giftedness included children and youth who gave "evidence of high performance capability in areas such as intellectual, creative, artistic, or leadership capacity, or in specific academic fields, and who require services or activities not ordinarily provided by the school in order to fully develop such capabilities" (Section 4103, Definitions, 102 Stat., pp. 237–238).

Silverman (1993b) suggested using a definition of giftedness proposed by the Columbus Group, which defines giftedness as "asynchronous development in which advanced cognitive abilities and heightened intensity combine to create inner experiences and awareness that are qualitatively different from the norm. This asynchrony increases with higher intellectual capacity. The uniqueness of the gifted renders them particularly vulnerable and requires modifications in parenting, teaching and counseling in order for them to develop optimally" (Columbus Group, 1991, p. 36).

Cline elaborated on Renzulli's "three ring" model (1977) of giftedness (above average ability, creativity, and task commitment). According to Cline (1989) the factors that work in combination include intelligence, creativity (internal and external states), task orientation and motivation, knowledge and/or background of experience, and the external environment or opportunity.

Coleman's research (1994) revealed eighteen primary identifiers of exceptional potential that he grouped into the following categories: exceptional learner, exceptional user of knowledge, exceptional generator of knowledge, and exceptional motivation.

Even though we have attempted to define and describe giftedness, identification of the gifted child remains problematic. No clear-cut method is available for identifying gifted students. We cannot predetermine who will make contributions to society. Intelligence to some extent is an inherited characteristic and is affected by environment (Blakeslee, 1990, 1995; Dehaene, 1998).

MULTIPLE INTELLIGENCE THEORY

Gardner's philosophy, as mentioned earlier, has provided a broader lens through which giftedness can be viewed. It provides an opportunity for the identification, expression, and development of a number of intelligences. He proposed seven candidates for intelligence (1983) and has recently expanded it to include two others, the naturalist and the spiritualist (1998). In this book, the seven initially proposed intelligences (verbal-linguistic, logical-mathematical, spatial, bodily kinesthetic, musical, interpersonal, and intrapersonal) will be used to guide teachers in recognizing the diverse talents students might bring to classrooms.

According to MI theory, each of the intelligences is a relatively autonomous potential and thus can function independently of the others. Each develops along its own trajectory. Support for the theory has been found in neuropsychological literature. Gardner (1975) in his research with brain-damaged adults found that specific faculties could be lost while others remained intact. Even though each is independent, they work in concert with one another in different domains. Profiles vary and individuals may possess strengths and deficits in each. Each intelligence has subcomponents:

- Verbal-linguistic intelligence can be broken down into components such as syntax and semantics and can include school-oriented tasks such as forms of expression in writing or oral ability.
- Logical-mathematical intelligence can include facility with numbers and/or reasoning abilities.
- Spatial intelligence involves the ability to observe, represent, and image in a variety of configurations.
- Bodily kinesthetic intelligence involves gestures and body movement.
- Musical intelligence includes sensitivity to music as demonstrated by composers and/or performers.
- Interpersonal intelligence involves an understanding of and ability to relate to others.
- Intrapersonal intelligence involves the understanding of oneself.

In content studied in school and in professional careers one intelligence may dominate as other intelligences are integrated in actual performance. Verbal-linguistic intelligence dominates for the writer and lecturer and combines with logical-mathematical intelligence for the lawyer. Logical-mathematical intelligence dominates for the mathematician and physicist but cuts across all domains. Spatial intelligence evidences itself in the work of the artist, navigator, and chess player, and works in concert with logical-mathematical intelligence for the architect. Bodily kinesthetic intelligence is demonstrated by the athlete and the mime and combines with musical intelligence for the dancer. Musical intelligence manifests itself in the singer, composer, lyricist, or performer as each works in concert with verbal or mathematical skills. Intrapersonal and interpersonal intelligences can be seen in religious leaders, politicians, therapists, and salespeople. Even though personal intelligences have been relatively ignored in schools, their importance cannot be underestimated (Goleman, 1995; Hacker, 1995; Hyatt and Gottlieb, 1987). Empathic understanding of others needs to be understood and encouraged so that students of all abilities and disabilities can be successfully included in the same classroom.

Verbal-linguistic and logical-mathematical skills have been the two intelligences that have been most valued in school settings and the two that intelligence type tests tap into, although a single score does not indicate that individuals perform equally in both areas (Kerr, 1992). One of the criticisms of Gardner's theory is that some of his candidates, that is, musical, spatial, or bodily kinesthetic, could be considered talents rather than gifts. But MI theory is very democratic and raises all of the intelligences to the same level. Each of the intelligences is a proclivity or potential that can blossom or not depending on the culture in which individuals are reared. Giftedness is seen as the ability to fashion products and solve problems in any domain that are of value in a cultural setting.

EDUCATION FOR THE GIFTED
IN THE INCLUSIVE CLASSROOM

Curriculum for the gifted needs to be viewed in the context of *inclusion*, which refers to the inclusion of students with both abilities and disabilities in the regular classroom. Public policy today requires that all students—average, above average, disabled, or disabled and above average—be placed together in classrooms. Instead of assessing student abilities in terms of deficits, multiple intelligence philosophy allows educators to view each child in terms of what he or she can do. Evaluation of intelligence takes place in each of the domains. The curriculum is the tool used to assess abilities. Assessment is ongoing. Tests are used to supplement data collection. Students are not expected to perform in areas that are too difficult for them. Strengths need to be noted and encouraged. This book has been written so that as students are allowed to choose the way they express themselves, teachers can identify and nurture special gifts in all children.

SPECIAL EDUCATION AND PUBLIC POLICY:
HISTORICAL OVERVIEW

The shift toward inclusion has its roots in the history of special education in the United States. It is the story of separate institutions for persons with disabilities. Initially built with humanistic purposes, the early proponents of asylums were considered principled social reformers seeking better treatment for the dependent members of society. The institutions existing at the turn of the century segregated individuals into categories of disability such as mental retardation and insanity and excluded them from the rest of society. As these institutions expanded, emphasis on concern for the deviant and disabled individual was shifted and replaced by an attempt to protect society from them (Taylor & Searl, 1987). By the early 1900s institutions served as a place to put individuals unwanted by the mainstream of society. As the populations in these asylums soared, conditions deteriorated to the point that the institutions became human warehouses: places filled with despair, disease, and often death.

The institutional model for providing services for individuals with disabilities went unchallenged for more than 100 years. However, in the 1960s and 1970s great changes occurred. A new era of normalization, first developed in Sweden, promoted the notion that people with disabilities could live as close to "normal" as the general population. At the same time, exposés, such as Geraldo Rivera's examination of the Willowbrook State School for the Mentally Retarded in Staten Island, New York, documented the horrible and shameful conditions that existed, stirring the American public to action (*New York State Association for Retarded Children v. Rockefeller,* 1973; referred to as the *Willowbrook* case). With more than 6,000 residents, Willowbrook was the largest institution for people with mental retardation in the world. Based on the landmark 1954 Supreme Court decision in *Brown v. Board of Education,* which outlawed racial separation in the schools, a series of major class action lawsuits was brought against state institutions on behalf of children with disabilities. In 1972 federal courts in Pennsylvania [*Pennsylvania Association for Retarded Citizens (PARC) v. Commonwealth of Pennsylvania,* 1972] and the District of Columbia (*Mills v. Board of Education of the District of Columbia,* 1972) ordered school authorities to educate students with disabilities in the same schools and programs as students without disabilities, with certain procedural safeguards (Turnbull, Turnbull, Shank, & Leal, 1995).

Both *PARC* and *Mills* were catalysts for many other lawsuits that followed, and the orders given in their decisions served as a model for Public Law 94-142, the Education for All Handicapped Children Act passed by Congress in 1975. In these decisions federal judges called for the "free and suitable publicly supported education" (*Mills*) for all children with disabilities in the "least restrictive" (*PARC*) setting possible. The law was reauthorized in 1990 and 1997 and is now called the Individuals with Disabilities Education Act (IDEA). IDEA defines special education as specially designed instruction to meet the unique needs of students with disabilities. It provides for "zero reject," a rule against excluding any student; nondiscriminatory evaluation; an individual educational plan based on the evaluation augmented by supplementary services as necessary; a least restrictive environment that requires students with disabilities to be placed with nondisabled students to the maximum appropriate; procedural due process; and parental and student participation.

In addition, Congress passed a series of laws to protect the rights of adults with disabilities. The Rehabilitation Act of 1973 offered funding for rehabilitation and more importantly contained Section 504, the civil rights bill for people with disabilities. Section 504 prohibits discrimination against individuals with disabilities and provides for many educational accommodations that enable children with disabilities to participate fully in our schools. The Americans with Disabilities Act (ADA) of 1990 expands these rights from the educational environment to all public places of transportation and employment.

INCLUSION AS A PHILOSOPHY

According to Hahn (1989, 1994) we need to change our paradigm and assume a humanistic approach and integrate individuals with disabilities into all aspects of societal life. He argues that the growth of the disability rights movement and the accompanying move toward inclusion of students with disabilities into general education emerges from a fundamental philosophical shift away from a "functional limitations" view of disability to that of a "minority group" model. He believes that special education was historically viewed from a medical and physiological perspective in which the persons with disabilities had to be "fixed" with therapies and rehabilitation. We now hold a more sociopolitical view of special education in which a disability is no longer a personal defect but rather the result of a disabling environment. In this model it is society's responsibility to provide remedies so that the children with disabilities can take their place in the general community of learners. From this civil rights perspective, the full inclusion of all children with exceptionalities into the educational mainstream is a fundamental right.

Therefore, inclusion is viewed as a philosophy around which appropriate strategies must now be devised. It encompasses a belief system that emphasizes individual worth and value and promotes a sense of belonging for all members of our society. These ideas apply to all students, whether "disabled," "average," "gifted," or "disabled and gifted."

> A first step to take, then, when planning for individual student differences is to identify the unique characteristics, skills, strategies, and knowledge each particular student brings to different learning tasks and to identify likely educational mismatches. (Villa et al., 1995, pp. 138–139)

Villa et al. (1995) point out that inclusive schooling does not "mean that children with gifts and talents will not receive focused attention in one-on-one or homogeneous group arrangements." They continue:

> On the contrary, both will be options, as needed for any student. Capitalizing on the multiple intelligences notion of human difference and potential, homogeneous groups could be arranged along any number of dimensions of interest or "intelligence" (e.g., musical preferences, recreational interests). (pp. 143–145)

Integrating MI theory into classroom practice provides teachers with ways in which giftedness can be expressed, assessed, and nurtured in domains that are not affected by a disability. As student potential is realized, MI theory needs to be joined with philosophies that guide the development of a differentiated curricula so that the level of challenge necessary for total involvement and success can be achieved (Csikszentmihalyi, 1990).

The philosophies guiding inclusion are sound, but obstacles exist that need to be overcome before full inclusion takes place. These obstacles include the following:

- Limited resources

- Variability of student behaviors
- Teacher attitudes
- Lack of teacher preparation
- Lack of systematic reintegration.

Advocates for special education fear that a continuum of services or a cascade model (Reynolds, 1962; Deno, 1970), which includes placements in resource rooms, special classes, special schools, or residential schools, will be replaced by a one-size-fits-all model. Proponents of inclusion have called for responsible inclusion. Responsible inclusion involves schools making individual case-by-case decisions. Failure to do this properly will cause great dissatisfaction with public schools.

Responsible inclusion involves building a vision; restructuring the roles and responsibilities of faculty; collaboration between schools, families, and community; and ongoing professional development (Muscott, 1991). Teachers need to be provided with the tools and strategies necessary to assess and meet the needs of the diverse population of learners that will be entering classrooms.

INCLUSION AND THE GIFTED

Public Law 105-17, the IDEA, guides educators in identifying and nurturing students with disabilities, but confusion abounds as to how to identify and nurture students with above average abilities. As a result, the degree of services provided for able students across the nation has been left to individual school districts that have attempted to meet the needs of children in their communities. Some states have mandates requiring that gifted students be served, while others do not. Policies among states vary greatly (Passow & Rudnitski, 1993).

MI theory is democratic in its approach and allows students to use their intelligences in a variety of ways. The gifts and talents of children with disabilities are often overlooked (Whitmore & Maker, 1985). Stereotypic expectations keep us from recognizing potential gifts that are domain specific. Some students with physical disabilities may display behaviors such as drooling or lack of eye contact that may be associated with mental retardation, when in fact these students are intellectually brilliant. Students with hearing impairments or who are visually disabled can be easily overlooked, as can the child with cerebral palsy (Willard-Holt, 1994) or the student who has a learning disability. Stephen Hawkings's brilliance could have easily been masked by his severe physical disabilities. There are many examples that are less dramatic, but we must begin to understand that many talents and abilities remain hidden because of apparent disabilities that have nothing to do with potential. Gardner's philosophy about this population is particularly appropriate because it enables professionals to view every aspect of the child's potential.

Teachers addressing the diverse populations entering classrooms today will need to provide opportunities for intelligences to be expressed in subjects across the curriculum. As precocity is exhibited, educators need to integrate theory involved in curriculum differentiation for the gifted.

MULTIPLE INTELLIGENCE THEORY IN CLASSROOMS

If we are to recognize and appreciate the many gifts and talents our students come to us with, we need to broaden the lens through which teachers view their students. Gardner's MI theory allows teachers to view all students positively in a variety of ways and to identify multiple intelligences in the classroom. This identification of various gifts in specific domains increases student self-esteem (Callahan, 1997). MI theory is not a curriculum but a philosophy. Dr. Gardner and his associates at Harvard have established educational settings based on this philosophy. This philosophy serves as a catalyst to assist teachers in providing opportunities so that giftedness can be identified, nurtured, and expressed. MI philosophy can be integrated into an existing curriculum. As potential is recognized, teachers can differentiate the curriculum so that students remain challenged and are rewarded in areas where potential gifts are observed, allowing talent to be nurtured and blossom.

Chapter 2

Applications of Multiple Intelligence Theory to the Curriculum

Typical questions a classroom teacher might ask include these:

How does multiple intelligence theory relate to classroom content?
How does one differentiate the curriculum?
What are some of the programming opportunities that can be provided?
Who should deliver services?

To answer these questions, this chapter does the following:

Links classroom content to multiple intelligence philosophy.
Outlines the principles involved in curriculum differentiation.
Suggests ways that services can be delivered in the classroom and beyond.

PRINCIPLES FOR DIFFERENTIATED CURRICULA

If all students with talents or gifts are to reach their potential, multiple intelligence (MI) theory needs to be integrated with philosophies that guide the development of curriculum for the gifted. Passow (1982a) and VanTassel-Baska (1988) have outlined principles for differentiated curricula. The principles apply across the intelligences or domains. These researchers believe the following:

- All learners should be provided curriculum opportunities that allow them to attain optimum levels of learning.
- Curricula must be adapted or designed to accommodate the learning needs of gifted learners, which are different from those of typical learners.
- The needs of gifted learners cut across cognitive, affective, social, and aesthetic areas of curriculum experiences.

Furthermore, they recommend that the curricula for gifted/talented learners accomplish these goals:

- Include more elaborate, complex, and in-depth study of major ideas, problems, and themes—those that integrate knowledge with and across systems of thought.
- Allow for the development and application of productive thinking skills that enable students to reconceptualize existing knowledge or generate new knowledge.

- Enable students to explore constantly changing knowledge and information, and to develop the attitude that knowledge is worth pursuing in an open world.
- Encourage exposure to, selection of, and use of appropriate and specialized resources.
- Promote self-initiated and self-directed learning and growth.
- Provide for the development of self-understanding and the understanding of one's relationship to persons, societal institutions, nature, and culture.
- Evaluate students with stress placed on their ability to perform at a level of excellence that demonstrates creativity and higher-level thinking skills.

MULTIPLE INTELLIGENCE THEORY AND CORE SUBJECTS

Principles for differentiation need to be integrated into all content areas. Each of the core subjects involves more than one intelligence, but one intelligence often predominates. Students need to be taught core subjects so that ability can be expressed in ways that tap into symbol systems that extend beyond the logical-mathematical and verbal-linguistic systems. Content beyond the core needs to be added to assist in the ongoing identification of the full range of gifts. What remains of primary importance is that students may possess gifts in one domain or in many.

Mathematics: Mathematics is currently a core subject. Precocity in mathematics is described by Gardner (1983) as logical-mathematical intelligence and will be evidenced as students are given the opportunity to work with mathematical problems or situations using logic. It is associated with scientific thinking and reasoning and is the capacity to recognize patterns, see relationships, and work with abstract symbols. It is evidenced in scientists, computer programmers, lawyers, mathematicians, and accountants. This intelligence can be seen as children pursue mathematical, scientific, and historical endeavors.

Language arts: Language arts ability is described by Gardner as verbal-linguistic intelligence and includes foreign language. Language arts is a core subject in schools. This intelligence can be seen in poets, playwrights, novelists, public speakers, and storytellers. This intelligence surfaces in the language arts curriculum.

Science: Science is a topic that is not always covered in any depth on the elementary level. Scientific precocity is identified with Gardner's view of mathematical-logical intelligence. It is also a core subject that provides students with the opportunity to use higher-order thinking skills. Scientific inquiry allows gifted thinkers to surface.

Social studies: Social studies is a part of the core curriculum. A combination of verbal-linguistic and logical thinking is evident in students who are potential historians. Personal skills are involved in political science and spatial skills in geography.

Physical education: Bodily kinesthetic intelligence involves the ability to use the body to express emotion or participate in sports. We see this type of intelligence at work in the performances of actors, athletes, professional dancers, and mimes. This intelligence surfaces in physical education classes, in dance classes, and in other activities involving bodily movement. Opportunities to demonstrate physical prowess are provided in schools in the form of athletics.

Art: Spatial intelligence describes the tasks involved in painting, drawing, architecture, and navigation and is used by graphic artists, cartographers, painters, and sculptors. Industrial arts and art classes tap into this intelligence. Artistic endeavors also depend on the opportunities afforded students in each school. Opportunities for artistic expression can be integrated into the classroom curriculum.

Music: Musical intelligence involves the capacity to recognize and use rhythmic and tonal patterns. It can be seen in musicians, composers, and music teachers. Music classes and musical activities assist this gift in surfacing. Opportunities to demonstrate musical ability vary from school to school. Opportunities to demonstrate can be provided in regular classroom settings.

Subjects not always considered core but which can assist in the identification of specific intelligences are described next. Classroom teachers can work with specialists such as school staff or professionals from the community. Students may be given the opportunity to present their work in artistic forms. These secondary topics include the following:

Dance: Dance is considered to be a part of bodily kinesthetic intelligence as defined by Gardner and is not an intelligence that is usually a part of the school curriculum. Opportunities to display talent can be integrated into classroom activities.

Drama: Opportunities for students to perform are sometimes provided in schools and by classroom teachers. The performing arts require a combination of verbal-linguistic intelligence, spatial intelligence, and bodily kinesthetic intelligence. Gifts will surface as students are provided with opportunities.

The following topics can be easily integrated into existing curriculum, such as the Social Studies curriculum:

Leadership development: Personal skills are essential to the identification and nurturance of effective leaders.

Values: Values and moral education need to be an integral part of leadership education for the gifted (Lindsay, 1988; Hegeman, 1997).

Lindsay (1988), Hegeman (1997), and Gallagher et al. (1982) stress the need to include leadership as a concept in the education of the gifted. Gallagher et al. define leadership as "the exercise of power or influence in social collectivities, such as groups, organizations, communities or nations, to meet the needs of the group" (p. 8). Leadership skills, personal skill development, and values education are closely intertwined. "Effective leadership in today's world includes the characteristics of self-understanding, self-expression, and openness to personal growth" (Sisk & Shallcross, 1986, p. 16).

Gardner and others have highlighted the importance of personal skill development. Robert Sternberg of Yale has acknowledged the importance of different kinds of "smarts." In their book *When Smart People Fail,* Hyatt and Gottlieb (1987) have attributed the failure of some smart individuals to their lack of social skills. In his recent book, *Money,* Andrew Hacker (1997) analyzes income levels in America and draws the conclusion that what individuals learn in their years spent in institutions of higher education is not important; rather, the factor that determines success is the modeling they receive in universities as to how to interact with others and appear successful. The area of the personal intelligences has attracted great interest with the appearance of Daniel Goleman's book, *Emotional Intelligence* (1995). The assessment and development of the personal intelligences have implications for all students.

Personal knowledge is intertwined with one's ethics and morals (Phenix, 1964). An individual is what he does. One knows himself by his decisions. According to Lindsay (1988), it is imperative that we begin to recognize the need to establish moral education at the core of the curriculum, especially for those children who are gifted in leadership:

> If we are to regain our national conscience, our sense of propriety, our hunger for excellence in every endeavor, we must begin with the design of a curriculum in moral education that will provide our future leaders with the appropriate models and methodologies for reestablishing these values at the center of our consciousness. (p. 9)

Lindsay warns us not to confuse moral education with indoctrination. Krathwohl, Bloom, and Masia (1956) outline a classification taxonomy for the affective domain. Their scheme describes the steps involved in establishing a value system. Raths, Harmin, and Simon (1966), Simon, Howe, and Kirschenbaum (1972), and Gailbraith and Jones (1976) suggest that this can be accomplished by including value clarification exercises in the classroom curriculum. The suggested approach does not aim to instill any particular set of values; rather it is designed to help students examine their own belief systems. According to Raths et al.:

> [W]e see values as based on three processes: choosing, prizing, and acting.
> Choosing:
>
> > (1) freely
> >
> > (2) from alternatives
> >
> > (3) after thoughtful consideration of the consequences of each alternative
>
> Prizing:
>
> > (4) cherishing, being happy with the choice
> >
> > (5) willing to affirm the choice publicly

Acting:

(6) doing something with the choice

(7) repeatedly, in some pattern of life. (1966, p. 30)

When values clarification exercises are incorporated into classroom activities, the thoughtful examination of decisions that affect others is stressed. Is this a decision you are proud of and would stand up for? Would you tell others? How do you let others know how you feel? Students can discuss current events in light of their own value systems or write their own moral dilemmas and open them up for discussion. Is it ever right to steal? Are there times when one's act might appear to betray a friendship? What if you were the mayor of a town and had to decide whether or not to allow a company to begin operations that would pollute your waters, but would provide unemployed members of your community with jobs?

As students in classrooms cover the prescribed curriculum, MI theory guides teachers in allowing students to express what has been learned in a variety of ways that allow innate proclivities to surface. For instance, to complete an assigned project, the logical-mathematical student might use charts and graphs; the verbal-linguistic student might wish to write prose or poetry, or choose to debate; the spatial child might create murals, dioramas, or models; the bodily kinesthetic student might choreograph an expressive dance; and the student with personal skills might create an empathic overview of events.

Students from culturally diverse populations or who are disabled should be assessed in each of the intelligences. A student who is physically disabled should not be expected to perform tasks involved in the bodily kinesthetic domain, but should be exposed to all of the other domains such as math, language, music, art, and leadership. A student with cerebral palsy might not be expected to debate a topic orally, but this would not preclude ability in written language or applications of assistive technology to facilitate debating.

The curriculum for the gifted should be qualitatively different, and its content, process, product, and the learning environment should be adjusted to accommodate the special characteristics of gifted students. Depending on the domain noted, specific strategies become appropriate.

CURRICULUM FOR THE GIFTED SHOULD ADDRESS CONTENT, PROCESS, AND PRODUCT

Defining Content

Content or *domain* refers to the body of knowledge to be learned. Content in schools touches on all of the intelligences. Chall and Conrad (1991) stress the importance of the match between a learner's abilities and the difficulty of the instructional task. In each of the domains, the optimal match should be slightly above the learner's current level of functioning, and the content should be sustained at a level that provides challenge and complexity. The nature of a discipline, as well as the scope and sequence involved, often dictates the nature of the differentiation that should take place. For example, acceleration is appropriate for mathematics; enrichment of or relating material to broad-based themes, problems, or concepts is appropriate for social studies; and employing the methodology of the professional is appropriate for all professions.

Defining Process

John-Steiner (1985) explores the creativity of the thinking of eminent individuals in different fields of study and examines the complex thought processes involved in creative production. As she analyzes the thought processes in each of the domains, she seeks to understand and reveal similarities and differences in the thought processes of extraordinary individuals. Potentially gifted students need to be involved in investigations that include higher level thinking skills and skills of inquiry, including higher levels of cognitive operations, creative thinking, and problem solving in specific domains. Whenever possible, the content should be problem based. Problem definition and attempts at problem solving should evolve as a result of research, whether it involves math, language, music, or art. Whenever possible, opportunities should be provided for thinking across the curriculum, providing for the use of complex thought processes.

Defining Product

In the classroom, students demonstrate their learning through their products. When they are allowed to select the way in which they wish to present their work, a variety of talents and abilities will surface. For example, a spatially gifted student might present an artistic work, a verbally linguistic child might present a play, and a logical-mathematical student might choose flowcharts or graphs.

When students are given choices, they can present their work in whatever forms they deem appropriate, such as projects, papers, presentations, or audiovisual programs. Products that are markers of giftedness should reflect in-depth research. When real-world problems are discovered through research, students can be exposed to problem-solving strategies that assist them in addressing the issues involved in specific domains. Students should be responsible for evaluating their work.

Identification of special talents and abilities sets the stage for meaningful curriculum planning. As teachers note abilities that are markers of giftedness, opportunities can be planned to ensure that students are challenged and are not languishing in their classroom as a result of being subjected to work they already know.

Identifying and planning for the needs of a diverse population will not happen overnight, but these changes can be implemented successfully over a period of time. Once "markers" of giftedness are noted and profiles established, a differentiated curriculum can be implemented. Markers may indicate that students are gifted in one area, in several, or in many, or that a particular student is capable of learning at a faster pace. Schools can arrange for programming alternatives that accommodate special needs.

DIFFERENTIATING THE CURRICULUM WHEN GIFTS ARE RECOGNIZED

If an inclusive classroom is to operate appropriately, classroom teachers need to integrate principles of a differentiated curriculum into domains of study and develop a repertoire of strategies that deliver information. When specific gifts are noted, different types of differentiation need to be implemented if the curriculum is to provide a level of challenge.

Curricular Modifications

Curricular modifications refer to ways in which the curriculum needs to be differentiated once areas of ability are noted. The domain noted dictates the strategy that is most appropriate. Curricular modifications or differentiation can take place in one domain or many, depending on the areas of ability noted (see Figure 2.1).

Depth   The term *depth* refers to researching a topic to allow for greater detail and deeper understanding. A student involved in learning about a subject may wish to select one aspect for in-depth investigation; for example, one student learning about the Civil War might become interested in learning about the causes of the war. A student interested in music might select a specific type of music.

Breadth   Sometimes students are introduced to a topic that stimulates their interest. Extending the topic and covering it in greater breadth might be appropriate. The following are examples drawn from classroom experience. One student reading about an American Indian child wanted to learn about American Indian children today. The student was connected via the Internet to an Indian tribe and began doing research on the Indian population today. The Internet provides a world of opportunities for students.

Curricular Modifications
Depth
Breadth
Tempo
Expansion of Basic Skills and Comprehension
Process Modifications (Greater emphasis is placed on Bloom's taxonomy, inquiry training, and creative thinking.)
Independent Study or Self Selected Content
Telescope or Compact
Add

Figure 2.1   **Types of curricular modifications**

Tempo   A characteristic that has often been observed with gifted children is the speed with which they are capable of learning. Some gifted students learn at a faster rate and need to be allowed to proceed at their own pace. Teachers can accommodate these students by compacting the curriculum and by providing them with self-pacing materials in the form of contracts, independent study, or computer-assisted instruction. (Compacting is described later in this chapter.) One fifth-grade student who had a particular affinity for mathematics was permitted to proceed through the curriculum for the year on his own. Work was monitored by the teacher and arrangements were made for him to work with a middle school teacher to continue the mathematics curriculum. Compacting can also provide for a student to pursue another interest.

Expansion of Basic Skills and Comprehension   If students are to be prepared to become producers of information in our society (Tannenbaum, 1983) and areas of precocity are noted, they need to be introduced to how professionals work in a particular domain. A budding writer needs to be introduced to professional writers and learn about the writing process. A would-be scientist should learn how scientists hypothesize and experiment. A student interested in history should learn early on about primary, secondary, and tertiary resources. Mentors and professionals can assist teachers as they introduce students to the life and work of the professional.

Process Modifications   One of the common identifiers of giftedness is the gifted child's ability to reason well and use complex thought processes. Process modifications include critical and creative thinking skills and have been included both in content and in curricular strategies. They are one of the keys to identifying and nurturing giftedness in children. Students may be identified as gifted by their ability to use higher level thought processes. An ability to think critically and creatively needs to be included in the curriculum in each of the domains. Some gifted students become bored when not presented with challenges. One gifted young man started becoming an observer in school rather than a participant. He found school to be boring and irrelevant and considered dropping out of high school. He was not happy until he reached college. At Columbia University he was introduced to the Socratic method of teaching. He did a complete about-face and became an interested—and interesting—student. Incorporation of process modifications such as Bloom's taxonomy, Taba's thinking strategies, or other inquiry models into classroom practice is especially helpful.

Independent Study or Self-Selected Content   When given the opportunity, children often select topics that indicate gifts in a specific domain. Independent study has been included both in content and in curricular strategies. As content, it allows students to select topics that might be indicators of domains of giftedness. One young woman chose creative writing as a topic of study in fifth grade. She had a very high IQ and to her parents high IQ meant "doctor." She was accepted into a university and began as a pre-med student. After two years she returned home and announced to her parents that she was not going to live their dream, but she was going to follow her own. She is now pursuing a doctorate in journalism.

As a curricular strategy it is important for students who are rapid learners to be allowed to master a topic independently. It can also be an option for students who exhibit precocity or have developed a passion in a particular domain and wish to explore a topic in greater depth and to continue on their own if needs are to be satisfied. It also provides the opportunity for students from diverse backgrounds to pursue individual interests that might be relevant to their culture. A description of how to implement independent study as a strategy is covered later in this chapter.

Telescoping or Compacting   This strategy recognizes those students who have a large reservoir of knowledge and eliminates boredom and unnecessary drill. It involves pretesting and post-testing to determine how much students know before the curriculum is presented. When students have been assessed as having mastered what is to be covered in advance, decisions need to be made as to how the student will be allowed to spend the time that is freed. Options include advancement in the content already known (and in which the student excels), allowing the student to accelerate in that domain, or allowing the student to select a topic not currently covered. Curriculum compacting is an eight-part process in which teachers do the following:

1. Identify the relevant learning objectives in a subject area or grade level.
2. Find or develop a means of pretesting students on one or more of these objectives prior to instruction.
3. Identify students who may benefit from curriculum compacting and should be pretested.
4. Pretest students to determine mastery levels of the chosen objectives.
5. Eliminate practice, drill, or instructional time for students who have demonstrated prior mastery of these objectives.
6. Streamline instruction of those objectives students have not yet mastered but are capable of mastering more quickly than their classmates.
7. Offer enrichment or acceleration options for students whose curriculum has been compacted.
8. Keep records of this process and the instructional options available to "compacted" students. (Reis, Burns, & Renzulli, 1992, p. 8)

Add   *Add* is a curricular option for students who can "test out" of parts or all of a curriculum or for students who move quickly. Teachers can use compacting strategies or, if the district provides these options, distance learning or other options that allow students to cover coursework independently to see who tests out. Teacher and student can add topics not covered, allow in-depth research in areas of interest, or allow study of topics not covered elsewhere. One fourth-grade youngster who was exceptionally bright was tutored in French by a community resident.

Programming Alternatives

Programming alternatives suggest ways in which school districts can begin to program for the gifted. Some may already be in place. Others may become possible in time. Administrators and teachers working together can remove barriers posed by classroom walls by accessing opportunities in the school and the community. Gifted students need to be provided with curriculum that is challenging and need to have the opportunity to interact with students of like ability for at least part of the time. The classroom walls often serve as boundaries to differentiated instruction. Current technology allows the use of on-line resources so that the world can be an encyclopedia for the gifted child. This section offers some of the options that might be put in place so that student instruction can be matched to ability.

As teachers observe currently available options for programming, they can begin to pursue others that can expand the classroom walls. Opportunities need to be sought so that students can be grouped with others of like ability so that they are challenged and do not feel out of step. These opportunities may be provided in the classroom or beyond. Some activities will require the cooperation of teachers or the administration. The goal is to find ways to meet the needs of each child. The options listed in Figure 2.2 are suggestions the authors brainstormed. The purpose of these suggestions is to "trigger" possibilities. As teachers assess their present settings, they can mix and match and creatively design ways that meet the needs of their students in their schools. The suggestions in Figure 2.2 can be viewed in terms of "How might I utilize _____?"

In Class   The classroom teacher is key to determining who the gifted are and in designing curriculum for them. The classroom becomes the place where students are provided with the opportunity to demonstrate potential gifts. Teachers can provide opportunities for students in the room in a variety of ways depending on available resources. Classroom management, which includes providing instruction in a variety of ways, takes time and effort. As gifts are noted, teachers can begin to establish a profile for a student and provide differentiated instruction in the classroom. When teachers identify a student whose gifts cannot be addressed in the regular classroom, they can enlist the support of additional personnel in and out of the school to help that student realize his or her potential.

Once differentiated curriculum has been designed, it can be used through the years. Teachers can share curriculum with each another. The following strategies can be implemented in the classroom to help identify the gifted child and to provide challenging opportunities and prevent boredom. Tomlinson (1995b) provides a variety of suggestions for teachers to use when differentiating instruction in mixed ability classrooms.

Tiered Assignments   Assignments can be structured so that they provide a variety of activities that allow students to explore knowledge by tapping into prior knowledge and allowing for continued growth. Incorporating activities that allow students to demonstrate the ability to respond to complexity and higher-level thought processes will allow gifts to surface. Students can begin learning where they left off

Figure 2.2 **Suggested programming alternatives**

In Class:
  Tiered Assignments
  Ability Grouping
    Flexible
    Clusters
    Cooperative Groups
  Learning Centers
  Interest Centers
  Contracts
  Intellectual Peer Teaching
  High School Students
  Computers, Technology, and Telecommunications
  Self-Paced Instruction
  Independent Study or Self-Selected Topic
Extending the Classroom Walls:
  Resource Room/Enrichment Center
  Revolving Door
  Acceleration
  Honors Class
  Advanced Placement
  Mentor
  Other Class
  Internship
  After School/Extracurricular
  Provisional Augmentation
  Community Resident
  Special School
  Credit by Examination (Testing Out)
  Grade Skipping
  Combined Classes
  Correspondence Courses
  Pull-Out Program

and choose work that is challenging, but not anxiety producing. Performance on tiered assignments aids in the identification of giftedness.

When creating tiered assignments, teachers need to do the following:

- Focus the task on a key concept or generalization.
- Provide a variety of resource materials at differing levels of complexity.
- Include tasks that require the use of advanced materials and complex thought processes.
- Pose questions that require problem-solving skills.
- Encourage students to broaden their reading and extend the assignment if they wish.

- Not specify who should take on the more complex aspects of the assignment. Students may surprise teachers and measure up to challenges if allowed to do so.
- Create open-ended assignments.
- Allow for creativity.
- Establish rubrics so that students understand criteria necessary for quality and success.

Ability Grouping   Ability grouping can take a variety of forms. The application of Vygotsky's (1978) zone of proximal development can benefit all learners. Mediated experiences enable the student to work at higher cognitive levels than they would be able to work independently. Students should be grouped together such that they are learning new material and have the opportunity to work with students of like or superior ability. The material to be learned can be mediated by the teacher or by other students. Students with disabilities can be placed in groups where they are intellectually challenged, keeping in mind that supports may sometimes be needed. For example, a student with a physical disability might require assistive technology and a student with a learning disability might require a note taker. Ability grouping aims to enhance strengths rather than remediate deficits. Emphasis needs to be placed on full participation.

Groups can be established in all of the content areas. The groupings should allow students to move quickly through basic skills, ensure that students who have mastered skills can move on, and provide for the development of advanced skills.

Flexible grouping allows students to move in and out of the group, working within a group or individually as needed. Groups should be created to match student need and/or interest and can be formed as students are pretested. Assumptions should not be made as to a student's ability or length of time needed for mastery. It is important that observations and testing remain current so that groups are constantly changing. As groups are formed based on the skills that need to be taught, they can be reconfigured once the skills are learned. Once students have achieved 85 percent mastery of a skill, they should be permitted to move on. Groups can allow students to accelerate in one or more content areas. Teachers need to make sure that gifted students are developing skills beyond the basics and that they are acquiring advanced knowledge in their areas of talent.

Clusters are another type of group. According to Hoover, Sayler, and Feldhusen (1993) gifted students benefit from cluster grouping. Cluster grouping can be arranged by administrators so that several identified gifted children in a grade are assigned to one classroom, rather than being dispersed among two or more classes. Clusters of students can also be formed within the class for short- or long-term instruction. Clusters can be based on interest or need and they also provide for flexible teaching. They can be formed or reconfigured based on teacher assessments of need.

Cooperative grouping can facilitate classroom management in a variety of ways. Cooperative groups can be formed with children of similar ability who may work together and provide stimulation and challenge for one another. Groups can also be formed with children of varying abilities; however, gifted students become easily bored when working in groups of mixed ability.

Cooperative groups may provide teachers with the opportunity to observe students for qualities other than academics. Leadership abilities may become apparent and social sensitivities may surface. Grouping can be especially helpful for the gifted child with a disability. It is critical that these students be placed in intellectually stimulating settings. Ensuring that there are other students in the group that can take on the roles in which they may have a deficit is essential. For example, a child with dysgraphia could be placed in a group where another student would take on the task of recording for the group. Cooperative groups can assist in assessing the development of interpersonal relationships that include the following:

- Analyzing situations
- Participating as a member of a team
- Being helpful to others
- Communicating thoughts, feelings, and ideas to justify a position
- Encouraging, persuading, or convincing others
- Motivating group members
- Negotiating and working toward consensus.

Learning Centers   Learning centers can house a collection of materials related to the units of instruction for core subjects. When children have completed their regular assignments, they can go to a learning center, where they are allowed to move at their own pace through the skills to be mastered. For the gifted, learning centers can include suggestions for exploring topics in greater depth or breath. Advanced reading materials should be provided. Suggestions that identify real problems should be included.

Whenever possible, a learning center should include the following items:

- Materials necessary for learning the topic on a level that provides a background and allows students to gain in-depth knowledge
- Written and audiovisual materials on the topic from which students can select to accommodate individual learning style preferences
- CD-ROMs for computers
- Puzzles and games that assist in assessing which learning strategies appeal to students.

Learning centers can also contain packets that provide opportunities to access different intelligences, for example, questions that address logical-mathematical inquiry, and opportunities for gifted writers or artists to evidence special capabilities. When they have completed these packets, students should have options for presenting what they have learned in various forms—in a logically written form (for the logical-mathematical child), as a creative piece (for the verbal-linguistic child), in diagrams (for the spatial child), or as plays that might include music or bodily kinesthetic performances.

A science learning center should include rules and supervision when necessary if safety is an issue (e.g., chemistry experiments), background information for a unit, materials that can be used for experimentation, and guidelines so that students can record their experiences in scientific laboratory reports.

A teacher covering a unit on American Indians might include materials on how to access information about how American Indians live today. Interviews might be arranged with local tribes or through the Internet. Questions might include these:

- What are some of the difficulties and challenges being faced by today's American Indians?
- Are all tribes faced with the same dilemmas?
- How might some of these challenges be addressed?

Interest Centers   Interest centers differ from learning centers. Learning centers address core curriculum, whereas interest centers expose students to areas not covered in the curriculum and are places that children can go to when other work is complete. They can serve as valuable tools for exposing students to content not covered in the curriculum. Commercially bought or teacher-made interest centers can be used.

Interest centers should provide opportunities for students to explore new areas of interest, enrich students who demonstrate mastery of required work, incorporate opportunities to become involved at all levels of thinking, and allow for in-depth study.

An interest center, also known as an interest development center (Burns, 1985), should include newspapers, magazines, books, videos, CD-ROMs, Internet addresses, manipulatives if needed, names and addresses of resources, etc. A center might be constructed around a famous person, for example, John F. Kennedy or Mother Teresa, or a topic not included in the curriculum such as lasers.

Questions investigating the life of a famous person might include analyzing the aspects of a person's life to determine what it was that made him or her "famous." Was the fame deserved? What constitutes fame?

A center for lasers might encourage students to investigate current uses of lasers today. What possible ways might they be used in the future? Visit or interview a physician who uses lasers in her practice. How has the laser changed our world? Are changes always positive?

Both learning and interest centers can be of an interdisciplinary nature and can allow for student choices. Opportunities to express areas of intelligence can be included. As students become involved, observations of their performance can provide additional markers of giftedness.

Once learning and interest centers are designed, they can be shared by teachers. They can be designed by individual teachers or teachers may work collaboratively.

Contracts   Contracts provide the opportunity for students to work at their own pace, completing assigned work according to certain specifications. Students who like to work independently will thrive on learning contracts. They allow the student to make decisions and encourage and recognize a student's ability to work independently. Students establish the appropriate pace at which to work. Contracts can blend skills and content. They can encourage extended learning and include questions that foster research and critical thinking. They can provide opportunities for creativity to surface. As students are involved, time is freed for the teacher to work with individuals or small groups. Rubrics for success need to be provided.

According to Winebrenner (1992) a learning contract should include these items:

- Clear instructions outlining the material to be covered
- Suggested resources
- Opportunities to go beyond the content required by the prescribed curriculum
- Material that focuses on concepts, themes, and problems.

Assignments to be covered should have a master contract and provide check points as concepts are covered. Enrichment or alternative activities should be provided as students work through the materials. Each section should include a pretest and post-test and assess mastery at 80 to 85 percent mastery. Students should be shown how to keep track of their work and teachers should make time periodically to discuss the material covered. Work should be evaluated by students and teachers.

Winebrenner (1992) suggests that working conditions such as the following be included in contracts:

1. No talking to the teacher while the teacher is teaching.
2. When you need help and the teacher is busy, ask someone else.
3. If no one can help you right way, keep trying yourself or go on to something else.
4. If you must go in and out of the room, do so quietly.
5. Don't bother anyone else.
6. Don't call attention to yourself. (p. 22)

Students who work quickly can cover required material easily, making time for in-depth research or independent study.

Intellectual Peer Teaching   Teachers may encourage peers who are of the same intellectual or academic level to work together on new learnings, accelerated learnings, or reviewed learnings. They may be in the same grade level, or well above.

High School Students   High school students can be used in any of the domains. High school staff can provide information as to which students can serve as mentors, tutors, or mini-course teachers. For example, when classroom teachers deem acceleration to be appropriate in areas where they do not have the expertise, such as higher mathematics, high school mentors can be used very effectively. High school mentors can also be used to teach mini-courses that expose students to topics such as biology or chemistry.

Mentors can work with students on topics related to student interest, introduce students to the mentor's area of expertise, or work with small groups of students.

Computers, Technology, and Telecommunications   Computers today have opened up a whole new world of instruction for students. As software becomes available, various programs can give students a great deal of independence in rate of instruction and quantity of information, allowing the student to move through content at a rapid rate. Telecommunications can make instruction available in any of the content areas for students who are advanced. School districts often discontinue or do not offer courses that are unusual or at advanced levels because there is not enough participation to support paying a teacher. Telecommunications makes it possible for a teacher at one location to teach students at any other location, provided appropriate hardware is in place. Current technology allows students with special needs, for example, those with visual or hearing impairments, to participate with intellectual peers when they are provided with the appropriate devices such as opticons or auditrons.

Computers allow classrooms and students to be connected to the Internet. Instruction can be provided by accessing different Web sites. Students and teachers can use directories and search engines to access information. Search engines are highly focused and directories are compiled by the computer or an individual. Here are some common WWW search engines and directories:

Alta Vista	http://www.altavista.digital.com
Dogpile	http://www.dogpile.com
Excite	http://www.excite.com
Lycos	http://www.lycos.com
Webcrawler	http://www.webcrawler.com
Yahoo (a searchable directory)	http://www.yahoo.com
Magellan	http://www.mckinley.com
Snap Online	http://home.snap.com

Surfing the net is a skill that requires students to select and weed out irrelevant information. It also can be very time consuming. Teachers can provide parents with a list of Web sites that can be explored at home, local libraries, or places that provide access to the Internet. Learning to surf and to distinguish relevant from irrelevant information is an important skill in the new information age.

One of the publications on the market today that assists teachers and students as they make their way through cyberspace is *Classroom Connect* (1866 Colonial Village Lane, P.O. Box 10488, Lancaster, PA 17605-9981). Issues provide information on how to connect to other classrooms, information about educational sites, how to teach with the Internet, etc.

Students and teachers can access sites that are domain specific. Reis and Gavin (1997) recommended several on-line resources for promising mathematics students:

ERIC	http://ericir.syr.edu
Math Forum	http://forum.swarthmore.edu
MathMagic Project	ahodson@tenet.edu

National Council of Teachers of Mathematics   http://www.nctm.org

National Science Teachers Association   http://www.nsta.org

Self-Paced Instruction   Computers are not the only way of providing students with self-paced instruction. Contracts might serve this purpose, commercial kits may be available, or teachers might design other ways for students to advance at their own paces. Are there materials available that can be used for self-paced instruction? Are parts of the curriculum organized so that students can move through quickly with appropriate check points?

Independent Study or Self-Selected Topic   Independent study can take a variety of forms. It can involve a student covering a course of study outside of the class, or can be a strategy guided by the classroom teacher. According to Renzulli (1977) independent study is a preferred learning strategy for the gifted. It can be used if content in other domains is compacted. Independent study is a strategy that demonstrates task orientation and can be used to accommodate learners who have completed other tasks. It can be used when teachers observe parts of the curriculum that have "turned a student on" so that the topic can be explored in greater depth or breath, or as an option for rapid learners who can cover specified curriculum independently or explore topics of interest that are not a part of the school curriculum. It can also identify potential areas of giftedness. For the classroom teacher, Cline (1986) recommends the following steps:

1. Student selects the topic to be studied.
2. Teacher guides the student as the student designs the study and formulates key questions.
3. Student learns the appropriate basic, expanded basic, and research skills relevant to the topic.
4. Teacher reviews the student's basic outline for the study and makes suggestions so that educational ideas that differentiate the curriculum are included.
5. Student and teacher locate appropriate resources for the study.
6. Student conducts necessary research.
7. Student is responsible for broadening or narrowing the topic. Teacher assists when necessary.
8. Student is allowed as much time as is deemed necessary to conduct the research.
9. If the student becomes aware of problems associated with the study, problem-solving strategies are taught which assist in seeking solutions.
10. Student is responsible for designing way in which he or she can communicate what has been learned. Various kinds of media are used. The student chooses the way in which material will be presented, for example, authors

a book, produces a slide-sound program, produces a video, makes a film-strip, presents a chalk talk, etc.

11. Student evaluates what has been accomplished in terms of individual capabilities and assesses independent study as an appropriate learning strategy, helping the students to become educational connoisseurs.

12. Teacher assists in seeking appropriate audiences for completed projects (i.e., classmates, peers, parents, professional publications, contests). (pp. 10–11)

Resource Room/Enrichment Center   Depending on the school, the term *resource room* can have a variety of connotations. It can be a place where children who require remediation are provided with additional instruction, or it can be a place where gifted students can work with a teacher in small groups or individually. If a resource room exists, does it accommodate gifted learners? If not, what needs to be available so that this is possible? Are personnel acquainted with the nature and needs of the gifted? If not, is someone available that can guide? Are the necessary materials available? Teachers and administrators can work together to assist in its development.

Revolving Door   In some school districts, students who are identified as gifted in the regular classroom "revolve" or spend time in a gifted program when they have topics they wish to pursue (Renzulli & Reiss, 1986). In some districts, a specially trained individual may be assigned the task of assisting gifted students in designing appropriate curriculum when they "revolve" in the program. A librarian in a school may be assigned the task.

Acceleration   Acceleration involves the speed at which a student may cover curriculum. It can take place within or outside of the classroom. Some school districts have classes in specific subjects that move through the curriculum more rapidly and may cover two years' worth of work in one year. In some schools, acceleration might involve "skipping" a year of content, moving to the next grade. For highly gifted children this might be a viable option. Domains of giftedness and level of ability should be the determining factors.

Social and emotional issues come into play. Parents, the child, and counselors need to evaluate each individual situation. Acceleration should not be limited by one year or to one subject. Acceleration in one domain can make room for other classes or additional advanced coursework. When acceleration takes place in the classroom, teachers have the responsibility of making sure that when students move into the next grade they will not have to repeat material already covered.

Honors Class   Some school districts group students homogeneously when they reach middle or high school. Honors classes offer students of like ability in particular domains the opportunity to learn an enriched curriculum together. The curriculum covers what has been prescribed for the "regular" class but teachers have the opportunity to accelerate and to enrich and incorporate materials from other disciplines. Honors classes are sometimes precursors to advanced placement classes.

Advanced Placement   Some school districts provide opportunities for students to take advanced placement courses. When students demonstrate the ability to move quickly and with great understanding, these classes allow students to take college-level courses while in high school. Not only does it allow students to maintain a level of challenge, but when college credit is given, it can save time and money later.

Mentor   A mentor is a special person who has expertise in a particular area and works with a student within or outside of the classroom. A mentor may meet with a student on a regular basis or may meet on an "as-needed" basis. Mentors allow learning to be extended beyond the classroom; they create a learning partnership. Mentorships can focus on the design and execution of advanced projects or the exploration of particular work settings. Mentorships are one of the most effective ways of influencing gifted students (Zorman, 1993). Mentors provide role models and are extremely effective when used with culturally diverse populations or populations with disabilities (Frasier, 1992). They may be parents, or they may be recruited from faculty, higher education, or from the community.

Goals of the mentorship need to be clearly stated for mentor, student, and teacher. Information about the student should be provided to the mentor. Progress should be monitored by the mentor and the student.

Other Class   When special abilities are noted, it behooves the classroom teacher to provide opportunities for students to continue to work at a level of challenge. Groups can be formed with students across the same grade, or students may be sent to grades above the chronological age. Students can be moved up in any of the domains.

Internship   The community should be viewed as a resource and companies canvassed to ascertain if internships are available. Internships might provide opportunities for gifted children to "shadow" or accompany professionals as they work.

After School/Extracurricular   If students take it upon themselves to study topics on their own or attend courses at other institutions after school or in the summer, credit should be given.

Provisional Augmentation   Provisional augmentation (Tannenbaum, 1983) refers to the opportunities that a particular teacher is already providing or might provide that are not presently a part of the school curriculum. Provisional augmentation can spark student interest or provide for additional instruction in areas of interest. It can also include topics that can be integrated into existing curriculum; for example, values or leadership education lend themselves well to provisional augmentation. A teacher might expose students to a unit that involves hatching chicks in the classroom.

Community Resident   Community residents can come to schools to speak on a variety of careers that can spark interest in students, or serve as mentors for students on a one-time or regular basis. They might offer to teach a mini-course to students. Certain professions, often those in the medical field, have a day during the week when they might wish to volunteer their services. They may be senior citizens or individuals of any age who have expertise in particular topics. They can work with a student on a one-on-one basis or work with a group of students. It might be a topic they have expertise in, or they might work with students to free up the teacher so that individual attention can be paid to one child.

Special Schools   Special schools might meet the needs of some gifted students. Special schools include those that specialize in particular domains, such as math, science, music, or art. This option depends on the community, available resources, and financial constraints.

Credit by Examination (Testing Out)   If students wish to cover curriculum on their own, and pass the required tests, they should be permitted to do so (AEGIS, 1998). Some states have developed formal policies for the procedure. For instance, West Virginia allows students to test out for credit (126 CSR 42, State Board of Education Policy 2510). Policy 2510 provides students the opportunity to earn credit for a course by demonstrating mastery of the content. It provides that the test be developed at the school or district level by the teacher(s) credentialed and assigned to teach the course. The test is comprehensive and provides students with an opportunity to demonstrate mastery of the entire course. Standards used to evaluate performance of students would be the same as those following the traditional course of study. Students may elect to test out of a maximum of one course per semester.

Grade Skipping   Grade skipping is different from acceleration in that a child actually "skips" a year, rather than moving through content at a faster pace. In some cases grade skipping may be a viable option. Depending on the district, the child, and the family, grade skipping can be considered. Questions to be considered: How mature is the student? Physical and emotional factors need to be considered. How advanced is the individual? What other options could be made available?

Combined Classes   Are there opportunities for teachers to work together and form groups so that each teacher can work with students in areas where gifts have surfaced and teachers are inclined to provide guidance?

Correspondence Courses   When correspondence courses are available and students avail themselves of the opportunity, and succeed in meeting prescribed requirements, students should be given credit. Here are two examples of these types of courses:

- High school and university math programs are available on CD-ROM and by mail from Stanford University. Contact Ted Alper, Mathematics Instruction Coordinator, EPGY, Ventura Hall, Stanford, CA 94305-4115; e-mail: alper@epgy.stanford.edu.

- High-level high school mathematics correspondence course from I. M. Gelfand, Rutgers University. Contact Harriet Schweitzer, Associate Director, Rutgers University Center for Math, Science and Computer Education, SERC Building, Room 239, Busch Campus, Piscataway, NJ 08855-1179; e-mail: harriets@gandalf.rutgers.edu.

Pull-Out Program   In some schools, students who have been identified as gifted are taken out of the classroom to work with a teacher. The amount of time varies from a few hours per week to a whole day. Sometimes cycles are used, where students will be placed in a program for a few weeks or months.

Combining Opportunities   One of the opportunities mentioned in the correspondence course section that combines opportunities is the mathematics program developed at Stanford University and available through John Hopkins. The EPGY program allows students to receive math instruction at home using CD-ROMs that track student progress. Students are provided with more challenging material as they achieve mastery of content. A tutor is assigned to the student and communicates with the student through the Internet and by telephone. How might teachers combine opportunities for students that might include books, computers, and/or mentors?

Teachers can develop a database for a class, or a schoolwide database can be developed to assist in the development of resources to assist in programming. When gifts are noted in areas not specifically provided for in the curriculum, specialists should be called and parents notified. If the school does not have a way of cultivating a particular talent, parents might wish to go outside of the school or seek special schools.

Finding Appropriate Audiences   Teachers can also seek appropriate audiences for students' work so that students are recognized and applauded for their efforts. One means of doing this is through participation in writing contests. Consider these examples:

- The "Publish a Book" contest for grades 2–3 and 4–5 is sponsored by the Raintree/Steck-Vaughn Publishing Company, P.O. Box 26015, Austin, TX 78755.
- "Written and Illustrated By" is sponsored by Landmark Editions, Inc., P.O. Box 4469, Kansas City, MO 64127.
- *Merlyn's Pen* is a magazine that publishes student writing in an attempt to broaden and reward young authors' interests in writing and to strengthen the self-confidence of beginning writers. *Merlyn's Pen,* P.O. Box 1058, East Greenwich, RI 02818.
- *Young Author's Guide to Publishers* introduces students to the writing and publishing process and lists possible sources for publication. This publication is distributed by Raspberry Publications, Inc., P.O. Box 925, Westerville, OH 43086-6925.

Math fairs, science competitions, art exhibits, and musical, dance, or dramatic performances are also venues for exhibiting student work. Local schools and communities often sponsor such events, as do some companies. For example, Westinghouse Awards are presented to students in both mathematical and science categories. Students enter the competition in high school and winners receive monetary awards.

If our children are to achieve in the particular domains in which they are gifted, they have to be introduced to those domains, learn the basic skills involved, be exposed to advanced basic skills, and be introduced to professionals in those fields and learn about their world of work. In this way, the gifted can be provided with an education that allows them to become producers of information in our society (Tannenbaum, 1983).

CONCLUSION

As teachers work with students in classrooms, it will become apparent that student profiles vary greatly. Some students will require minor modifications to the curriculum that can be accommodated in the classroom. For others, meeting their needs might present greater challenges and might not be accomplished all at once. Exceptionally gifted students should surface as challenging materials are presented. Individual intelligence tests may provide clues as to the gifts of a special child, but the tests must be structured such that they are not negatively influenced by culture or disability. Physical and educational accommodations need to be made in and out of the classroom, sometimes requiring more than one option or more than one opportunity for acceleration.

Teachers need to determine how to begin to structure classrooms so that they are comfortable. Resources and support need to be sought and evaluated. The classroom can be structured so that strategies for differentiation and programming are integrated, maintaining a comfort level for teacher and student.

If we are to help the gifted reach their potential in an inclusive classroom, we need to weave appropriate curricula for the gifted into the fabric of the school. To do so, we need to assess each student in terms of individual potential in each domain, as we develop a continuum of services that provides able students with challenging educational opportunities in all content areas. This task cannot be accomplished without including the classroom teacher in the process of identifying problems and finding solutions. Furthermore, research indicates that many veteran teachers lack the skill and/or the will to design educational settings that can accommodate gifted learners (Archambault et al., 1993; Tomlinson, 1995a; Westberg, Archambault, Dobyns, & Slavin, 1993). All teachers—veterans, newcomers, and those studying to enter the profession—need to be introduced to the many faces of giftedness, to learn how to identify the gifted, plan for them, and provide optimal matches between students and curriculum. Research supports the effectiveness of trained teachers in gifted education (Karnes & Wharton, 1996). Every teacher wants to meet the needs of all of the children in the classroom—and they can do so when provided with the appropriate educational background and administrative support!

Section 2

Twice Exceptional: Gifted Children with Disabilities

Chapter 3 : **Gifted Children with Physical Disabilities**

Chapter 4 : **Gifted Children with Sensory Impairments**

Chapter 5 : **Gifted Children with Learning Problems**

Some populations have been underrepresented in programs for the gifted (Whitmore, 1987). These underrepresented populations include students with physical disabilities, those with sensory impairments, and those with learning problems.

In Chapter 3, we discuss the need to include gifted children who are physically disabled in the regular classroom when the appropriate supports are provided. Physical disabilities do not necessarily affect intellectual ability. With the appropriate physical and emotional support, gifted children who are disabled should have the same opportunities as other gifted children.

Gifted children with hearing impairments are the subject of Chapter 4. Gifted children who are hearing impaired should have special supports, depending on the degree of impairment. Teachers need to keep in mind that students with hearing impairments born to hearing parents are deprived early on of the metacognitive interaction with parents that fosters intellectual development. Furthermore, American Sign Language has no relationship to the English language and presents additional challenges for these students.

Chapter 4 also considers gifted children with visual impairments. In this chapter the challenges involved in educating visually impaired gifted children are discussed. Conventional IQ tests will not reveal the intellectual abilities of gifted children with sensory impairments. Some of the obstacles to identification include developmental delays and incomplete information about the child. Gifted children who are visually impaired require a dual curriculum to compensate for challenges presented by the impairment.

Challenges involved in educating children with learning disabilities are discussed in Chapter 5. IQ profiles of intellectually gifted children with learning disabilities will reveal discrepancies between verbal and performance scores. These discrepancies can serve to identify gifted children with learning disabilities. When strengths are noted and accommodations made, these children are capable of achieving at high levels.

Chapter 5 also includes a discussion of gifted students who have been diagnosed with attention deficit hyperactivity disorder (AD/HD). Gifted children with AD/HD can be cognitively able, while children with learning disabilities have specific deficits that interfere with performance. Qualified professionals need to be consulted inasmuch as there is no single test to diagnose AD/HD. Once identified, special accommodations should be made.

CHALLENGES INVOLVED IN IDENTIFICATION OF GIFTED CHILDREN WITH DISABILITIES

According to Whitmore and Maker (1985), the following obstacles might prevent gifted individuals with disabilities from reaching their potential:

- *Stereotypic expectations:* Misconceptions concerning the gifted have been created by the Terman studies. Lewis Terman insisted on asserting that the IQ was the determiner of future eminence even though there were critics who repudiated the notion.

Terman's work has been difficult to refute even though the debate continues today as to whether the selected sample achieved eminence. Five volumes have been published to verify and confirm his ideas (Burks, Jensen, & Terman, 1930; Cox et al., 1926; Terman, 1925; Terman & Oden, 1947, 1959). Terman and Oden (1959) studied the mental and physical traits of 1,000 gifted children. He selected and conducted follow-up studies of nearly 1,500 children from California. He gathered data that included racial and social origin, intellectually superior relatives, vital statistics about families, anthropometric measurements, health and physical characteristics, medical examinations, school and educational history, school accomplishments, specialization of abilities, scholastics, occupations and other interests, play interests (including sociability), reading interests, influence of interests on school achievement, and character and personality traits.

Volume II (Cox et al., 1926) addressed the early mental traits of 300 geniuses. Using eminence as a criterion for genius, Terman rated 301 men and women on behavior and performance in childhood and early youth. These individuals were given a perceived IQ. In Volume III (Burks et al., 1930), Terman retested his subjects and noted educational progress, scholastic achievement by grade and by Stanford Achievement scores, scholastic and other interests, vocational plans and vocational achievements, social and personality traits, health history and vital statistics, family statistics and sibling tests, and special ability groups. He included case studies and concluded with a composite portrait of the gifted child that is often quoted in the literature, leading us to believe that gifted children exceeded norms in all areas of development, were good looking, and were motivated and mature.

- *Developmental delays:* Depending on the disability, cognitive development and intellectual performance may limit a child's ability to respond to stimulation. For instance, children with visual impairments show some developmental delay in abstract thinking that is related to the absence of visual images.

- *Incomplete information about the child:* Complete information about health, home, extra school activities, and performance in school is necessary to properly diagnose intellectual giftedness.
- *No opportunity to develop superior mental abilities:* A large segment of the population is overlooked because of a lack of opportunity to develop and demonstrate exceptional abilities.

Discussions with professionals reveal that individuals in segregated settings can develop a learned helplessness, can be sheltered, so that they do not develop simple, everyday problem-solving skills.

Looking at giftedness through another lens reveals that accurate identifiers of abilities would include the following: aptitude in a specific domain, ability to communicate ideas (providing communication devices or support when necessary), problem-solving skills, creative production or thought, and retention and use of knowledge.

INTERVENTIONS FOR INTELLECTUALLY GIFTED CHILDREN WITH DISABILITIES

Intellectual giftedness in individuals with disabilities can be identified when students are provided with instruction that facilitates exposure to each of the domains. Supports and devices that allow disabilities to be overcome, such as hearing devices, supportive equipment, optical devices, communication devices, and wheelchairs, as well as instructional accommodations, are needed.

If potential talents are to be identified in children with disabilities, these students should be placed in environments that stimulate performance. Subsequent assessment should not be clouded by the disabling conditions. Disabling conditions might include sensory impairments, such as hearing or visual problems.

HOW TO ESTABLISH GENERAL GUIDELINES FOR INCLUDING INDIVIDUALS WITH DISABILITIES IN REGULAR CLASSROOMS

If intellectually gifted disabled students are to be placed in regular classrooms, administrators and teachers need to do the following:

- Determine if children and parents are emotionally ready to support the transition.
- Assess the disability and determine whether the school environment can physically support the disability; for example, can hallways, bathrooms, and tables accommodate wheelchairs?
- Assess the school's ability to support the psychological needs of students with disabilities.
- Obtain any supports, material resources, physical adaptations, and human resources necessary to support the condition.
- Provide sensitivity training for students and teachers. Children with disabilities should not be placed in settings where teachers and students have not been sensitized to the condition. Role playing and simulation games concerning the affective needs of students with disabilities are some of the important strategies that can be used to ensure success, allowing individuals to look beyond the disability. A disability does not necessarily affect intellectual functioning.
- Establish connections and enlist ongoing support of specialists and agencies that have expertise in special areas.
- Establish networks of support from home and community for staff and students.
- Evaluate and assess success for the student, the teacher, and the class.

With the appropriate staff development, training, and support, whenever feasible, including all members of society in an inclusive classroom is necessary if gifts are to be identified. Inclusion must take place on a case-by-case basis and will take time. In special cases, meeting the needs of the individuals involved might still require segregated settings. Teachers in regular classrooms or in segregated settings need to view students in terms of what they can do and then plan in areas of students' strengths. The IQ test and the myths created over the years as to who the gifted are must be dispelled if gifted children are to meet their potential.

Chapter 3
Gifted Children with Physical Disabilities

Typical questions a classroom teacher might ask include these:

How do physical disabilities affect performance?

What special provisions should be made?

Is my school and, in particular, my classroom designed to accommodate intellectually gifted persons with disabilities?

Do I need special training?

Will my students be accepting?

To answer these questions, this chapter does the following:

Discusses challenges involved in identifying gifted persons with physical disabilities.

Outlines appropriate physical accommodations.

Outlines curricular modifications.

DEFINITION

The range and variety of physical disabilities is extensive. Children can be born with physical disabilities or acquire them after birth through disease or accident. Children with physical disabilities are served through the Individuals with Disabilities Act (IDEA) under three categories: (1) orthopedic impairments, (2) multiple disabilities, and (3) health impairments.

Although special and general educators and state and local agencies use the term *physical disabilities* to describe students with neural motor problems, IDEA defines this group of students as orthopedically impaired. Orthopedic impairments are defined by the IDEA as follows:

> Orthopedic impairment means a severe orthopedic impairment that adversely affects a child's educational performance. The term includes impairments caused by congenital anomaly (e.g., club foot, absence of some member, etc.) impairments caused by disease (e.g., poliomyelitis, bone tuberculosis, etc.), and impairments from other causes, (e.g., cerebral palsy, amputations, and fractures or burns that cause contractures).

Multiple disabilities refers to concomitant impairments that cannot be addressed singly. Other health impairments (OHI) are defined by IDEA as follows:

> Having limited strength, vitality, or alertness due to chronic or acute health problems such as a heart condition, tuberculosis, rheumatic fever, nephritis,

learned how to write fast to try to keep up. I learned my math. I used to take down as much as I could by dictation whenever the teacher was kind enough to read out loud.

I didn't have any assistance and I ran into a lot of social problems. There was never anyone to intervene on my behalf. In sixth grade, I didn't make the SP (Special Progress) because my parents were told that my IQ was too low. I had to be two years ahead in math and reading. I was over the cutoff point in reading but missed the math. I took the test when I had just returned to school after an ailment and they wouldn't retest me. My IQ test was a group test with standard print. I couldn't finish it. My parents were told that my score was low and that they were pushing me. They were told to back off, when they weren't pushing me at all.

In eighth grade I was put into a sight conservation class, which encouraged students with vision problems not to use their sight. I was placed in regular classes and they helped me along, but I did not make the SP. In eighth and ninth grades, a resource teacher was assigned to help me who didn't know what to do. They read my visual report and said that it must be a mistake. They couldn't believe my vision was that bad and that I was able to keep up. They would not allow me to take any of the tests for the special schools in New York City for bright students. I was told that I shouldn't want to do that because of my vision.

In ninth grade, I made Arista [an honor society for academic achievement in the public schools] because I had over a ninety average. One of the strongest memories I have is of a contest I entered. Students were asked to write essays regarding citizenship, scholarship, and service. We were told that the three top essays would be read to the assembly. We weren't supposed to put our names on them. When the assistant principal found out that mine was one of the three chosen, and that I was in sight conservation, she called me into her office and told me that I wouldn't want to do it because it would be embarrassing. She told me to read it to her so that she could see how it would look at the assembly. She told me how awful it looked because I held the paper right up to my face and that I wouldn't want to embarrass everybody. I refused to back down, so I memorized the entire essay and pretended to read it. After that experience I lost my voice for a few days. Even though I was provided with a resource teacher, it was of no help because she wouldn't even run interference for me. She even allowed the school to kick me out of a sewing class.

In ninth grade I was given a hand two-and-a-half magnification monocular optical device which allowed me to see the chalkboard in front of me. I also started using magnifiers. Today I use much more powerful instruments.

located in because I required special transportation. I enjoyed being in the program. It provided me with a sense of choice, control, and challenge. I enjoyed participating in the stimulating discussions that took place.

I was accepted as a student at a university that is friendly to individuals with disabilities. I am enjoying attending. I am doing well and am actively involved in the school. I would like to pursue a doctorate in English.

I asked Amanda about her social life.

I really didn't have much of a social life until I was sixteen or seventeen. I don't have any problems now. I have friends on campus that have disabilities and some who don't. I am friendly and get along well with others. I notice that there are some students here with disabilities that are still harboring some anger and resentment and do not have very good social skills.

asthma, sickle cell anemia, hemophilia, seizure disorder, lead poisoning, leukemia, or diabetes that adversely affect a child's educational performance.

CHARACTERISTICS

Medical conditions, health problems, and physical limitations are the distinguishing characteristics of children with physical disabilities. Figure 3.1 lists some of the many types of physical disabilities experienced by our school-age children. Unfortunately, individuals having any of these conditions in regular classrooms, or in segregated settings, are often viewed in terms of their disability, thus hiding potential gifts. Remediation of deficits takes precedence over developing areas of strength.

IDENTIFICATION

There is a paucity of literature regarding the identification and nurturance of intellectually gifted individuals with physical disabilities. Johnsen and Corn (1989) reported that a review of the literature for students with sensory or physical disabilities revealed fewer than ten articles had been written since 1981 about gifted students with sensory and physical disabilities. A recent search for research involving gifted and physical disabilities revealed very little. The only case cited involved gifted students with cerebral palsy.

The customary identification methods such as standardized tests and observational checklists are not adequate. Problems involved include these:

- Inability to respond to tests requiring verbal responses.
- Limited mobility, which can inhibit performance on tests requiring hand manipulation.

Anomalies: Congenital malformation, such as the absence of a limb or the presence of an extra finger

Arthrogryposis: A birth defect characterized by joint rigidity or limitations in joint movement

Bronchopulmonary dysplasia: A chronic lung disorder that might require ventilator support

Cerebral palsy: Spastic or loss of voluntary motor control, which may cause difficulties in speaking

Dermatomyositis: Inflammation of the skin and tenderness and weakness of the muscles

Dwarfism: Forms of dwarfism include achondroplasia (bulky forehead, saddle nose, lumbar lordosis, bow legs), hypochondroplasia (milder degree of achondroplasia), dystrophic dysplasia (severe dwarfing with rigid hitchhiking thumbs)

Dysautonomia: Disorder of the autonomic nervous system, which controls such essential body functions as digestion, blood pressure, and temperature control

Dystonia: Dystonic movements that result in sustained, often bizarre postures

Lamellar ichthyosis: Excessive accumulation of scale on the skin surface, which can cause restriction in mobility

Morquio syndrome: Abnormal musculoskeletal development in childhood, which can cause dwarfism, hunchback, enlarged sternum, and knock-knees

Muscular dystrophy: A group of hereditary muscle-destroying disorders

Myasthenia gravis: Disorder of neuromuscular transmission

Osteogenesis imperfecta: Bones do not grow normally in length and thickness and break easily

Polio: Viral infection that affects cells of the spinal cord and can cause paralysis

Prader Willi syndrome: Tendency toward severe obesity

Respiratory conditions: Complications from respiratory conditions that may require tracheostomies, continuous oxygen, or dependance on a respirator

Spina bifida: A nonprogressive malformation of the spinal cord frequently accompanied by hydro-cephalus; the higher the spinal defect the more severe the loss of function

Spinal muscular atrophy: Disease that affects the spinal cord, resulting in degeneration of nerve cells and causing weaknesses in muscles

Spinal cord injuries: Generally caused by accidents, paralysis and lack of sensation can result in paraplegia or quadriplegia

Tar syndrome: Absence of lower arm bone usually accompanied by a blood disorder

Traumatic brain injury: Traumatic situation causing damage to the head that may result in coma and cause a lowered level of intellectual functioning, at least temporarily

Figure 3.1 **Physical disabilities experienced by school-age children**
Although IDEA refers to physical disabilities as orthopedic impairments, most practitioners in special education use the term physical disabilties to refer to a very broad range of students.

- Limited life experiences due to impaired mobility, which can artificially lower scores.
- Attempts to compare them with "average" students. Because gifted children attempt to compensate for their weaknesses, they may appear closer to "average." Whitmore and Maker (1985) recommend they be compared to children with similar disabilities to properly assess levels of giftedness.

Willard-Holt (1994) cites two case studies which found that gifted students who have cerebral palsy exhibit indicators of cognitive ability similar to nondisabled gifted students, but recognition is inhibited by communication barriers. When alternative forms of communication were established, subjects learned quickly and displayed a sophisticated sense of humor. They exhibited maturity beyond their years and exhibited characteristics of motivation, persistence, determination, patience, and goal orientation. One of the subjects showed gifts in art and the other in writing and math. Both students were in mainstreamed settings where they interacted with nondisabled students.

Whitmore and Maker (1985) cite a case study of Herb, an individual with quadriplegia. Interviews with Herb revealed his aptitude for science and writing. The principal of the school was not supportive of his entry in the science fairs but allowed him to do so. He won high awards in two state-level science fairs. In addition to his scientific aptitude, they reported Herb to be a persistent individual who always sought ways of accomplishing a higher quality of work. His persistence helped him to complete a college education and to obtain employment in his field even though he had many obstacles to overcome. Herb attributes part of his success to being involved in a school that included students with and without disabilities. He reported that one of the greatest obstructions to success in his life was his parents. Fortunately, their low expectations served to motivate him to attempt to reach higher heights.

Whitmore and Maker (1985) make a case for additional research that would benefit the development of intellectual giftedness in disabled persons.

INTERVENTIONS

According to Willard-Holt (1994), the two major obstacles to programming for gifted students with physical disabilities are (1) identifying the student's need for services and (2) designing the context and content of educational interventions that address cognitive and physical needs.

Interventions for the physically disabled need to begin with providing necessary supports for them.

ASSISTIVE TECHNOLOGY FOR INDIVIDUALS WITH PHYSICAL DISABILITIES

The IDEA defines an *assistive technology device* as follows:

Any item, piece of equipment or product system, whether acquired commercially off the shelf, modified or customized, that is used to increase, maintain, or improve the functional capabilities of children with disabilities. (IDEA, Public Law 101-476, 20 U.S.C., Chapter 33, Sec. 1401 (26))

Assistive technology can be considered "low" technology (for example, the everyday simple device such as a pencil grip) or "high" technology, such as sophisticated computerized voice synthesizers.

Assistive technology can include aids such as supportive equipment that helps individuals adapt to their environment, assistive equipment that partially or fully replaces the lost capability in order to assist people in increasing their functional capability, or rehabilitative equipment used in therapy or rehabilitation to help regain lost physical functioning.

Assistive devices might include the following:

- Devices necessary for feeding, grooming, fastening clothing, or sleeping
- Communication devices, which might include special typewriters, hearing aids, machines for dialing telephones
- *In situ* motion such as braces or splints
- Travel accommodations such as wheelchairs, canes, walkers, or crutches
- Adaptation devices, such as cooking utensils for people with one hand or driving aids
- Rehabilitation devices used to exercise body parts and measure physical functioning.

Assistive technology redefines what is possible for students with disabilities and increases their ability to realize their full potential. It increases self-esteem because it allows the student to be more independent and productive and integrated into the school environment. By lessening the impact of the disability, assistive technology can enhance social acceptance with peers through increased social interactions. The technology can provide the opportunity for potential gifts in students to surface.

ISSUES AND CONCERNS

Including students with giftedness and physical disabilities in the regular classroom involves special considerations concerning assistive technology and medical concerns.

Medical Concerns

- In addition to the child's primary disorder, does the child have additional problems, such as seizures, diabetes, sensory disorders?
- Does the child take medication? If so, how frequently and in what amounts? Are there any possible side effects? Who is authorized to dispense medication?
- What procedures should be followed in the event of a seizure, insulin shock, diabetic coma, or other problem with regard to contacting the child's parents or medical personnel?
- Should the child's activities be restricted in any way?

Travel

- How will the child be transported to school?
- Will the child arrive and leave at the usual times?
- Will someone need to meet the child at the entrance to school?
- Will the child need special accommodations to travel within the school building or classroom?

Transfer and Lifting

- What is the preferred way to lift and transfer the child into and out of a wheelchair?
- What cautions or limitations are there regarding transfer and lifting?
- How much help does the child really need with movement and transfer?

Communication

- Does the child have a speech or language problem? Consult the speech–language pathologist.
- If the child does not communicate verbally, what particular or unique means of communication does the child use?
- Can the child write or type? Is specialized equipment required?
- Can the child make his or her needs known to the teacher? How?

Self-Care

- What type of help does the child need with daily living skills such as feeding, toileting, dressing?
- What equipment does the child need (i.e., straws, special cup, metal utensils, extensions of utensils)?

Positioning

- What positioning aids or devices does the child use (i.e., braces, wedges, pillows)?
- What particular positions are most useful for specific academic activities?
- What positions are useful for resting, toileting, feeding, dressing?

Intervention involves sensitizing other students in the class to the social and emotional concerns involved. Discussions with individuals with physical disabilities reveal sensitivities that should be addressed. Individuals with disabilities should be spoken to directly. They should not be stared at or ignored. They should not be pointed at, pitied or spoken about behind their backs. They should be treated fairly—not ridiculed or embarrassed. In other words, they should be treated like any other child.

If an individual with a disability needs help, offer assistance. Include students with disabilities in activities whenever possible. Underneath the disability they are just as human as you are.

Reviewing the biographies of gifted individuals with disabilities reveals that they may have gifts in one domain or many. They can be included in the regular classroom with the appropriate support. If the appropriate support is not available, and they remain in segregated settings, attempts should be made to link the students with students in regular classrooms through telecommunication or e-mail. Exposure to all of the intelligences (except those that might be limited due to the disability) will allow gifts to surface. Activities that support inter- and intrapersonal skill development should be emphasized to increase sensitivity for teachers and students.

Strategies for differentiating the curriculum would take the same form as with any other gifted individual. Provisions should ensure that appropriate devices that support the requirements of the disability are in place.

Support staff, which includes counselors, physical therapists, emergency services, physicians and nurses, should be provided. When groups are formed, care should be given to placing children in settings where the disability is supported. For example cooperative grouping might allow one student to compensate for the disability of another. Whenever possible, mentors should be provided.

Chapter 4

Gifted Children with Sensory Impairments

Typical questions a classroom teacher might ask include these:

How do sensory impairments affect performance?

What special provisions should be made?

Is my school and, in particular, my classroom designed to accommodate intellectually gifted persons with sensory impairments?

Do I need special training?

Will my students be accepting?

To answer these questions, this chapter does the following:

Discusses challenges involved in identifying persons with sensory impairments.

Outlines appropriate accommodations.

Outlines curricular modifications.

THE GIFTED CHILD WITH A HEARING IMPAIRMENT

Definition

Hearing loss is difficult to define because one cannot be certain at which time one's hearing stops being normal and becomes a disability. However, the most commonly accepted set of definitions regards hearing impairment as a generic term indicating a hearing disability that may range in severity from mild to profound. It includes the subsets of deaf and hard of hearing. The IDEA defines deafness as a hearing impairment that is so severe the child is impaired in processing linguistic information through hearing, with or without amplification, which adversely affects a child's educational performance. Turnbull, Turnbull, Shank, and Leal (1995, p. 554) cite Moores' definitions as follows: Being deaf means that "hearing is disabled to an extent that precludes understanding speech through the ear alone, with or without a hearing aid. . . . " Being hearing impaired or hard of hearing "makes difficult, but does not preclude, the understanding of speech through the ear alone, without or with a hearing aid" (Moores, 1987).

Disorders of hearing are described as conductive impairments, sensorineural impairments, or mixed impairments (Hallahan & Kauffman, 1997). *Conductive impairments* include any dysfunction of the outer or middle ear in the presence of a normal inner ear. Acquired hearing losses in children are most often of the conductive type. Individuals with a conductive impairment can understand what they hear, provided that speech is made loud enough.

PERSONAL INTERVIEW
John's Story

John is a gifted child with a severe hearing loss. John went to a private nursery and kindergarten where he had received speech therapy. He was always in a regular classroom but was pulled out for speech therapy. John's elementary school had a program for the gifted, but he was not placed in a gifted program until middle school. At the time of this interview, John was a senior at Skidmore College majoring in biochemistry. He planned to interview for placement at Cornell Medical School. At this time he had a 3.75 grade point average and had received departmental honors in biochemistry. He would be graduating magna cum laude.

When did you become interested in medicine?

My grandfather and uncle were both doctors. I have always been fascinated with medicine.

Are there any aspects of school that are difficult for you because of the hearing loss?

No.

What kind of supports do you use at school?

An auditory trainer; an auditory trainer is a transmitting device. The professor wears a microphone and I wear a receiver. I hear the professor without any background interruptions.

Has anyone taught you to lip read? Are there any other supports that you use?

I taught myself how to lip read. The people at Skidmore have constantly inquired to see if there was anything else that I needed, but I don't. Even before I entered they inquired as to my needs.

Does Cornell have any special programs for persons with hearing impairments?

No, but they know about me.

When did you become aware that you had a hearing problem?

I remember that I was quite young. I was not aware, but my parents were. A construction worker was working with a jackhammer and I didn't hear him. I had learned how to read lips so the loss was not too evident. I remember when they first gave me hearing aids. I went outside and started hearing things. I became frightened and started crying.

Does your hearing loss present any problems for you?

No.

What advice would you give to others who work with individuals with hearing impairments?

Treat them normally. Don't underestimate people with disabilities. So many do. I just know. I felt there were individuals who were uncomfortable with me.

Did you have any experiences where you felt the hearing loss was a problem?

I have felt that some people have been uncomfortable. I had one teacher in high school who was very uncomfortable using the auditory trainer. It worked out, but it took some convincing.

Did anyone in school ever let you know they thought you were bright?

The teachers I had for speech therapy thought I was bright, but it was not until I got to college that anyone else took notice. I wondered why. In college my teachers and other students have remarked about my abilities. Now my peers come to me for help and make comments like "I can't believe how smart you are." The difference is dramatic. Until college people didn't seem to care. Maybe they are fascinated. At Skidmore they want to write an article about me. I conducted a session for students in the Honor Society and the school newspaper received messages asking that they write an article about me.

What advice would you give to someone with a hearing loss?

Don't let anything stand in your way. If you set your mind to do something, then go for it. If you need help along the way, ask for it. People will help you.

We also interviewed John's mother, who has a younger son with a minimal hearing loss.

When did you become aware that John might have a hearing disability?

Probably when he was a year and a half old. He was making sounds but he really wasn't saying any words and the few words he did say were not correctly said. He would refer to "light" as "ite." His vocabulary was very small. We started testing him when he was almost two. We took him to different physicians. Looking back now, I see that this was the wrong approach. We should have gone directly to the Hearing and Speech Center. We tried different physicians. The comments that we got were that he was not ready to speak yet, or he had nothing to say. One doctor took a spoon and banged the leg of a table that had chrome legs. John reacted and he told us that he heard. Whether he heard the vibration or the actual sound, I don't know, but that wasn't the answer we were looking for.

We then took him for a hearing test and he was smart enough to fool them. Unfortunately, he tested borderline normal. He was about two to two and a half. From there we took him to a neurologist who gave him an EEG. It came out normal. We then went upstate to see a pediatric neurologist. He looked at the results of the hearing test and he interviewed us. His diagnosis was congenital aphasia. He told us that day, when John was two and a half years old, that he would never speak. That was his diagnosis. I went home and went to sleep. My husband said that the diagnosis was ridiculous; he must be wrong.

We went to Long Island Jewish Hospital. John was tested psychologically. The psychologist was astounded at how quickly John was able to complete puzzles. She was sitting there with a stopwatch. He was so fast that she couldn't believe it. She sent us to a speech pathologist who tested him. She couldn't figure out what was wrong. She told us we had nothing to lose by sending him for speech therapy.

After one session the speech therapist came back to us and told us that there was nothing wrong with our son other than he had a severe hearing loss. This was without any formal tests. She said she would work with him so that he would not be able to fool the audiologist. She worked with him. He was tested and has been tested since then. From that test on, each test he was diagnosed as having a severe hearing loss. I don't know what happened the first time.

As a result, they recommended two hearing aids. John was almost four years old. It was the most amazing thing to behold. He was frightened as they put the wax in his ears for the molds. He cried and cried. He absolutely refused to put the hearing aids on. We came home and literally forced him. He walked outside and it was unbelievable. For the first time he heard the birds and the cars. He was frightened. He went to private nursery school and kindergarten. A speech therapist at the school worked with him, and he went to a private speech therapist three times a week.

Did anyone ever tell you how bright he was?

No. No one ever discussed any scores with me that indicated he was gifted. When I look at his college grades, it is unbelievable. At one time we went for counseling. The one thing that was emphasized was that our child was normal. He had a hearing loss but that was it. We were told we must treat him normally. Sometimes I feel guilty that we never said, "Poor John." Maybe we should coddle him more.

What were some of the challenges you faced?

It can be very frustrating. I remember vividly one day he wanted "bird" for lunch. I couldn't figure out what he wanted. Was it chicken? Egg? I finally took him to the refrigerator. He wanted Friendship cottage cheese. It had a blue bird on the container. I would never have figured it out. It wasn't easy. It was very frustrating. Teachers have not always been sensitive to John. We had an incident in elementary school where he had a teacher who criticized him continuously. She never had anything good to say. We both felt so uncomfortable all year. I have found that having two hearing-impaired children results in certain problems that we had as parents that fortunately my friends did not have. I would relate certain instances to tell how I was feeling and they just couldn't understand.

Is there any advice you would give to others who face a similar challenge?

Give the child whatever extra help he needs in term of the disability. John never needed tutors or help in class. But it should be provided when necessary. Recognize and reward the abilities. His intellectual capabilities were not recognized until he got to college. Only his speech therapists appreciated him.

Next, John and his mother (Mrs. S) responded to questions about John's social life. His mother reported that John's social life has always been a problem. John had told the interviewer earlier that he was very sensitive to those around him in terms of how they handled his disability.

What were some of the difficulties you encountered?

I always had a hard time socially in school. Kids can be mean. In a group or in a loud room where you can't hear someone, you keep saying "What? What? What?" The other person gets discouraged and won't talk to you anymore. That discourages me. It makes me withdraw. I back away. I don't deal with it anymore. I should explain to that person that I can't hear in this setting and they need to speak up or we need talk outside.

Should the school help with social aspects of development?

No one has ever tried, but they should. The awareness of the staff has to be elevated. If they are unaware of the problems then they don't know how to treat you.

Have you developed ways of compensating for your hearing loss?

Because one of my senses is impaired, my other senses are keener. I believe my sense of smell and sight are very keen. I was a very good lip reader. I picked this up on my own. I could read a conversation taking place across the room.

The following excerpt is a report from a speech therapist who worked with John from preschool through elementary school.

My experience with John was unlike any other in my career. I have never met a brighter person. John demanded to be taught. He grasped ideas and concepts rapidly—sometimes before his language had caught up to the pace of his thinking. I have never seen anyone synthesize information the way John did. I was lucky to be around early on when much of what John learned was a first presentation, unadulterated by repetition. It made it easy to see the process of comprehension, retention, and application in its purest form. John was amazing.

Hearing-impaired children do not learn abstractions—concrete concepts are where most of them get stuck. John grasped abstract concepts quite early. He was able to have a metalinguistic conversation (I think while he was still at private nursery or kindergarten) and we would spend a great deal of time discussing word meaning.

Hearing-impaired children do not recognize subtlety. Humor is often difficult for them to grasp. John was a very serious boy, but he did get jokes and occasionally would make some of his own. There was nothing about John that suggested a handicap except his hearing aids. However, he was so obviously exceptional that another child in his class requested hearing aids so he could be as smart as John. Teaching John was a combination of remediation and enrichment. I needed to make sure that he didn't miss classroom instruction and I filled in the gaps when they existed. On the other hand, I also had to respond to John's demand for information. He did what you have told me gifted children do; he would wring every last drop from a subject. My sessions with him were frequently a mixture of teaching vocabulary so he could keep up with the class, and probing the depths of some subject. We hit the library often to do research. By third grade, John had exhausted my fund of information on most topics.

I consider myself lucky in my career choice. I have been enriched by my association with children, and I have learned much from each of them. John was by far my best tutor. He showed me that the word handicap *is a relative term, and that what you learn in graduate school is only the loosest of guidelines. His success in academia and in his personal life does not surprise me. I could have predicted it in kindergarten.*

Hearing loss due to pathology in the inner ear or along the nerve pathway from the inner ear to the brainstem is referred to as a *sensorineural impairment*. A "pure" sensorineural impairment exists when the sound-conducting mechanism, that is, the outer and middle ear, is normal in every respect. Sound is conducted properly to the fluid of the inner ear, but it cannot be analyzed or perceived normally (Newby, 1964). This individual does not hear his own voice or the voices of others normally and may speak in a loud voice that is inappropriate.

A *mixed impairment* refers to the combination of a conductive and a sensorineural hearing loss.

Table 4.1 is a general classification guide to the degree of severity of hearing losses.

Table 4.1   **Relationship of degree of impairment to understanding of language and speech**

Average of the Speech Frequencies in Better Ear (dB)		**Effect of Hearing Loss on Understanding of Language and Speech**
Slight	27–40	May have difficulty hearing faint or distant speech. May experience some difficulty with language arts subjects.
Mild	41–55	Understands conversational speech at a distance of 3–5 feet (face to face). May miss as much as 50 percent of class discussions if voices are faint or not in line of vision. May exhibit limited vocabulary and speech anomalies.
Marked	56–70	Conversation must be loud to be understood. Will have increased difficulty in group discussions. Is likely to have defective speech. Is likely to be deficient in speech and language usage and comprehension. Will have limited vocabulary.
Severe	71–90	May hear loud voices about 1 foot from the ear. May be able to hear environmental sounds. May be able to discriminate vowels but not all consonants. Speech and language defective and likely to deteriorate.
Extreme	91 or more	May hear some loud sounds but is aware of vibrations more than tonal patterns. Relies on vision rather than hearing as primary avenue for communication. Speech and language defective and likely to deteriorate.

Source: Adapted from Report of a Committee for Comprehensive Plan for Hearing-Impaired Children, May 1968, Office of the Superintendent of Public Instruction, Title VI, Elementary and Secondary Education Act, and the University of Illinois, Division of Services for Crippled Children. Reprinted with permission from Hallahan, D. P., & Kauffman, M. J. (1997). *Exceptional children: Introduction to special education* (p. 321). Needham Heights, MA: Allyn and Bacon.

Other terms used by educators include these:

- *Congenitally deaf:* Born deaf.
- *Adventitiously deaf:* Born with normal hearing, but sense of hearing becomes nonfunctional later through illness or accident.
- *Prelingual hearing loss:* A hearing loss at birth or before the child has learned language.
- *Postlingual hearing loss:* A hearing loss that develops after the child has developed language. (Hallahan & Kaufman, 1997)

Characteristics

Whitmore (1981) identified a set of characteristics that might reveal giftedness despite the intervening impairment. Those children who have an absence of oral communication skills might reveal their giftedness through communication by alternative modes: visual, nonverbal and/or body language, and might exhibit superior memory and problem-solving ability, or an exceptional interest and drive in response to challenges.

Yewchuk and Bibby (1989) emphasize the need to include parent information, teacher observations, and the nonverbal portions of IQ scores as sources of information for identification when determining giftedness.

Identification

Even though Furth (1966, 1973) showed that deaf students are as intelligent as hearing students, it is estimated that only 15 percent of the U.S. gifted population with hearing impairments is enrolled in special programs for the gifted (Gamble, 1985). This special population is not being properly identified and nurtured. Vernon and LaFalce-Landers (1993) followed fifty-seven gifted deaf and hard of hearing people longitudinally to determine educational, career, and mental health status. They collected data from forty-nine who were old enough for postsecondary schooling and for whom data were available: 86 percent had attained some postsecondary education; 43 percent graduated from a four-year college; and 18 percent attended graduate school. Thirty-nine percent experienced mental illness requiring hospitalization or therapy; 33 percent were in professional or supervisory roles; and 30 percent were unemployed.

Identification and nurturance of this special population is of great concern. For children with hearing impairments to perform at grade level would be a remarkable achievement and an indicator of brilliance, but schools have failed to recognize this. In a major court decision involving P.L. 94-142, the *Rowley* case, it was ruled that because a very bright young deaf girl was achieving at near grade level, she was not entitled to an interpreter (Board of Education of the Hendrick Hudson Central School District, 1982). Turnbull (1986) comments on the Supreme Court's decision and reports that evidence in the trial showed that only 59 percent of what occurs in a regular classroom would be available to a deaf child without an interpreter. Children with hearing impairments would have no way of achieving their potential without the appropriate support services.

Interventions

According to Mykelbust (1964), special considerations should be taken into account when determining the intelligence of a deaf individual. The way in which mental abilities are measured is of critical importance. Identification of a gifted child with a hearing impairment is extremely difficult when the usual instruments are administered. Nonlanguage tests should be used with those whose deafness dates from the prespeech language age. For children with hearing impairments, a global IQ score is inappropriate. The most acceptable measures would include individually administered tests with nonverbal content.

The use of standardized achievement tests poses another problem. On average, the academic achievement of students with hearing impairments compared with their hearing agemates can be delayed by four or five years (Bess & McConnell, 1981). According to Mykelbust in 1964, when nonverbal criteria are used, deafness does not influence cognition. This still holds true today. Memory and convergent thinking may be affected, but only selectively. Divergent thinking and evaluation ability appear to be affected by deafness. These mental functions entail a broader background of experience. Enrichment that addresses higher-order thinking skills is essential for students who are deaf if they are to actualize their potential. Specialized training can be given.

John's history, detailed at the beginning of this chapter, indicates that students who are deaf can succeed in a hearing school, but teachers and students should be sensitized to their special needs. Provisions should be made early on to expose children who are deaf to all domains and thinking skills so that giftedness can be identified and nurtured. Exposing students with hearing impairments to all of the domains will assist in revealing gifts in one domain, or in many.

Special emphasis should be on critical and creative thinking skills and on inter- and intrapersonal skill development. A focus on inter- and intrapersonal skill development for the students with hearing impairments as well as other students in the class will provide sensitivity training for all, thus preventing gifted children who are deaf from losing self-esteem.

As areas of special ability are noted, strategies that differentiate the curriculum should take place. Special attention needs to be paid to including critical and creative thought processes into content areas.

Auxiliary personnel should accommodate the special needs of intellectually gifted students with hearing impairments. These personnel might include speech–language pathologists, teachers of sign language, or audiologists who see to it that the proper hearing aids are provided. New technologies are now being developed that combine computers and televisions. Individuals are being trained in a new methodology called *C Print* or real-time captioning. This involves words appearing on a television screen which are being typed by a trained typist using abbreviated forms of language. Students can read most of what is being said in a lecture while it is taking place and receive a printed copy immediately following the lecture. Research indicates that more information becomes available in printed English to deaf students as opposed to sign language (Everhart, Stinson, McKee, & Giles, 1996).

Interventions need to address social and emotional concerns. This includes counseling of the hearing parents of children who are deaf. "Hearing loss may be especially frustrating and difficult to cope with in gifted people, because it can stand in the way of intellectual development and career opportunities" (Vernon & LaFalce-Landers, 1993). Most children who are deaf are born to hearing parents. As a result the child is deprived of sensory input from normal mother/child interactions. Hearing parents do not always learn to sign. Those that do may not become proficient, preventing children who are deaf from having access to available information, which can cause developmental delays.

Cognitive development is impacted by limited parent/child metacognitive interactions. "The origin of cognitive and metacognitive strategies is to be found in an individual's interactions with knowledgeable others, within the contexts of sign-mediated, goal-oriented activity" (Akamatsu, 1996). In addition, sign language does not have the same connection with the written word as does the spoken word. Learning to sign and read presents children with two entirely different languages. Turnbull, Turnbull, Shank, and Leal (1995) aptly quote Helen Keller as she emphasizes the plight of the individual with a hearing impairment: "Blindness separates people from things, but deafness separates people from people" (p. 551).

Individuals who have progressive and/or late-onset hearing losses often face significant emotional problems. Individuals who reject sign language and who reject and associate failure with becoming members of the Deaf Community, may suffer greater psychological problems as a result of lack of stimulation and social support. Such isolation can lead to depression and negative feelings.

Looking to the Future: Controversies Regarding the Education of Children with Giftedness and Hearing Impairments

An ongoing controversy concerns whether or not children with hearing impairments should be educated in regular classrooms or in segregated schools.

Public Schools as Settings for Gifted Students with Hearing Impairments   Yewchuk and Bibby (1989) report the results of a study involving students with hearing impairments. The study compared 120 students enrolled in a school for the deaf and 58 enrolled in a public school. Teachers identified a total of 36 students in both settings. Teachers in the public school identified a proportionately higher number of students (36 percent) than the teachers at the school for the deaf (12.5 percent). This finding was surprising inasmuch as teachers in the mainstream setting had little experience working with the hearing-impaired population.

A mainstream setting with the appropriate support services would ensure that gifted children with hearing impairments would receive the stimulation required to challenge and develop their gifts. In segregated settings such as schools for the deaf, there is little emphasis on detecting and developing potential gifts (Yewchuk and Bibby, 1989). Teachers in segregated settings are expert in signing, but may not have the same degree of expertise in content areas. Emphasis has focused on remediation or normalization related to aspects of the disability. Because gifted students with hearing impairments are typically identified and labeled only in terms of their disability, there exists a pressing need to identify and recognize potential gifts so that prevailing stereotypes can be eliminated.

Polsky (1996) reports on the Cleary School where a unique high school program was instituted. Twenty-two deaf and hard of hearing students were placed in a mainstream secondary education program with assistance provided by sign language interpreters, tutors, and therapists. Two of the students reported that the education was better than in a segregated school. "'I was thrilled to arrive here,' said Velasquez, who like Keefe, speaks through a sign interpreter. 'Between body language and lip-reading, we manage to communicate'" (p. B4).

Segregated Settings for Gifted Students with Hearing Impairments   Interviews with professionals who work with the deaf community reveal concerns relating to the social and emotional lives of students. For deaf children who are a little reticent, the hearing world can be intimidating and lead to social isolation. Deaf students in hearing schools encounter their share of hostility and mimicking of their sign language.

In a 1996 interview with Dr. Frank Bowe, a professor at Hofstra University in the Department of Counseling, Research, Special Education and Rehabilitation and a recognized authority on education of the deaf, he voiced his belief that including gifted students who are hearing impaired in regular classrooms is important to their intellectual development. The stimulation and competition prepares them for work in a hearing society. He added a note of caution: The regular classroom might not be for all children with hearing impairments. Some might be overwhelmed and need to be sheltered.

THE GIFTED CHILD WITH A VISUAL IMPAIRMENT

PERSONAL INTERVIEW
Barbara's Story

Now we turn to a discussion of students with visual impairments. Consider Barbara, who is an intellectually gifted individual with a visual impairment.

In first grade my parents were given the option of putting me in a self-contained class. We visited the class and realized that students with all kinds of disabilities were included. At six years old, I knew there were disturbed children in the class, and I shuddered. I didn't want to be put into the class. I was put into a regular classroom and received no assistance until eighth grade. There was no provision made for magnification. I couldn't see the chalkboard. I couldn't read for more than ten to fifteen minutes at a time. It took me a long time to learn to read. Once I caught on, I shot ahead.

Math was always easy for me because you didn't have letters next to each other, but I couldn't see the chalkboard. I would have to rush up to the chalkboard after the teacher finished lecturing and rush to copy it down. I learned how to write fast to try to keep up. I learned my math. I used to take down as much as I could by dictation whenever the teacher was kind enough to read out loud.

I didn't have any assistance and I ran into a lot of social problems. There was never anyone to intervene on my behalf. In sixth grade, I didn't make the SP (Special Progress) because my parents were told that my IQ was too low. I had to be two years ahead in math and reading. I was over the cutoff point in reading but missed the math. I took the test when I had just returned to school after an ailment and they wouldn't retest me. My IQ test was a group test with standard print. I couldn't finish it. My parents were told that my score was low and that they were pushing me. They were told to back off, when they weren't pushing me at all.

In eighth grade I was put into a sight conservation class, which encouraged students with vision problems not to use their sight. I was placed in regular classes and they helped me along, but I did not make the SP. In eighth and ninth grades, a resource teacher was assigned to help me who didn't know what to do. They read my visual report and said that it must be a mistake. They couldn't believe my vision was that bad and that I was able to keep up. They would not allow me to take any of the tests for the special schools in New York City for bright students. I was told that I shouldn't want to do that because of my vision.

In ninth grade, I made Arista [an honor society for academic achievement in the public schools] because I had over a ninety average. One of the strongest memories I have is of a contest I entered. Students were asked to write essays regarding citizenship, scholarship, and service. We were told that the three top essays would be read to the assembly. We weren't supposed to put our names on them. When the assistant principal found out that mine was one of the three chosen, and that I was in sight conservation, she called me into her office and told me that I wouldn't want to do it because it would be embarrassing. She told me to read it to her so that she could see how it would look at the assembly. She told me how awful it looked because I held the paper right up to my face and that I wouldn't want to embarrass everybody. I refused to back down, so I memorized the entire essay and pretended to read it. After that experience I lost my voice for a few days. Even though I was provided with a resource teacher, it was of no help because she wouldn't even run interference for me. She even allowed the school to kick me out of a sewing class.

In ninth grade I was given a hand two-and-a-half magnification monocular optical device which allowed me to see the chalkboard in front of me. I also started using magnifiers. Today I use much more powerful instruments.

Optical devices were not what they are today. In high school I was provided with more powerful optical devices. I still couldn't read more than ten to fifteen minutes at a time. My mother started recording textbooks for me. I used the recorded texts and was able to see the chalkboard. In tenth grade I was assigned an itinerant teacher. At the beginning of eleventh grade he was taken away and I was told I could go to a resource room in another school, but I chose not to go because I knew they wouldn't help me anyway.

In my senior year, because of my grades, it was recommended that I go to a good girls school which my parents couldn't afford. I visited a college in Massachusetts where I was told that they did not advise anyone with a visual impairment to go into teaching. New York City had provisions for obtaining teaching licenses for individuals with disabilities. Because I failed the vision part of the exam, I was told that I had to do a demonstration lesson, which I believe was set up so I would fail, but I passed.

This is the kind of experience that many people with disabilities who are in education today went through. Children today should not have to go through the kinds of experiences I had. I remember not finishing tests and handing them in, hoping I had answered enough questions to pass. You shouldn't have to worry about those things. I graduated from a university cum laude. By the time I was in college I was able to use a tape recorder and optical devices. I was able to read for a longer period of time. Today I use a computer with enlarged fonts and other optic devises. I am also driving with the use of an optical system. There are only thirty-five states where visually impaired persons are allowed to drive. If I lived in Alabama I couldn't drive.

I believe I was able to survive in spite of my early experiences because I had supportive parents and a supportive ophthalmologist.

Barbara has a doctorate from an Ivy League university, is teaching at a major university, and has made many contributions to her field.

Definition

Visual disability, including blindness, is defined by IDEA as impairment in vision that, even with correction, adversely affects a child's educational performance. Students with visual impairments represent a wide range of visual functioning:

- *Visually impaired:* Requires special educational provisions because of visual problems (Barraga & Errin, 1992).

- *Blind:* Has either no vision or, at most, light perception (Barraga & Erin, 1992). Students learn through the use of Braille or related media without the use of vision.
- *Low vision:* Has severe visual impairment after correction but visual function can be increased through the use of optical aids and environmental modifications (Corn & Ryser, 1989). Students with low vision have the benefit of some vision as well as their other senses. Functional vision will depend on factors such as lighting, use of optical aids and devices, tasks, and personal characteristics. Modifications in lighting, size of print or objects, and distance may be required.

Characteristics

Some of the characteristics of visually impaired students may mask potential gifts. Whitmore and Maker (1985) address some obstacles to identification: developmental delays, incomplete information about a child, and lack of opportunity to evidence superior mental abilities.

In addition, other concerns involve learned helplessness; problems with communicating, understanding, and attending; need to learn two curricula (the mainstream core curriculum and a special core that provides strategies to assist in everyday functioning); and a critical shortage of teachers. Caseloads for teachers of persons with visual impairments are great. Students do not always get the necessary attention.

Identification

Corn (1986) speaks to the difficulties involved in identifying a child with two exceptionalities:

- Gifted students and students with disabilities possess a range of physical and intellectual functions.
- A delay in concept development may be related to a lack of experience, rather than a lack of abilities.
- Lack of prior experience may inhibit the emergence of gifts and talents.

Corn cites the biography of "Laura," who was born with congenital cataracts and was legally blind. She was diagnosed as being mentally retarded but was later diagnosed as being neurologically impaired without retardation. She tested in the "low average" range on an IQ test and was considered to have emotional reactions with neurological involvement. At age 10, based on her sculpture and drawings, she received a scholarship at a nationally known art institute for a summer workshop. She was also selected as the youngest member of a city-wide choral group even though she was unable to read music. She sang at a nationally known center for the performing arts. She attended a self-contained public school class until sixth grade and attended a private high school that allowed flexible scheduling with tutoring. In order for gifted visually impaired students to be properly identified, proper services should be provided early.

Interventions

Appropriate interventions need to begin with outlining of goals. Corn, Hatlen, Huebner, Ryan, and Siller (1995) have outlined the following goals for the visually impaired, including those with multiple disabilities:

1. Students and their families will be referred to an appropriate education program within thirty days of identification of a suspected visual impairment.
2. Policies and procedures will be implemented to ensure the right of all parents to full participation and equal partnership in the education process.
3. Universities, with a minimum of one full-time faculty member in the area of visual impairment, will prepare a sufficient number of educators of students with visual impairments to meet personnel needs throughout the country.
4. Service providers will determine caseloads based on the needs of students and will require ongoing professional development for all teachers and orientation and mobility instructors.
5. Local education programs will ensure that all students have access to a full array of placement options.
6. Assessment of students will be conducted, in collaboration with parents, by personnel having expertise in the education of students with visual impairments.
7. Access to developmental and educational services will include an assurance that instructional materials are available to students in the appropriate media and at the same time as their sighted peers.
8. Educational and developmental goals, including instruction, will reflect the assessed needs of each student in all areas of academic and disability-specific curricula. (p. 5)

Academically oriented students with visual impairments have been mainstreamed successfully with support from specially trained teachers. Meeting the needs of the visually impaired child in the regular classroom might include teaching them to read and write using Braille, use of books on tape, teaching listening skills, personal/social and daily living instruction in the use of special aids and equipment and instruction in the use of optical aids, and a core curriculum that addresses the special needs of students with visual impairments, as discussed next.

Core Curriculum for Students with Visual Impairments   For students with visual impairments, there is a core curriculum, which is the existing core curriculum developed for sighted students and an expanded curriculum to cover additional areas of learning. The expanded core curriculum for these types of students is larger and more complex and includes experiences and concepts incidentally learned by sighted students.

The core curriculum for children who are blind or visually impaired covers these subjects: mathematics, science, social studies, history, health, physical education, fine arts, economics, business education, vocational education, English language arts, and other languages to the extent possible.

Expanded Core Curriculum for Students with Visual Impairments   Hatlen (1996, p. 4) provides an example of the expanded core curriculum for students with visual impairments:

- *Compensatory academic skills, including communication modes:* Compensatory and functional skills include concept development, spatial understanding, study and organizational skills, speaking and listening skills, and adaptations necessary for accessing all areas of the existing core curriculum.
- *Orientation and mobility:* Teachers specifically prepared to teach orientation and mobility to learners who are blind or visually impaired are necessary for this curriculum to be delivered. The expanded core includes emphasis on the need of persons with visual impairments to be as independent as possible and learn from the environment through which they are passing.
- *Social interaction skills:* Social skills, which are casually and incidentally learned by sighted individuals, must be taught to individuals with visual impairments.
- *Independent living skills:* These skills include tasks and functions involved in personal hygiene, food preparation, money management, time monitoring, organization, etc.
- *Recreation and leisure skills:* Even though many of the physical education activities are appropriate for visually impaired students, they need to be taught to develop lifelong leisure skills.
- *Career education:* Expanded opportunities to experience career opportunities firsthand are essential for the visually impaired.
- *Use of assistive technology:* Technology can serve as a great equalizer for the individual with a visual impairment. Braille for the student can be transformed to print for the teacher. A myriad of other tools involving opticons and computers can help bring sight to those with visual impairments.
- *Visual efficiency skills:* Thorough systematic diagnosis and training of students with functional vision can be taught so that they can efficiently utilize their remaining vision.

The importance of teaching the expanded core curriculum to gifted students with a visual disability was confirmed by professionals in the field. Gifted students with visual impairments have dropped out of programs because of their inability to problem solve on a daily basis, not because they are not intellectually capable.

The Expanded Core Curriculum for Blind and Visually Impaired Students will be difficult to complete in 12 years of education, especially for students who are high academic learners. Special approaches for fitting the Expanded Core Curriculum into a normal education career have been suggested. One possibility that has been used is to depend on the infused competencies contained in the Existing Core Curriculum for providing the additional skills and knowledge needed by the visually impaired learner. (Hatlen, 1996, p. 8)

Concerns for the development of gifted students with visual impairments extend to social and emotional development. Appropriate guidance and counseling is an essential component of assisting the student with a visual impairment to develop inter- and intrapersonal skills. Instruction should include preparation for work experiences. "Topics such as going for interviews and explaining one's abilities and disabilities, knowledge of laws for rehabilitation, and information related to specialized vocational preparation are among those which may be included in career education" (Corn, 1986, p. 77). Leadership skills can also be developed and enhanced as gifted students with visual impairments are placed in situations in which they learn that helping and being helped works both ways.

Content for the gifted student with a visual impairment includes the content to be learned by all students, plus the expanded core. Including students with visual disabilities in the regular classroom allows children to share in the exposure activities provided for all students, that is, multiple intelligences and higher level cognitive abilities. Content to be learned should be available in Braille and/or be tape recorded. Teachers should plan well in advance so that materials can be ordered and students can have them available in time. Materials can be ordered by registering for the National Library Service for the Blind and Physically Handicapped (see Resource list at end of chapter).

Strategies for differentiation should be incorporated into the curriculum depending on areas of abilities noted. Room should be made to ensure that the expanded core curriculum is being covered either programmatically or provisionally.

The regular and core curriculum for students with visual impairments should be presented not only in an accessible manner, but also at a pace appropriate for the students' learning. For example, acceleration may or may not be considered for the general or core curriculum, whereas other students might be directed toward acceleration. Individuals and organizations who assist in serving this population include guidance counselors, special teachers of the visually impaired, and the American Foundation for the Blind.

Mentors and role models should be made available. Volunteers should be utilized as needed to record materials.

RESOURCES

National Library Service for the Blind and Physically Handicapped, The Library of Congress, Washington, DC 20542; phone: (202)707-5100.

Textbooks on Tape, Recording for the Blind and Dyslexic, 20 Roszel Road, Princeton, NJ 08540; phone: (609)452-0606.

Chapter 5

Gifted Children with Learning Problems

Typical questions a classroom teacher might ask include these:

How do I recognize intellectually gifted children with learning problems?

How does a learning disability affect intellectual functioning?

What can I expect of a child with a learning disability?

What modifications do I need to make in my classroom?

How can I accommodate a child with attention deficit hyperactivity disorder (AD/HD)?

To answer these questions, this chapter does the following:

Describes the characteristics of gifted children with learning problems.

Outlines special needs.

Discusses ways in which curriculum can be differentiated.

CHILDREN WITH GIFTEDNESS AND LEARNING DISABILITIES

Definition

Gifted children with learning disabilities present unique challenges to educators. In order to examine the needs of this population, it is helpful to review definitions accepted by people in the field. Marland (1972) provides the following definition of *giftedness:*

Gifted and talented children are those identified by professionally qualified persons who by virtue of outstanding abilities are capable of high performance. These are children who require differentiated educational programs and/or services beyond those normally provided by the regular school program in order to realize their contribution to self and society.

Children capable of high performance include those with demonstrated achievement and/or potential ability in any of the following areas, singly or in combination.

1. General intellectual ability
2. Specific academic aptitude
3. Creative or productive thinking
4. Leadership ability
5. Visual and performing arts
6. Psychomotor ability [psychomotor was subsequently dropped]. (p. 10)

PERSONAL INTERVIEW
Gary's Story

Gary's story is told from his mother's point of view.

Gary—who, because of being born a month early, entered kindergarten a year earlier than he would have, as the "youngest boy."

Gary—who was speaking complete, compound sentences at a year and a half old.

Gary—who would sit for hours to be read to from the age of one.

Gary—who at age three, watched and loved a science program aimed at eight-year-olds.

But, by age four, when I tried to interest him in learning letters and written words, he walked away—I didn't think much of it.

People were always getting a laugh hearing such big words from such a small child. He was my child and I talked to him all the time and thought nothing of it.

By the middle of first grade his reading ability indicated problems. His vocabulary and comprehension were high even though he couldn't decode the actual words. His teacher remarked that he had such a thirst for information. Learning how to read and get this knowledge for himself would be so satisfying to him. His second-grade teacher suggested he be tested. She said that in conversations, he spoke like a middle schooler, but he wasn't reading or writing at grade level. The testing showed a 147 IQ with clearcut learning disabilities.

With third grade came resource room time—one hour each school day. He needed the specialized instruction, but being grouped with four others was very frustrating because the pace was much too slow for him. He was also very unhappy about not being in a reading group in class, reading and analyzing stories. Resource was his reading time. He complained all year about this. Third grade also meant admission to the program for the gifted children in the school district. His teachers told me that he would not be recommended, even though his IQ was superior. Taking care of his deficits was more important.

At this point his disability was being accentuated and his intelligence ignored. Despite having one of the best and most loved teachers in the school, I would say third grade was his unhappiest year. I asked about the school's program for the gifted and was told by his teacher that it wasn't a good idea now. I could see his enthusiasm waning. He hated resource room and there *were no outlets for his mental alertness. I didn't realize how much he needed an outlet. I just thought he wasn't the student I had thought he could be. In retrospect I can see that extra mental stimulation was necessary.*

For fourth grade I spoke with the school personnel to discuss the possibility of Gary having the opportunity to participate in the gifted program, even though I thought it might actually be too much for him with his "problems" and while still going five hours a week to resource room. I spoke to the teachers in the program, who reassured me that Gary's positive attributes would be emphasized, and that compensation would be provided for his deficits. He was not only OK, he thrived. During the year he didn't even complain about resource room as much. He was proud and excited about his work in the gifted program, something he loved. The program was designed around independent study and Gary chose chemistry. In the library he showed me how to find research material—he learned to use the tools during his time in the gifted program. Fourth grade was a pivotal year. His reading and writing were becoming functional and I also saw the light return in his eyes. Gary is an information person not a paper person. The gifted program not only gave him the opportunity to pursue his interest but also gave him a break from what was most frustrating to him. It gave him a feeling of learning with pleasure, not pressure. His success in the program, unlike regular gifted students, gave him a self-image of "I can" which had been badly damaged. Self-image of abilities is important and his was falsely too low. Participation in the gifted program gave him the confidence to know he could succeed in spite of his disabilities, which he will always have to some extent.

In fifth grade his project for the gifted program was on physics. In seventh grade, he was an A-plus science student and attained a qualifying grade point average so that he was admitted into the national Junior Honor Society. When things get messed up in writing, spelling, or math because of his disabilities, we can laugh about it because he has confidence in knowing that he is "gifted" and will succeed in spite of himself.

Gary's profile truly reflects "a paradoxical combination" of exceptionalities (Tannenbaum & Baldwin, 1983). A review of Gary's test scores in third grade revealed that he had a verbal score of 149, a performance score of 115, and a full-scale score of 137. A breakdown of the test is shown in Figure 5.1.

Gary fit the definition and description of a gifted child with a learning disability in a number of ways. Gary was capable of comprehending and thinking on high levels. His problems manifested themselves in his reading ability and written expression. He could not decode or spell. In addition, he had problems with his motor systems. Because of his lack of coordination,

```
              INDIVIDUALIZED EDUCATION PROGRAM
                        PHASE ONE
                       1991/1992

                       Reason.:   Annual Review
                       CSE Date....:  05/20/91

STUDENT DATA:
   STUDENT NAME ...........................:                           ID....: 1168
   DOB  ...................................:
   PARENT/GUARDIANS .......................:
   ADDRESS  ...............................:

   HOME TELEPHONE NO. .....................:
   DOMINANT LANG. HOME  ...................:
   DOMINANT LANG. STUDENT .................:
   DATE ENTERED PROGRAM ...................:

CURRENT PLACEMENT DATA:
   CLASSIFICATION .........................:  Learning Disabled
   GRADE  .................................:  05
   PLACEMENT  .............................:  Resource Room
                                               30 min/sess, 3.0 sess/wk
   CLASS SIZE/RATIO .......................:  5:1
   LENGTH OF PROGRAM  .....................:  10 Months
   SCHOOL .................................:
   TEACHER  ...............................:
   DIPLOMA  ...............................:  Local Diploma
   TRANSPORTATION .........................:  per district policy
   ANNUAL REVIEW  .........................:  05/91
   TRIENNIAL  .............................:  02/91,
   IQ TEST  ...............................:  WISC-R- 2/88
                                               149 Verbal, 115 Performance, 137 Full Scale
   FOREIGN LANGUAGE EXEMPT  ...............:  Not Applicable

RECOMMENDATIONS:
   CLASSIFICATION .........................:
   GRADE  .................................:
   PLACEMENT  .............................:
   CLASS SIZE/RATIO .......................:
   LENGTH OF PROGRAM  .....................:
   SCHOOL .................................:
   TEACHER  ...............................:
   PROGRAM INITIATION DATE: ...............:  09/01/91
```

Figure 5.1 **Gary's test scores**

he was allotted extra time for physical education. He had problems with self-esteem and would turn away from frustrating situations. He exhibited signs of hyperactivity which are still present today. Gary's scores revealed a large discrepancy between subsections. He was very aware of being different and suffered a great deal of frustration both in the regular classroom and in the resource room. He was capable of understanding concepts beyond those being taught in the regular classroom but could not be included in reading groups. The students that he worked with in the resource room were far below him intellectually. He reported the pace to be far too slow.

Gary had advanced verbal abilities and showed evidence at home of scientific problem-solving ability. He had quick recall of information and was involved in many academic activities outside of school. He was a highly motivated child except when it came to reading and writing. His self-concept was affected because of his inability to read or write. He still has difficulty with handwriting.

Gary's mother reported that he blocked out a lot of emotion because of his sensitivities. Until he was admitted into the gifted program he was socially isolated and still lacks social skills. His hyperactivity was evidenced more at home than at school, although teachers at school reported that Gary needed to get up and walk around the room. His psychomotor skills are still poor and he does not participate in sports. He does not like drill and repetition and experienced a great deal of difficulty learning multiplication tables. When knowledgeable about a topic he does have a tendency to dominate discussions.

Gary is in tenth grade now. He is an A-plus student in science and has maintained an A average in all of his subjects. He has had to drop Spanish. He still cannot decode and has learned to read by memorizing words by sight. Learning another language would place too great a burden on him. He still cannot spell and his mother edits all of his work. The challenge now is finding an appropriate college placement for Gary.

The federal definition of a learning disability under P.L. 94-142 (Education for All Handicapped Children Act of 1975, which became IDEA, P.L. 101-476 in 1990 and was reauthorized in 1997 as P.L. 105-17) is as follows:

> . . . those children who have a disorder in one or more of the basic psychological processes involved in understanding or in using language, spoken or written, which disorder may manifest itself in imperfect ability to listen, think, speak, read, write, spell or do mathematical calculations. Such disorders include such conditions as perceptual disabilities, brain injury, minimal brain dysfunction, dyslexia and developmental aphasia. Such a term does not include children who

have learning problems which are primarily the result of visual, hearing, or motor disabilities, of mental retardation, of emotional disturbance, or of environmental, cultural, or economic disadvantage.

As cited by Baum, Owen, and Dixon (1991, p. 8) a team may determine that a child has a specific learning disability if (1) the child does not achieve commensurate with his or her age and ability levels in one or more areas that include oral or written expression, listening comprehension, basic reading skill or comprehension, and mathematics calculation or reasoning when provided with learning experiences appropriate for the child's age and ability levels; and (2) the team finds that a child has a severe discrepancy between achievement and intellectual ability in one or more of (these) areas (U.S. Office of Education, 1977, p. 65).

As early as 1964, Johnson and Myklebust described children with learning disabilities as having integrity emotionally, motorically, sensorially, and intellectually. Despite these integrities they are deficient in learning and cannot learn in the usual manner. It is possible that children with learning disabilities might also have other deficits. There are times when disabilities overlap.

When children exhibit characteristics of the gifted and the learning disabled, they pose a special challenge for the classroom teacher. Baum, Owen, and Dixon (1991) suggest the definition proposed by the Association for Children and Adults with Learning Disabilities (1985) with clarifying points as appropriate:

> Specific Learning Disabilities is a chronic condition of presumed neurological origin which selectively interferes with the development, integration and/or demonstration of verbal abilities. . . . Specific Learning Disabilities exists as a distinct handicapping condition in the presence of average to superior intelligence, adequate sensory and motor systems, and adequate learning opportunities. The condition varies in its manifestations and in degree of severity. . . . Throughout life, the condition can affect self-esteem, education, vocation, socialization and/or daily activities. (p. 10)

Baum, Owen, and Dixon (1991) make these clarifying points:

1. These students are able to learn and accumulate knowledge in ways not traditional in academic settings.
2. The disability is of a more permanent nature whose compensation techniques are of primary importance.
3. Because these students have normal or above average intellectual functioning, the learning disability causes the individual to face frustration and failure in specific areas which require learning inputs, strategies, or products that may be directly opposed to the individual's natural learning style. This in turn may cause failure and frustration for students. Results from these unsuccessful learning experiences are often manifested in disruptive behavior, poor self-efficacy, short attention span, and hyperactivity. These characteristic behaviors are thought to interfere with learning. However,

because they are often situation specific, we do not view them as causes, but in many instances as effects (Baum, 1984, 1988; Baum & Dixon, 1985; Baum & Owen, 1988; Dixon & Baum, 1986; Whitmore, 1980).

Characteristics

Possible characteristics of an intellectually gifted child with a learning disability might include (Hughes, 1995; Udall & Maker, 1983) strong verbal language (i.e., vocabulary, ability to express one's self); strong problem-solving skills; extreme curiosity; leadership abilities; an unusual imagination; capable of original thought or ideas in art, music, or other nonacademic areas; creativity and/or divergent problem-solving ability; and quick recall of factual information verbally. This type of child also is apt to have avid outside interests.

Some characteristic weaknesses of this type of child include lack of attention, motivation, and self-concept; deficiencies in academic areas (spelling, math, reading); poor handwriting; inability to stay focused on a task; poor memory (long and/or short term); poor auditory, motor, or visual perception; lack of a realistic self-perception; unorganized; easily frustrated, and sensitive to criticism.

In addition, Udall and Maker (1983) report that gifted students with learning disabilities demonstrate the following:

- Discrepancies between tested potential and school performance
- Discrepancies between subsections on standardized tests (i.e., WISC, WRAT, Stanford–Binet)
- An attempt to hide or "mask" the disability
- An awareness of being "different"
- A high level of frustration (p. 228).

Hughes (1995) described the paradoxes faced by intellectually gifted children with learning disabilities:

- Has a poor memory for facts but excellent comprehension
- Prefers complex and challenging materials, but is easily distracted and sets unrealistic goals
- Becomes bored with rote or memorization tasks, but is unorganized in behavior
- Cannot read, write, or spell, but has excellent oral language skills
- Can be manipulative of people and situations, but has poor people skills
- Performs poorly on "simple facts," such as addition and subtraction, but is capable of complex, conceptual manipulations, such as algebraic concepts
- Has a strong sense of humor, but is unable to judge appropriate times to display it
- Comes up with penetrating insights, but is unable to determine cause and effect related to own actions

- Able to concentrate for unusually long periods of time when the topic is of interest, but is unable to control actions and attention when the topic is not of interest.

Silverman (1989) compares the characteristics of underachievers as listed in Joanne Whitmore's 1980 text, *Giftedness, Conflict and Underachievement,* with the characteristics of gifted students with learning disabilities as cited in the literature to find an identical set:

- Perfectionistic
- Supersensitive
- Lacks social skills
- Socially isolated
- Unrealistic self-expectations
- Low self-esteem
- Hyperactive
- Easily distracted
- Psychomotor inefficiencies
- Chronically inattentive
- Frustrated by the demands of the classroom
- Fails to complete assignments
- Excessively critical of self and others
- Rebellious against drill and excessive repetition
- Disparaging of the work required
- Becomes an "expert" in one area and dominates discussions with that expertise. (p. 37)

Identification

To establish the definitional requirement of "discrepancy," identification of gifted children with learning disabilities should also include an individual IQ test and standardized tests; records of school performance and achievement; observations by teachers, counselors, or other school professionals; and interviews with the parents and the child. Inasmuch as there is no clear-cut profile or description of a gifted child with a learning disability, the information gathered should provide a picture of strengths and deficits.

IQ tests are appropriate and useful when used for diagnostic purposes. As in Gary's case, this type of profile will indicate areas of giftedness as well as areas of deficit.

Barton and Starnes (1989) report that an analysis of the Weschler Intelligence Scale for Children–Revised (WISC-R) reveals a distinctive cognitive pattern for the gifted child with a learning disability. Test results reveal commonalities with the gifted population and with the learning disabled population. Gifted students with learning disabilities receive the highest scores on the similarities, vocabulary, and comprehension sections. This is congruent with parent and teacher descriptions. They grasp concepts readily and excel in creative problem solving and abstract reasoning. The gifted child with a learning disability scores lowest in the areas of arithmetic, digit span, coding, and sequencing. This matches the patterns found in the population of those with learning disabilities. Patterns in group achievement test scores should target students who require in-depth evaluation for early identification and preventive intervention.

Interventions

The characteristics cited earlier can signal the need for testing to determine if learning disabilities are present. If this is the case, the classroom becomes the place where the environment can be modified to accommodate the needs of the learner. Opportunities to display areas of strength should be provided and adaptive techniques should be implemented in areas of deficit.

When the diagnosis is complete and the profile established, areas of strength can be highlighted as opposed to deficits. Inasmuch as underachievement and low self-esteem often result from frustration and failure, the teacher's role becomes one of accentuating the positive.

Barton and Starnes (1989) emphasize the need to program appropriately for this population by providing materials and instruction individualized to accommodate the disability while recognizing academic strengths. Activities, materials, and knowledge should be at the level of cognitive ability, not skills. Principles of gifted education should be incorporated with the most effective strategies and techniques appropriate for the disability.

In Table 5.1, Baum et al. (1991) cites Whitmore (1980) and compares the strategies that would be used for the traditional special education setting with the environment appropriate for gifted children with learning disabilities.

Baldwin and Garguilo (1983) and Baum et al. (1991) suggest that for children with learning disabilities, teachers should use a prescriptive approach, narrowing the focus of instruction to specific tasks. The classroom should not be overly stimulating or cluttered. Learning centers should have explicit instructions at the level of the student. Whenever possible, instruction should take place in small groups or on a one-on-one basis with the teacher. Multisensory materials should be used. Lessons should be timed (fifteen to twenty minutes) depending on the abilities of the child. Independent work should be structured and monitored. Students should be helped to organize their work. Learning style should be noted and accommodated. Creative problem-solving strategies should be taught. Positive feedback should be given whenever possible and as soon as possible.

Tobin and Schiffman (1983) advocate the use of computer technology with gifted children who have learning disabilities. Computer technology can be used as an instructional tool to assist in individualizing a program for a student in areas of both strengths and weaknesses. The computer can also provide immediate positive reinforcement. Kleinman, Humphrey, and Lindsay (1981) found that students with learning disabilities spent more time working out problems on microcomputers than with pencil and paper.

If there is a deficit in the area of reading, while remediation is taking place, students should be provided with materials that will give the necessary information.

Table 5.1   Traditional educational interventions versus modification necessary for gifted students

Needs	Traditional Special Education Interventions	Necessary Modifications for Students with High Intellectual Potential
Rational approach for emotional adjustment	Decisions made for student	Student encouraged to confront the duality of his learning behaviors and to help decide on coping strategies
Classroom organization	1. Structured; designed to minimize student interaction and maximize work 2. Teacher-centered 3. Opportunities for verbalization are minimal	1. Self-directed 2. Engage in active inquiry 3. Stimulating intellectual activity
Instructional style and curriculum	1. Modality-based 2. Devices for increasing memory 3. Basic skills focus	1. Methods of inquiry 2. Problem solving 3. Creative thinking 4. Student interaction maximized 5. Emphasis on advanced thinking skills (analysis, synthesis, and evaluation)

Source: from Baum, S. M. (1984). Meeting the needs of learning disabled gifted students. *Roeper Review, 7*(1), 6–9. Used by permission of Roeper Review.

Students can be provided with audiovisual materials. If possible audio tapes of textbooks should be made or material can be presented orally. Reading materials should be rich and rigorous but at a low enough level that they do not cause frustration.

In the area of mathematics, students should be allowed to use calculators. Montague (1991) studied how gifted students and gifted students with learning disabilities use mathematical problem-solving strategies. Their results indicated that gifted students are well aware of their cognitive and metacognitive knowledge. They were systematic in their approach and used a variety of problem-solving strategies. Gifted students with learning disabilities showed some evidence of cognitive and metacognitive strategy knowledge, but were not aware of their knowledge, were less refined in their approaches to problem solving, and as a result were less successful. They might have been taught strategies but were unable to call on the appropriate ones to solve a problem not posed before. Montague suggests that new strategies be taught and old strategies be refined and reinforced. Instructional techniques such as modeling, verbal rehearsal, prompting, performance feedback, reinforcement, and mastery learning should be included in their instruction. Students should have the opportunity to practice the strategy independently and in small groups.

Hughes (1995) suggests that the reading program for the gifted student with a learning disability should be designed to move the student beyond literal understanding. Skills should include extending vocabulary and exploring issues, with an emphasis on higher levels of thinking. Rich, complex, culturally diverse literature should be presented. Strategies should include vocabulary webs, whole language, cooperative groups, and interdisciplinary units. Writing should include the use of graphic organizers. The use of colors to differentiate groups of related concepts can assist learning. For example, a group working with the principle of change can begin by listing all things related to change. The activity can become more complex as the group lists examples of nonchange. Place these students in cooperative learning groups where they do not need to perform in areas of deficit but can demonstrate their strengths. Hughes (1995) also suggests using advance organizers for students. Modeling examples of what is expected and what is going to take place is important for the gifted student who has a learning disability.

Adaptive techniques should be used for writing. Students should be permitted to use tape recorders and computers and to have other students take notes for them. When work is written, it should be edited without penalty. Students should be exposed to all of the content, assessing areas of strength. Content presentation should allow for the disability. Presentation methods should accommodate the child with a learning disability. If necessary, books on tape should be ordered, which are available from the National Library Service for the Blind and Physically Handicapped (see Resource list at end of chapter).

When areas of strength are noted, appropriate differentiation should be planned. A level of challenge should be maintained. Grouping should be planned so that students have the opportunity to work with intellectual peers. Adaptive strategies, such as having students who are not capable of writing placed in groups where other students may write for them, are appropriate. Tape recordings of materials should be provided whenever necessary. Editing should be done for students without penalty.

If a child has been identified as having a learning disability, the school district needs to provide support services. As we move to more inclusive classroom settings, teachers need to consider the answers to these questions as they work with students with learning disabilities:

- Who can assist you as you plan programs for gifted students with learning disabilities?
- Who in your district has been assigned the task of remediating in areas of deficit?
- How might you work with this faculty member to bring the appropriate materials to the students that accommodate specific learning needs?
- Are there volunteers or parents who can assist in making tapes for the classroom?
- What about the physical setting? Is there a place where the student can do her or his work and not be distracted? If not, can you provide a study carol?

CHILDREN WITH GIFTEDNESS AND ATTENTION DEFICIT HYPERACTIVITY DISORDER

Many children with learning disabilities also display attention deficit or attention deficit hyperactivity disorders. The interrelationships among attention deficit disorder, learning disabilities, and hyperactivity can be seen in Figure 5.2.

Definition

AD/HD is a disorder that is commonly inherited (Zametkin, 1995). Lovecky's (1994b) research reveals that gifted children with attention deficit disorder (ADD) have a difficult time during childhood years. Their behavioral symptoms can inhibit academic success and have emotional and social consequences.

In 1902 Dr. George Still, a British pediatrician, published a study he had conducted involving twenty patients in his practice. He noted that they followed a similar pattern of defiance. They appeared to lack inhibitory volition. He thought the answer might lie in the depths of the mind and not in the environment. This theory received greater acceptance when, following the influenza epidemic of 1918, doctors discovered a pattern of postencephalitic behavior disorder, characterized by an inability to concentrate or control impulses. In 1937 a Rhode Island pediatrician found that by giving amphetamines to children with these symptoms, a calming effect was realized, allowing individuals to focus for greater lengths of time. These studies were brought to the fore when the symptomology was included in the broad labeling of *minimal brain damage,* later changed to *dysfunction* in the 1950s. Once labeled, the medical community began to focus on the cause and the cure.

"Despite the declaration by some critics that attention deficit disorder is a 'fad disability' and simply the latest excuse for parents who do not discipline their children, scientific research shows that ADD is a neurobehavioral disorder that is biologically based, says the U.S. Department of Education" (*American Teacher,* 1995, p. 1).

Figure 5.2 **Interrelationships among attention deficit disorder, learning disabilities, and hyperactivity. Children with attention deficit disorder tend to have learning disabilities; some are also hyperactive (AD/HD). However, not all children with hyperactivity or learning disabilities have attention deficit disorder.**
Source: Reprinted with permission from Batshaw, M. L., & Perret, Y. M. (1982). *Children with disabilities.* Baltimore: Paul H. Brookes Publishing Company.

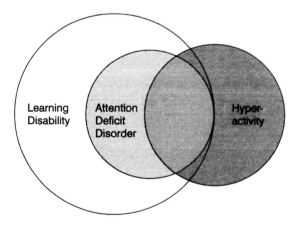

PERSONAL INTERVIEW
Anthony's Story

In the following excerpt, the mother of a child diagnosed as having attention deficit hyperactivity disorder (AD/HD) relates her experiences.

I know you asked me to do this some time ago. I've had a very difficult time getting myself to do just that. I don't know if there is still some part of me that is in denial about Anthony or would just like it all to go away. As a mother it is very hard for me to see my son struggle with life the way he does, and the guilt that goes along with that is sometimes overwhelming. As a counselor who works with other parents whose children are in similar situations and who has been successful at it, it makes my own personal and family failings even more frustrating. Sometimes I am too emotionally tied to Anthony to help.

Anthony is a very strong-willed child. We noticed that, even as an infant, we would sometimes be engaged in power struggles with him. Our pediatrician was the first to even broach the subject that there might be a problem. He thought that there was a possibility that Anthony was ADD. He thought we should keep an eye on it and see what happened. Midyear in kindergarten his teacher suggested that we have him tested because he seemed unable to stay on task and socially he was having problems. One on one he was fine, but in group situations he seemed to do things that annoyed other children. We were skeptical since we were beginning to believe we had made a bad choice of preschool and private kindergarten, having chosen a Montessori setting run by nuns. But we took him to be tested to be sure. There were many family issues we also felt might be contributing to his inability to focus.

In November of his preschool year, Anthony's maternal grandfather died after a fifteen-month-long bout with cancer. Anthony was extremely close to my father and we spent much of our time at my parents' home. This left little time for social interaction for Anthony with his peers. He spent a great deal of time around the adults in his life. During this time, his father was going to school at night and I was pregnant with his sister Katie. The pregnancy was not easy and Katie's first six months of life were colicky. After the testing we went to the therapist suggested by the school. I was not comfortable with him and neither was Anthony. His office was not geared for a child at all. We stopped therapy because Anthony was very upset by it. He is a very closed child who does not share his feelings easily. Yet it was becoming apparent that his self-esteem was very low and his behaviors were overshadowing his other gifts—of which there are many. Anthony is a sweet boy with a good heart who takes life and things that are said to him very hard, very personally, and to heart. He is a child who doesn't understand how his own actions cause his worst fears—being in trouble and not being liked.

First grade was a difficult time but he had a wonderful teacher who adored him and who worked hard with him and with us. She unexpectedly became pregnant and in January of that year left her position due to complications. This devastated Anthony, who is not a child who transitions well, and this was sudden. He had a horrible couple of weeks and I spoke to the new teacher and asked her to be patient. She came back to me a few weeks after and said she would never believe it was the same child. He had settled down. We went in search of a new therapist and chose someone who specialized in children. The outcome was much the same. Anthony was happy to go and play, but there was no way he was going to talk to this person. We stopped going after three months of therapy because he didn't seem to change much. Anthony also seemed to be falling into a pattern of becoming a victim at school and at camp. He was not equipped to deal with this and to this day still has trouble standing up for himself.

Anthony's second-grade year was a very hard one. His teacher disliked him and only found him to be a problem. She could never see the child behind the behavior (Figure 5.3). She humiliated him in front of the class whenever she could, all of which I learned about too late to do anything about and from friends of Anthony, not from Anthony himself. Sometimes the information would come from a classmate's mother. Anthony worked so hard to earn her praise but he failed at every turn and his self-esteem plummeted even more.

After a bad experience in camp the summer of second grade, I was at my wit's end and my husband and I decided to look for a new therapist. Money was a problem so I searched for someone who took our insurance. It was Dr. G. who put a label on Anthony's behavior, saying that he was an ADD child. After seeing him for a couple of months, she suggested placing Anthony on Ritalin. She said we had time to think about it. My husband was reluctant at first because he was concerned about side effects. I, on the other hand, wanted to give Anthony a fresh start in third grade and because I knew testing was in November for the gifted program, I wanted Anthony to have the best shot he could; if the medicine helped him, then great. If it didn't, we hadn't lost anything. As it turned out, Ritalin has helped Anthony to focus. The fact that he has had wonderful teachers in both third and fourth grade and in the program for the gifted has been a tremendous help as well (Figure 5.4). Unfortunately, I still don't think Anthony has been able to get a handle on his impulsive behavior and his need for negative attention. While we have allowed him to take a break from Dr. G we will start again in the New Year.

Child _____						

Child _____
Teacher _____ Grade _2_

November 19 _93_

School _____

Effort: 1 = outstanding
2 = satisfactory
3 = improvement needed
N.A. = not applicable

Comments

	Effort	Outstanding Progress	Satisfactory Progress	Can do this with Teacher Assistance	Improvement Needed
Language Arts					
Reading	1-2				
Uses word attack skills		✔			
Increases word knowledge		✔			
Comprehends materials read			✔		
Writing	1-2				
Uses correct sentence structure			✔		
Expresses original ideas in writing			✔		
Writes neatly and legibly			✔		
Spelling	1				
Learns assigned words		✔			
Spells words correctly in written activities		✔			
Listening & Speaking	3				
Listens attentively					✔
Expresses idea effectively		✔			
Mathematics	1-2				
Knows basic facts		✔			
Understands concepts		✔			
Applies knowledge to solve problems			✔		
Social Studies	1-2				
Understands concepts		✔			
Participates constructively in activities					✔
Science and Health	1-2				
Understands concepts		✔			
Participates constructively in activities					✔
Special Area Subjects					
Art	2-3				
Applies skills and expresses ideas creatively			✔		
Approaches art tasks constructively			✔		
Music	1-2				
Understands concepts and applies skills			✔		
Participates in class activities			✔		
Physical Education	1				
Unless otherwise specified child is performing well			✔		

Comments

Anthony is adjusting to second grade and learning to be responsible for his behaviors. He performs best when he listens attentively and works carefully.

Anthony needs additional practice with social skills: cooperating with others, respecting others, following classroom rules and controlling outbursts.

Anthony often has difficulty responding to authority B.G.

Anthony calls out often and it becomes a distraction to others in class. M.D.

Social Development	Usually	Sometimes	Rarely	Work Study Skills	Usually	Sometimes	Rarely
1. Is sensitive to the needs of others		✔		6. Follows directions	✔		
2. Accepts responsibility		✔		7. Completes work on time	✔		
3. Works cooperatively		✔		8. Works independently	✔		
4. Exercises self-control		✔		9. Uses time constructively		✔	
5. Respects property		✔		10. Works neatly and carefully	✔		
				11. Contributes to class discussions	✔		

Absent	1
Late	0

Parent's Signature _____

Figure 5.3 **Progress report, second grade**

Child_____

Teacher_____ Grade __3__

Effort: 1 = outstanding
2 = satisfactory
3 = improvement needed
N.A. = not applicable

November 19 _94_

School _____

	Effort	Outstanding Progress	Satisfactory Progress	Can do this with Teacher Assistance	Improvement Needed	Comments
Language Arts						
Reading Below__ At__ Above ✔ Level__	1					
Uses word attack skills		✔				
Expands vocabulary		✔				
Comprehends materials read		✔				
Reads with expression and fluency		✔				
Shows interest in independent reading		✔				
Writing	2					
Uses correct sentence structure			✔			
Expresses ideas clearly			✔			
Writes neatly and legibly			✔			
Spelling	1					
Learns assigned words		✔				
Spells words correctly in written activities			✔			
Mathematics Below__ At__ Above__ Level__	1					
Knows fundamentals		✔				
Computes accurately			✔			
Solves problems			✔			
Social Studies	1					
Identifies and locates sources of information			✔			
Interprets information			✔			
Applies acquired knowledge			✔			
Science and Health	1					
Obtains, organizes and applies information acquired			✔			
Understands concepts relating to health needs		✔				
Participates constructively in activities		✔				
Special Area Subjects						
Art	1-2					
Applies skills and expresses ideas creatively			✔			
Approaches art tasks constructively			✔			
Music	1					
Understands concepts and applies skills			✔			
Participates in class activities			✔			
Physical Education	1-2					
Unless otherwise specified child is performing well			✔			

Comments

Anthony is an intelligent student. He participates in our class discussions and offers thoughtful ideas. He pulls an experience and his knowledge to help make him a terrific problem solver.

He is an enthusiastic learner—eager to join in and accomplish the given task.

His ability to focus and succeed have greatly improved.

Anthony has shown much better focus. B.G.

I'm glad Anthony is in my third grade.

Social Development	Usually	Sometimes	Rarely
1. Is sensitive to the needs of others	✔		
2. Accepts responsibility	✔		
3. Works cooperatively	✔✔		
4. Exercises self-control	✔		
5. Respects property	✔		

Work Study Skills	Usually	Sometimes	Rarely
6. Follows directions	✔		
7. Completes work on time	✔		
8. Works independently	✔		
9. Uses time constructively	✔✔		
10. Works neatly and carefully	✔		
11. Contributes to class discussions	✔		
12. Listens attentively	✔		

Absent	5
Late	0

Parent's Signature _____

Figure 5.4 **Progress report, third grade**

My husband and I are still very frustrated, as is Anthony. While his life has moved forward in many ways, in many more he still has a long way to go. His self-esteem is still a big concern as are his impulsive behaviors. We are still looking for answers on how to make Anthony's life as normal as possible. Our biggest heartbreak is knowing that for Anthony life as a child is hard, very hard, and not much fun and that is just not the way it should be. All we have ever wished for our children was that they be happy and healthy, but in Anthony's case we are having a hard time making him happy.

The exact causes of AD/HD are unknown. There is no evidence of brain damage. There is a genetic component as indicated by the fact that one in every four children with AD/HD has a biological parent with AD/HD who is similarly affected. The symptoms of AD/HD persist into adulthood for many students but not necessarily all (Zametkin, 1995). Talan (1996) reports that federal researchers completed a five-year study at the National Institute of Mental Health and found that precise areas of the brain were smaller and more symmetrical in boys with attention deficit hyperactivity disorder, suggesting that there are functional differences in how information is processed. It appears that there is a problem with neurotransmissions across cells. The area of the brain that inhibits behaviors is not functioning properly, causing impulsivity. In 50 percent of the AD/HD population, onset occurs prior to age 4. In most cases it becomes recognizable in school. It is a chronic condition that can diminish over time. Twenty to 50 percent of children continue to have symptoms such as restlessness and fidgeting into adolescence and adulthood (Cohen, 1995). Early intervention is critical because of the impact of the behaviors on academics and social development. Multimodal treatment is often necessary, such as medication, therapy, and behavior modification (Zametkin, 1995).

Characteristics

The following list of common symptoms of attention deficit disorder with hyperactivity have been adapted from the *Diagnostic and Statistical Manual of Mental Disorders,* fourth edition (American Psychiatric Association, 1994):

Inattention

1. Often does not give close attention to details or makes careless mistakes in schoolwork, work, or other activities.
2. Often has difficulty sustaining attention in tasks or play activities.
3. Often does not seem to listen when spoken to directly.
4. Often does not follow through on instruction and fails to finish schoolwork, chores, or duties (not due to oppositional behavior or failure to understand instructions).
5. Often has difficulty organizing tasks and activities.

6. Often avoids, dislikes, or is reluctant to engage in tasks that require sustained mental effort (such as schoolwork or homework).
7. Often loses things necessary for tasks or activities, such as toys, assignments, books or tools.
8. Is often easily distracted by extraneous stimuli.
9. Is often forgetful in daily activities.

Hyperactivity

1. Often fidgets with hands or feet or squirms in seat.
2. Often leaves seat in classroom or in other situations in which remaining seated is expected.
3. Often runs about or climbs excessively in situations in which it is inappropriate (adolescents or adults may have feelings of restlessness).
4. Often has difficulty playing or engaging in leisure activities quietly.
5. Is often "on the go" or often acts as if "driven by a motor."
6. Often talks excessively.

Impulsivity

7. Often blurts out answers before questions are completed.
8. Often has difficulty awaiting turn.
9. Often interrupts or intrudes on others, such as butting into conversations or games.

If six or more symptoms of inattention or hyperactivity–impulsivity have persisted for at least six months in more than one setting, to a degree that is maladaptive and inconsistent with developmental level, the patient should be evaluated.*

AD/HD children may not seem to listen to what is being said to them. They may be distracted by a noise or activity in the room that causes them to lose focus. They might engage in physically dangerous activities without considering possible consequences (not for the purpose of thrill seeking); for example, runs into the street without looking.

Children with AD/HD are cognitively able, as opposed to students who have specific disabilities that interfere with the acquisition of skills such as reading or writing. Children with learning disabilities can be diagnosed with the aid of an IQ test (discrepancy in verbal and performance scores); there is no one definitive diagnosis tool to determine AD/HD in children.

Parents and teachers should become aware of the behaviors that describe AD/HD children. It is important that a diagnosis be made early so that children are not reprimanded for behaviors beyond their control. This causes children who are AD/HD to lose self-esteem.

---

* Reprinted with permission from the *Diagnostic and Statistical Manual of Mental Disorders*, fourth edition. Copyright 1994 American Psychiatric Association.

Identification

Webb and Latimer (1993) emphasize the difficulties involved in determining whether children are AD/HD and gifted and suggest the use of many instruments, including intelligence tests (which should be administered by qualified professionals), achievement and personality tests, and parent and teacher rating scales. Portions of the intellectual and achievement tests will reveal attention problems or learning disabilities, whereas personality tests may indicate depression or anxiety. Evaluation should be followed by appropriate curricular and instructional modifications, which include areas of strength and learning style. For AD/HD children, performance on a WISC will often indicate weaknesses in the arithmetic and digit span subtests.

Under the IDEA (P.L. 105-17), these children are entitled to special education services as determined by their Individualized Education Plan (IEP). These laws guarantee appropriate public education for all children with disabilities regardless of degree of severity from ages 3 to 21. The special services include the spectrum of special education and is IEP dependent. Children may receive a multitude of related services, such as a resource room or an aid. Children and young adults who do not qualify for services under the Individuals with Disabilities Education Act can receive

In speaking with Anthony's mom, she reported the following with regard to his educational evaluations.

In Anthony's case he had difficulty attending during testing so the testing was conducted over many sessions.

According to the test results (Wechsler Preschool and Primary Scales of Intelligence), Anthony attained a verbal IQ of 156 (99th percentile), a performance IQ of 127 (96th percentile), and a full-scale IQ of 149 (99.95th percentile). The examiner reported that Anthony's anxiety and self-distracting behaviors affected his performance on timed tasks. He also appeared to be experiencing a developmental lag in the acquisition of visual perceptual motor skills, relative to his verbal abilities. The examiner summarized Anthony as having an overall level of intellectual functioning in the very superior range. While Anthony's verbal abilities were clearly better developed than his nonverbal skills, it is important to recognize that even his nonverbal abilities fall within the superior range. Anthony was experiencing some visual perceptual motor immaturity's that negatively impacted his performance, which might interfere with his smooth acquisition of basic reading skills. He also had difficulties with attention and concentration that might have a neurological basis. He was reported to be an anxious, insecure child who used many self-distracting behaviors, along with excessive verbalization and constant activity, to avoid his feelings of anger, sadness, and frustration.

accomodations under Section 504, the National Rehabilitation Act, which defines disabilities more broadly, and affords more flexibility to the local schools.

Identifying and classifying children with AD/HD can be extremely important. Under the IDEA and Section 504, test accommodations, such as extended time, can be made. Time constraints in testing situations placed on students with AD/HD can mask the students' true potential.

Intervention

Webb and Latimer (1993) and Wolfle and French (1990) point out striking similarities in characteristics of AD/HD and gifted children that cloud the identification of the gifted student with AD/HD. Typical gifted children who daydream may be viewed as being reflective or engaged in creative thought. Gifted students with AD/HD might be chastised in the same situation for being off-task. Gifted children might be expected to question rules and resist authority. This would be considered unacceptable for gifted students with AD/HD.

Wolfle and French (1990) suggest the use of a *five M model*. The five M's stand for (1) medication, (2) management, (3) modification, (4) modeling, and (5) mothering.

Many medications are on the market today that have been proven to be very effective. Decisions as to whether they should be used can only be made by the parents with the advice of physicians and counselors. One parent reported that her son was on the verge of being kicked out of school. Under the care of a psychopharmacologist, the child was put on a combination of medications and became an A student.

Using good classroom management strategies is perhaps the most effective way of working with AD/HD students. Some options include these:

- Seat AD/HD students in an area with few distractions.
- Provide a free-range area where they can move around as they need to release excess energy.
- Outline the rules and regulations to be followed in the room.
- Reiterate the rules throughout the year.
- Outline respective rewards and/or punishments for appropriate and inappropriate behaviors.
- Provide a time-out area where they can reflect on their actions.
- Outline the course work.
- Use visuals and manipulatives as well as oral and written materials to promote attentiveness and retention.
- Allow additional time on tests.
- Review instructions or assignments on the board. Be specific.
- Review previous lessons.
- State needed materials.
- Ask questions of the student to determine if he is staying focused.
- Ask and wait. Probe for the correct answer before calling on another student.
- Try to keep the noise level down in the classroom.
- Provide immediate feedback.

- Provide advance warnings. Let the student know that a lesson is about to end.
- Preview lessons to come. Let students know what they will learn, and how they should participate.

Because children with AD/HD are impulsive, it is helpful to outline techniques that will assist them in monitoring and controlling their attention and behavior. Consider these suggestions:

- Look for the instructions on the blackboard.
- Raise your hand if you have something to say.
- If help is needed and the teacher is not available, quietly ask another child.
- When necessary, ask the teacher to repeat instructions, rather than guess.
- Break large assignments into smaller tasks. Set a deadline for each task and reward yourself as you complete each one.
- Each day, make a list of what needs to be done. Plan the best order for doing each task, then make a schedule for doing them.
- Work in a quiet area. Do one thing at a time. Give yourself short breaks.
- Write things you to need to remember in a notebook with dividers. Write different kinds of information such assignments in different sections.
- Post notes to remind yourself of things to do. Tape the notes to places where you are likely to see them.
- Categorize and classify your belongings and keep similar things together.
- Create a routine. Get yourself ready for school in the same way, every day.
- Exercise, eat a balanced diet, and get enough sleep.

As children find ways of coping, interruptions lessen.

Make sure you praise a student when appropriate strategies are used. Wolfle and French (1990) included evidence that behavior modification is an effective non-medical treatment that can help students to control behavior. Positive reinforcement or token reinforcement was found to reduce activity levels, increase attention span, and increase academic performance. Using a contract in combination with a token system can be effective. Teachers and students may write the contract together, outlining in specific, concrete terms the work to be completed, the behaviors to be demonstrated, the reward for displaying the behavior, and the cost for not fulfilling the contract. Set time limits for satisfying the contract.

Modification refers to altering the classroom environment depending on the needs of children. For some children with AD/HD it is important that stimulation be kept to a minimum. This includes room decorations. Children with AD/HD tend to perform better when seated close to the teacher in front of the classroom where there are apt to be fewer distractions. If there are some students who appear to provoke children with AD/HD more than others, see to it that these children are not seated close to the child. Children with AD/HD need to be able to move around. Possible ways to provide for needed movement in positive ways might include allowing the student to assume positive roles in the classroom such as passing out paper, erasing the blackboard, and taking messages to the office.

Modeling appropriate behavior is another important essential. Teach children to become aware of their feelings and practice verbalizing them before their impulsive behavior takes over. What situations cause the child to feel angry? Practice in advance: "When I have completed my work and have to wait I get angry." Teach children to choose positive activities that will not disturb others in this situation: "I will take a book out." "I will go over to the art center and take out a piece of paper and draw." Teach children to reinforce their own positive actions. Teach them to think to themselves, "I did a good job!" Teachers can reinforce positive behaviors when they are observed. Both teachers and parents can model behaviors that illustrate that they too become frustrated at times. Verbalizing these feelings and not acting out can help children with AD/HD to gain control. Teaching and modeling social skills is an integral part of their development.

When working in areas of curriculum, teachers should present content as prescribed for all students, noting areas of strength. Present information in settings that are appropriate using interactive materials to maintain focus. Differentiation should be implemented as gifts surface. Depending on the severity of the problem, special accommodations may need to be made. Providing one-on-one mentoring will help to maintain students' focus.

Teachers can help parents to understand their child. Demonstrating unconditional love and acceptance of a child displaying the symptoms of AD/HD can be difficult. As adults, it is imperative that the behavior not be confused with the child. The actions demonstrated cannot be controlled and should not be punished, although they cannot go unnoticed. When admonishing a child, the child should not become the object. Telling a child that certain behavior is not appropriate or acceptable is totally different from telling them that they are not accepted. Explaining to the child that his actions are causing other children to dislike him avoids personalization and diminishment of self-esteem. Children's strengths must be emphasized and rewarded.

Administrators need to help teachers understand the nature of the problem. Lack of understanding can be detrimental to the child's performance.

The following excerpts are progress reports from teachers about Anthony, the child we met at the beginning of this section.

Anthony's second-grade report card and, in particular, the teacher's comments underscore the need to prepare general classroom teachers to work with children with AD/HD. Anthony clearly demonstrates the characteristics of this disorder and is not just being a "bad boy." Consider this November 1993 progress report:

Anthony is adjusting to second grade and learning to be responsible for his behaviors. He performs best when he listens attentively and works carefully.

Anthony needs additional practice with social skills: cooperating with others, respecting others, following classroom rules, and controlling outbursts.

> Art: Anthony often has difficulty responding to authority.
> Music: Anthony calls out often and it becomes a distraction to others in the class.

The teacher went on to say that Anthony needs improvement in the following areas: listens attentively, participates constructively in activities in social studies, participates constructively in activities in science and health, rarely exercises self-control, and sometimes uses time constructively.

The following progress report was written in March 1994:

Anthony works successfully through the curriculum areas. He is proud of his success. Anthony continues to be reinforced in social skills. He is reminded of appropriate behavior and encouraged in his efforts.

> Music: Anthony is a good student, but at times his calling out and moving about is distracting.
> Physical Education: Anthony's behavior is distracting and disruptive at times.

Anthony's mother reports that this was a terrible year for Anthony. . . .

In third grade Anthony had a teacher who was more tolerant and accepting of Anthony. This is reflected in his November 1994 progress report in her room and in other settings.

Anthony is an intelligent student. He participates in our class discussions and offers thoughtful ideas. He pulls on experience and his knowledge to help make him a terrific problem solver. He is an enthusiastic learner—eager to join in and accomplish the given task. His ability to focus and succeed have greatly improved. [There were no needed improvements listed.]

> Art: Anthony has shown much better focus.
> Music: I'm glad Anthony is in my third grade.

In March 1995, the same teacher wrote:

Anthony is continuing to show good growth. He is becoming a good leader. Anthony has been accepted in our district's gifted program and he has made a fine transition into his participation. I know he enjoys being a part of the program. Anthony has continued to be an enthusiastic class member. He has especially enjoyed our science unit on buoyancy, "Boats Are Us!" Keep up the excellent work!! I enjoy our little daily chats!!

Anthony received "Satisfactory in Art and Music" and "Outstanding in Physical Education." He also received "Great!" for the areas of works cooperatively, exercises self-control, and respects property.

What becomes clear is that the classroom teacher can positively impact the child's behavior.

RESOURCES

Attention Deficit Information Network (Ad-IN), 475 Hillside Avenue, Needham, MA 02194. Provides up-to-date information on current research, regional meetings. Offers aid in finding solutions to practical problems faced by adults and children with an attention deficit disorder.

Children and Adults with Attention Deficit Disorders (CHADD), 499 NW 70th Avenue, Suite 109, Plantation, FL 33317; phone: (954)587-3700; www.chadd.org. A major advocate of and key information source for people dealing with attention disorders. Sponsors support groups and publishes newsletters concerning attention disorders.

National Information Center for Children with Disabilities, P.O. Box 1492, Washington, DC 20013-1492.

National Library Service for the Blind and Physically Handicapped, The Library of Congress, Washington, DC 20542; phone: (202)707-5100.

Textbooks on Tape, Recording for the Blind and Dyslexic, 20 Roszel Road, Princeton, NJ 08540; phone: (609)452-0606.

Section 3

Special Populations of Gifted Children

Chapter 6 is concerned with gifted children who come from minority and disadvantaged populations, such as African Americans, Alaskans, American Indians, and immigrants. The special challenges presented in nurturing and identifying children from culturally diverse backgrounds are discussed. The classroom is an important place in which to begin to acknowledge differences and provide for environmental deficits.

Chapter 7 addresses the concerns involved with identifying and planning for exceptionally gifted children. The exceptionally gifted child should be identified and nurtured early in life. When a child's intellectual abilities far surpass that of peers, accommodations should be made

so that boredom, underachievement, acting out, and withdrawing do not become issues.

The young gifted child is the subject of Chapter 8. Challenges involved in the identification and nurturance of young gifted children are discussed. Uneven development between social, emotional, intellectual, and gross or fine motor skills can cause frustration for young gifted children. Recognition of the dyssynchrony assists in providing appropriate opportunities for these students.

Chapter 9 includes a discussion of the nurture and support needed by gifted females in order to cultivate their gifts. Gifted females present unique challenges because of the nature of differences. They need support and encouragement to develop areas of strength.

Chapter 6

Gifted Children from Diverse Backgrounds

Typical questions a classroom teacher might ask include these:

What are some of the specific characteristics of gifted students from diverse and minority backgrounds?

Why have students from diverse and minority populations been so under-represented in gifted programs?

How can we effectively identify these students?

How can I accommodate these students in my classroom?

To answer these questions, this chapter does the following:

Discusses students from minority and disadvantaged populations.

Introduces special concerns for identifying gifted students from minority and disadvantaged populations.

Presents the concerns involved in engaging and maintaining gifted minorities in academic pursuits.

DEFINITION

Populations of culturally diverse individuals have been underrepresented in programs for the gifted. Culture is defined as the "unique manner by which diverse groups of human beings organize and actualize their physical and mental lives in dialectical confrontation with biological survival, oppression, resistance, the struggle for human dignity, self-determination and fulfillment" (Weill, 1993). The definition includes discussions regarding gender, race, age, and socioeconomic class. Cultural differences exist in each of the diverse populations. These differences can affect classroom performance and lead to cultural conflict or misunderstandings, preventing identification of giftedness.

The United States is comprised of diverse ethnic groups. The country has been referred to as "A Nation of Immigrants" on more than one occasion, yet our educational system does not reflect the diversity of thought and knowledge which encompasses American Indians (sic). The "Americanization" of the public school system needs to occur. This transition must include cultural diversity and will most certainly promote equity in educational opportunity. When this occurs, problems relating to American Indian education will decrease and understanding will be promoted between diverse peoples. (Michigan State Board of Education, 1987, p. 15)

Populations that have not been served and that have been underrepresented in gifted programs include those variously labeled culturally deprived, educationally

PERSONAL INTERVIEW
Dana's Story

Dana is a gifted woman of African American descent whose story reveals many of the stresses encountered by students from disadvantaged backgrounds.

I was born in the South. My father was a jealous husband, perhaps with cause, and was abusive to my mother, who was ten years younger than him. My mother abandoned our family when I was four years old. I have one sister. We moved north and my father remarried a women who had two children of her own—a daughter nine years my senior and a son seven years my senior. When we moved north, my father took a job as a chauffeur for a family where my stepmother worked as a cook and a domestic, sleeping in.

My father was very weak and left control of the home to my stepmother, who was not happy to have two additional children to care for. We were cloistered in our house and lived in a ghetto surrounded by derelicts. We were not allowed out unless we were going to school or church. We lived in a totally secluded environment. The center of our lives was our church, where there was a total sense of community.

My childhood was not a happy time in many respects. I was required to assist with work my stepmother brought home such as laundry and had chores at home to pay my way. I was not treated well. Church and school were my salvation. Education was valued by everyone I knew. Even though there was no active help with homework or projects, we were told that education was important and the key to success in life. Professionals were respected and admired at home and at church. I was happy that we had moved because we were given free books. In the South we had to pay for them. I was an excellent student and was skipped in fourth and seventh grades. I was always a voracious reader. I loved books. I was reading by the time I entered school. Even though no one at home took an interest in my little sister and me, they approved of reading, art, and sewing. These are the things we busied ourselves with.

My teachers recognized my abilities and supported me. Knowing I was badly treated, two teachers offered to adopt me. My home life was miserable so I believe I had perfect attendance at school. Sick or well I went. My teachers attended the same church as I did. I didn't dare misbehave for fear they would tell my parents at church. I read eight to nine books a week. The city librarian at school would choose books for me that were appropriate even though they were far beyond my grade level. I was the salutatorian in junior high school and I graduated from high school at sixteen years of age.

I went to a free four-year college and worked while going to school from four to eleven at night each day. I contributed half of my salary to my home for room and board and helped my little sister. She was exceptionally bright but only got to complete two years of college. I married and moved and went to a college in New York City part-time. This was the first time that I attended an educational institution that was not segregated. I studied speech and drama, then psychology and education. I went back home to complete my education. I was awarded scholarships to complete a master's and doctorate at a fine Southern university. I always wanted to be a teacher. My teachers literally saved my life. They had recognized special talent in me. They were wise and caring people and made a lasting impression on me.

In one word [I attribute my success to] tenacity. I knew I was smart. I also knew that educated people were respected. There were many obstacles along the way with little help. The struggle has taken its toll. It took me a lot longer than my colleagues to get where I am today.

deprived, underprivileged, low socioeconomic status, inner-city dwellers, culturally impoverished, culturally handicapped, educationally disadvantaged, children of the poor, culturally impoverished, culturally different, and culturally diverse.

Children who are at risk may include students from foreign countries but can also include Native Americans and Alaskan students (Tonemah, 1991).

CHARACTERISTICS

If we are to accurately assess potential giftedness in culturally diverse populations, we need to gain a greater understanding of the differences or special characteristics prevalent among each of the groups. Their culture may impact language, behavior and personal interactions, learning style, and values.

Research regarding cultural and environmental factors that have shaped behaviors in specific populations is discussed in the following subsections.

Asian Americans

Hasegawa, Gallagher, Kitano, and Tanaka (1989, p. 152) report on the unique behaviors of gifted Asian American students in Table 6.1.

American Indians

Knutson and McCarthy-Tucker (1993, p. 5) report that for the Native American, the cultural differences can be delineated as follows:

Table 6.1   Characteristics of giftedness and cultural values of Asians, and the behaviors resulting from their interactive influence

Absolute Aspects of Giftedness	Cultural Values Often Characteristic of Asians	Behavioral Differences
Strong need for consistency between abstract values and personal actions	Arugama or akirame (mature self-control or resignation)	Passivity, lack of assertiveness
High expectations of self	Confucianistic ethic (people can be improved by proper effort and instruction)	Academic orientation and achievement
Unusual sensitivity to expectations and feelings of others	Family honor and tradition, personal responsibility	Self-discipline, self-motivation, preference for structure and defined limits
Perfectionism	Conformity, correctness, respect for and obedience to authority	Patience with and willingness to do drill and rote exercises; decreased risk taking and creative expression
Persistent, goal-directed behavior	Educational achievement of the work ethic	Concentration and persistence on academic tasks

Source: Reprinted with permission from Hasegawa, C., Gallagher, R., Kitano, M., & Tanaka, K. (1989). Asian Americans: The problem of defining Asian Americans. In C. June Maker & Shirley Schiever (Eds.), *Critical issues in gifted education: Defensible programs for cultural and ethnic minorities.* Austin, TX: PRO-ED.

Traditional Native American Values

- Speaking: softer, slower, interject less, delayed responses
- Emphasis on nonverbal communication
- Avoidance of speaker or listener
- Cooperation, sharing, anonymity, humility, privacy
- Control of self, discipline, patience, harmony with nature
- Holistic
- Participation after observation
- Present orientation

Contemporary Anglo-American Values

- Speaking: louder, faster, interrupt often, immediate responses
- Emphasis on verbal expression, use verbal encouragement
- Directly address speaker or listener
- Competition, personal goals, fame, recognition, expressiveness
- Control of others, blame others, aggressive, competitive, subjugation of nature
- Analytic, inquisitive
- Trial-and-error learning
- Future orientation

African Americans

Cultural differences cannot be ignored as a factor in underachievement in African American students. According to Ford (1992), blacks have distinct cultural values that may conflict with the dominant culture and can therefore obstruct the educational process and hinder achievement. "Underachievement is more likely to occur when the values, beliefs, norms and attitudes of members of the Black culture are inconsistent with those established by the majority White culture, which controls most systems" (p. 130). African American children may hide their academic abilities by becoming class clowns, purposefully underachieving, and dropping out of school to avoid negative peer pressure.

Gifted African American students share the same concerns as gifted students in general: poor peer relations, negative peer pressures, perfectionism, heightened sensitivity, concern about social and world issues, and excessive expectations from others. However, their concerns are compounded because they contend with social and environmental issues such as racism and discrimination, lowered teacher expectations, and high rates of poverty. Cultural conflict over differences relative to values and learning style preferences and psychological issues (that is, racial identity, self-concept, and locus of control) exacerbates underachievement among gifted African American students. All of these factors hinder effective identification and placement.

Puerto Ricans

Diaz (1996) reports on factors affecting the underachievement of Puerto Rican students. The major finding of her investigation was the lack of students' exposure to early appropriate academic or curricular experiences. Other inhibiting factors included these:

Family Factors
- A strained relationship with one or both parents, and one or more siblings
- Unhappy home climate because of illness or other factors
- Minimal parental academic guidance or support
- Inconsistent monitoring of student's achievement-oriented activities at home
- Inappropriate parental expectations.

School Factors
- Lack of early exposure to appropriate academic or curricular experiences
- Absence of opportunities to develop and/or improve a schoolwork discipline
- Negative interactions with teachers
- Unrewarding curriculum and questionable counseling experiences.

Community Factors
- Hostile environment including gang-related incidents, ethnic prejudice, and few opportunities for constructive entertainment

- Personal factors
- Insufficient perseverance
- Low sense of efficacy
- Inappropriate coping strategies.

DIFFERENCES IN LEARNING STYLES AMONG DIVERSE POPULATIONS

Teachers need to become sensitized to the different learning styles that are prevalent in different groups. The literature on culturally diverse populations points to the difficulties involved in accommodating all of the variables involved. Different theorists define and diagnose learning style preferences in a variety of ways. Different populations demonstrate different preferences. A review of some of the conclusions drawn from research includes the following studies.

Ewing and Lan Yong (1992) reported on the learning style preferences among gifted African American, Mexican American, and American-born Chinese middle grade students. Chinese students indicated significant group differences in preferences for noise, light, visual modality, studying in the afternoon, and persistence.

Gifted American-born Chinese were found to prefer the visual modality to a greater degree than their American and Mexican American counterparts (Ewing & Lan Yong, 1992). Gifted Mexican American students indicated that they did not prefer auditory modality. Chan (1986) also found that Chinese children prefer the visual mode of learning. African American students preferred a kinesthetic modality.

Researchers have found that American Indian students prefer a visual approach to learning. For example, Navajo children learn by visualizing carefully formed impressions (Swisher & Deyhle, 1989). Walker, Dodd, and Bigelow (1989), in their study of the cognitive patterns of Yakima Indian students, concluded that spatial ability appears to be a relative strength. In addition, Kleinfeld (1973) found that Eskimos evidence a pattern of high figural ability and low English verbal ability.

Patton (1994) reported on the cognitive strengths and preferred learning modes of African American gifted learners and the implications for learning (see Table 6.2).

IDENTIFICATION

If appropriate interventions are to be put in place, specific issues involved in identification need to be addressed; specifically, lack of services due to financial problems, racial bias among educators, culturally biased standardized tests, and lack of parent participation (Knutson & McCarthy-Tucker, 1993).

Harris (1993) addresses the challenges involved in identifying gifted children who come from families that are recent immigrants. Problems involved language, culture, as well as possible "hidden" factors. The process of acquiring a second language is a long and complex one. Assessment of abilities using English-based instruments can lead to erroneous conclusions. Intellectual potential may not be revealed.

Table 6.2   **Cognitive strengths/preferred learning modes of African American gifted learners and related implications for construction of appropriate learning experiences**

Cognitive, Psychomotor, and Creative Strengths AND Preferred Modes of Learning	Effective Teaching/Learning Methodologies to enhance and positively develop strengths and complement preferred modes of learning
S Verbal fluency, stylistic, charismatic language use	Language arts emphasis on literature, reading, oral discussion, debates, public speaking, poetry reciting, drama
S Advanced kinesthetic ability	Emphasis on use of technology, experimentation with puzzles, manipulatives; frequent movement in class allowed
PM Verbal, physical movement	Organization, utilizing hands-on learning
S Creative, resourceful, advanced aesthetic sensibilities, inventive	Emphasis on integrating the arts with core content instruction; utilizing problem-based learning; opportunities for developing new solutions to old problems; synthesizing
PM Interest/concern for humankind; prefers person-to-person interaction/contact (over person-to-object interaction)	Emphasis on development of social interaction skills; leadership development opportunities, anthropology; world affairs; utilizing cooperative learning as an instructional strategy
PM Belief/interest/value for the relationship of human beings with nature	Focus on science; ecology; outdoor field experiences; study of other cultures with similar values (i.e., Native American, Asian American)

Source: Reprinted with permission from Patton, J. M. (1994, April 7). African American students with gifts and talents in an inclusive classroom. Paper presented at the Annual 72nd International Convention of the Council for Exceptional Children, Denver, CO.

Customs and sex-role behaviors may differ greatly. Learning styles, listening behaviors, and response patterns may also differ. "Hidden factors" might include illegal immigrant status and limited knowledge about social and health care services and could impede educational progress. Children who are capable of achieving may experience feelings of guilt for family members who have been left behind. They may fear forming close associations with teachers and other potentially helpful adults. As they grow, they may take on the role of interpreter for the family and begin resenting the responsibility.

Factors affecting poor performance among diverse populations might include the following:

- Experiential deprivations, especially in childhood, which would include lack of cognitive stimulation
- Limited language development
- Differences in learning styles
- Lack of role models

- Low expectations on the part of parents and teachers
- Peer pressure
- Lack of parental involvement
- Strained relationships with one or both parents or siblings
- Cultural differences
- Racial bias
- Lack of opportunity

In addition to the biases listed earlier, standardized tests are also biased in that test items are not based on any definite theory of cognitive or intellectual functioning. Gifted students are most often identified by standardized intelligence and achievement tests (Archambault et al., 1993). For gifted culturally diverse students, standardized tests are often ineffective for identifying and assessing giftedness (Miller-Jones, 1981). In addition, achievement tests cater to those who understand how to take tests.

According to Alexander and Muia (1982), standardized tests are normed on white middle-class values and life experiences, rely heavily on the English language, and require experiential knowledge. Tonemah (1991, p. 5) also addresses the limits imposed by using standardized tests:

1. Standardized test scores by themselves cannot measure total achievement of a school, of a grade, or of a discipline in a grade.
2. Standardized tests cannot be used as a sole source of evaluation of student performance, particularly that of gifted and talented students.
3. The use of standardized tests, for special populations, particularly Native Americans, may be discriminatory.

Insufficient familiarity with the English language can create problems for immigrant children and some Eskimo groups. Even those who have learned English often use their native thought processes and formulate their speech accordingly (Department of Education, 1990). Even speech therapists can have difficulty detecting the difference between dialect and speech problems. Tonemah (1991) emphasizes the importance of a relevant curriculum for students from diverse backgrounds.

INTERVENTIONS

What becomes clear is that classrooms today should reflect the needs of all learners. Factors that need to be addressed include involving parents in the education of their children, sensitivity to behaviors, assessment of ability, and delivery of instruction.

Alternatives to Standardized Tests

Alternatives to standardized tests have been developed and include the following:

- AIGTAM, American Indian Gifted and Talented Assessment Model (Tonemah & Brittan, 1985)

- GAIN, the Gifted Attitudes Inventory for Navahos (Abbott, 1983)
- The Baldwin Identification Matrix Inservice Kit for the Identification of Gifted and Talented Students (Baldwin & Wooster, 1977)
- SOMPA, System of Multicultural Pluralistic Assessment (Mercer & Lewis, 1978)
- Raven Progressive Matrices (Raven, Court, & Raven, 1985), also known as the Standard and Progressive Matrices.

Identification and education of young, economically disadvantaged, potentially gifted students should include the use of portfolios as suggested by Wright and Borland (1993). They suggest that teachers collect examples of students' work in response to one or more activities in which all students have participated. The activity should be curriculum based and grounded in work being done in the classroom. It should be developmentally appropriate and representative of a specific domain. This would provide a standard that can be used to compare and identify exceptional ability. A teacher-selected sample should be included that demonstrates a student's ability, potential, or growth in a domain. This is especially helpful for the child whose tests do not reflect abilities. Students should be asked to select work that has a special meaning for them citing why this work had been selected. Notable moment cards should be used by teachers for capturing special moments. These are recommended, but not exclusively, for affective and social development. Teachers can also request that parents supply information about the individual youngster.

Information gathered as part of a portfolio can take a variety of forms: written samples, photographs (for example, pictures of artwork, sculptures, or structures), audiotapes, videotapes, anecdotes, awards received, and computer disks. Portfolios can be compiled over time using computer disks that can incorporate photographs with written and spoken words.

According to Weill (1993), providing bilingual education to students limited in English is theoretically sound. Those who are not capable of speaking English are too often viewed as deficient and are relegated to performing remedial activities. Krashen (1988) believes that developing literacy in a primary language contributes to superior levels of cognitive development.

Attempts should be made to provide materials that deliver instruction in written and audiovisual forms. Lessons should be varied to accommodate different modalities by incorporating hands-on experiences whenever possible. The classroom should be designed so that students can work independently and in groups. Group work should be balanced with opportunities for individual learning. Because teachers note that students perform better when using a particular style of learning, this information should be discussed with children and parents so that they can share in the responsibility for the child's learning.

Instruction needs to bolster the development of cognitive processes. Bereiter and Engelmann (1966) studied the cognitive processes of children of poverty. They believed deficiencies in reasoning manifested themselves in two ways: (1) Their background had not taught them to perform operations such as comparing, combining, and translating; and (2) children had not experienced verbal interactions that required them to inquire, analyze, explain, or deduce.

Earlier studies reported similar findings. Klaus and Gray (1968) worked with youngsters from socioeconomically depressed homes and found the children had not developed the concepts involved in classifying or generalizing. Teachers began working with the children and paid a great deal of attention to developing perceptual discrimination, concept formation, number ability, and language and continuously encouraged the development of attitudes toward learning such as persistence, achievement motivation, and delaying gratification. At the end of a three-year program, the youngsters scored nine points higher on an IQ test as compared with a matched group that had no such exposure. Lewin's (1996) research confirms data collected so far. A new study of 790 families receiving welfare warned of problems for schoolchildren. "Most of the homes in the study were rated as safe and orderly. But most were also characterized as providing little cognitive stimulations and emotional support to young children, based on both independent interviewers' findings and the mothers' own reports on indicators like how often they read to their children or spanked them" (p. A14).

Giftedness is not solely a cognitive phenomenon (Sternberg & Davison, 1986). Cognition, metacognition, and motivation interact. According to Kurtz (1990), metacognition is a complex system including cognitive and motivational components, with cultural–environmental factors as mediators. Metacognitive functioning is required in outstanding music performance (Bemberger, 1986) and in nonacademic performance areas (Bloom, 1985). Development of cognitive and metacognitive abilities should be stressed so that gifted students can achieve their potential in any of the domains.

As Whimbey and Whimbey (1975) state in their book *Intelligence Can Be Taught:*

> Intelligence is an attention/processing skill used in analyzing and mentally reconstructing relations. The distinguishing feature of this skill is breaking complex relations (or problems) into small steps that can be dealt with fully. The major components of the skill are extensive search and careful apprehension of all details relevant to the relation through utilization of all available information including prior knowledge; accurate comparisons; and sequential, step-by-step analysis and construction. (p. 120)

When skills are taught, intelligence as measured by tests improves. This was demonstrated in research reported by Peterson (1995). For example, when the U.S. Military Academy Preparatory School, the major avenue for black applicants to reach West Point, was in danger of having its funding cut back, access to higher learning for disadvantaged students was threatened.

Jabari Miller had managed a C+ average in high school, Nathaniel Edwards scored 740 on his SAT, and Katina Manning had math skills that were so poor that she gave up on college and enlisted in the army.

> The best these three Army recruits—all of them black—might have hoped for academically after high school was a community college or a lesser state school. But all of them got the same break—acceptance into the U.S. Military Academy

Preparatory School here, 10 months of intensive class work in just two academic subjects, English and math. The Army prep score raised Mr. Edwards's SAT score more than 300 points; it set Miss Manning on her way to becoming a top calculus student. (Peterson, 1995, p. A1)

All three of these students are now studying at the United States Military Academy at West Point.

Teachers should compensate for the lack of cognitive stimulation by incorporating questions in discussions and on tests that address higher levels of thinking (Bloom, 1956) and provide for complexity. Assessment includes taking note as students interact with curriculum and responses indicate an interest in understanding underlying concepts, ability to analyze information, and reasoning.

Emphasis on Creativity and Leadership

Frasier (1992) reviewed the difficulties involved in identifying and educating gifted children who are either economically disadvantaged or members of a culture other than the dominant culture. Diversity within cultural groups, as well as differences between groups, should be recognized when designing identification procedures, curricula, and instruction. When identifying children from other cultures, the focus should be on assessing abilities valued by that culture and should include data regarding creativity and leadership. Torrance (1977) purports that the greatest strengths of disadvantaged and culturally diverse students are the creative skills and motivations. Data should be gathered from a variety of sources (Williams & DeGateano, 1985).

Importance of Parental Involvement

Parents should be brought into the educational life of their children (Freeman, 1993). They should feel and see a sense of entitlement in their children's education. Children need to be nourished and encouraged. The importance of parental involvement was confirmed by Terwilliger (1934, as cited in Kearney & LeBlanc, 1992). A study of ten black gifted students with IQs of higher than 125 found that they came from superior homes and chose careers from the professional occupations. Parents of less affluent economic backgrounds, parents living in different family/household structures, or parents with lower educational levels may be apprehensive about becoming involved in school, thus hindering the success of their children.

Patton (1994) urges empowering families of African American families. Parents of African American students should be advised of the potential gifts and concomitant behaviors to be expected at home and school. Parent sessions can be conducted to assist families in counteracting the negative pressures placed on their children by society. Parents should be trained in the development of advocacy skills. Services should be extended to parents, extended family members, churches, community leaders, and agency personnel to assist in the formation of a collaborative support model to enhance services for African American gifted learners. As content is introduced and potential giftedness noted, parents should be notified. Bringing parents into the educational setting in a positive manner is important in the development of student potential.

Emphasis should be on cognitive development and independent study. Independent study is a curricular option that can allow investigation of meaningful topics. Content should include exposing students from different cultures to all of the domains. Exposure to all of the intelligences in each of the domains is essential to the identification and nurturance of students from culturally diverse populations. As they are allowed to express themselves in ways that remove the barriers presently existing, potential giftedness will surface, allowing teachers to differentiate the curriculum for them based on abilities noted. Culturally diverse students would benefit greatly from programming that includes a mentoring component (Zorman, 1993). Teachers need to seek instances in which gifted students can be provided with mentors and role models. The importance of mentoring has been highlighted by Wright and Borland (1992), Tillman (1996), Frierson (1996), and Plummer (1996). At the Wadleigh School in Manhattan, black students are selected in sixth grade and receive special instruction in grades six, seven, and eight in tasks required to take SAT-type exams. In ninth grade, they are accepted into prestigious private boarding schools. While attending these schools, they are mentored by previous graduates of the school. Parents are involved in planning for their children. Graduates of the program include fifty-five students who are in universities and preparatory schools. At the present time students from Wadleigh have graduated from Lawrenceville, Hotchkiss, Deerfield, Proctor, St. Paul's, St. George's, Dalton, Lenox, Fieldston, Verde Valley, Tilton, Collegiate, Phillips Andover, Exeter, Milton, Brooks, and Portsmouth Abbey. Over the years, 280 Wadleigh students have graduated from Harvard, Yale, Dartmouth, Williams, Massachusetts Institute of Technology, Union, Wesleyan, Trinity, University of Pennsylvania, Princeton, Columbia, Bucknell, Mount Holyoke, Brown, Sarah Lawrence, Tufts, Smith, Vassar, Lehigh, Duke, and Cornell. One of the keys to success for this program has been the existence of an effective support network. From their initial entry into a preparatory school until they graduate from a university, there is ongoing communication among students, parents, and Christopher Plummer, the founder of the program. The alumni of the program are actively involved in mentoring and working one on one with students. The graduates of the program serve as excellent role models and mentors.

Project Step-Up (Systematic Training for Education Programs for Underserved Pupils) is another program that provided successful interventions. Professionals worked collaboratively with twelve school districts in four states (Texas, Arizona, Arkansas, and Florida) and three universities (Lamar University in Beaumont, Texas; the University of Arizona in Tucson; and Arkansas State University in Jonesboro) to plan, implement, and evaluate a comprehensive three-year demonstration project (1990–1993) for 216 minority, economically disadvantaged children who would have normally been overlooked as candidates for their gifted and talented program. Approaches were based on the structure of the intellect (SOI) model of Guilford and the multiple intelligences (MI) of Gardner. In addition to training teachers, the program developed new methods of locating and involving community members as mentors, role models, and instructors. Methods and materials were developed and implemented to actively involve parents of at-risk children in their children's education.

LOOKING TO THE FUTURE: NEED FOR TRAINED TEACHERS

According to Tonemah (1992), for Native Americans and Alaska Native students, stereotypes among colleagues should be dispelled and teachers sensitized to the needs of this special population. Teachers should be taught to value intelligence and creativity, to understand the implications of giftedness, and how to nurture gifted Indian students. Tonemah (1990) makes a case for training Native Americans as teachers of gifted Native Americans. His research revealed the great extent to which Indian students were inappropriately assessed, underserved, and overlooked by tribal, state, and federal education programs. A master's program for Native American teachers focused on teaching gifted and talented Native Americans. "We feel that Indian educational service providers have greater insights into the concerns, issues, problems, and nature of Indian students than do non-Indians" (p. 5). It is essential that teachers be aware of the differences that exist between populations. Lowered expectations may result from a lack of sensitivity, causing underachievement.

In light of the diversity that can exist in classrooms today, it is unrealistic to expect that teachers be culturally matched to students, if diversity is a societal value. Teachers should increase their awareness and sensitivity to the many differences that exist between and among populations. It behooves teachers to find out about the cultural backgrounds of students in their room and possible differences that might impact learning, including cultural backgrounds and learning styles.

The lack of training received by classroom teachers inhibits their effectiveness in identifying and educating gifted students (Ford, 1994; Rhodes, 1992). "The belief systems of teachers, administrators, parents, and the learners, themselves must be analyzed and shaped in ways that expect and assume that these learners exist and their gifts and talents identified" (Patton, 1994, p. 4). Teacher expectations play a large part in the identification and nurturance of gifts and talents. The majority of teachers have received little or no training in multicultural education. The combination of not having received training in either gifted or multicultural education hinders them significantly in their ability to identify and plan for gifted students from diverse ethnic backgrounds.

When gifted minority children are exposed to teachers who are empathetic and accepting and who provide a caring curriculum designed to identify domain-specific gifts, the children can be expected to make gains in academic achievement, self-concept, and intrinsic motivation.

FOR FURTHER READING

Banks, J. A. (Ed.). (1995). *Handbook of research on multicultural education.* New York: Macmillan Publishing Company.

Williams, L., & DeGaetano, Y. (1985). *ALERTA: A multicultural, bilingual approach to teaching young children.* Menlo Park, CA: Addison Wesley Publishing Company.

Chapter 7

Exceptionally Gifted Children

Typical questions a classroom teacher might ask include these:

> Are there levels of giftedness?
>
> How might I recognize the exceptionally gifted student?
>
> What are some of the sensitivities and challenges involved in meeting the needs of the exceptionally gifted child?

To answer these questions, this chapter does the following:

> Discusses the development of exceptionally gifted children.
>
> Speaks to their special sensitivities.
>
> Suggests ways to plan for them.

DEFINITION OF LEVELS OF GIFTEDNESS

Morelock and Feldman (1997) have created a *taxonomy of extreme precocity*. They have separated giftedness into levels. An *extraordinarily high IQ, omnibus prodigy* exhibits an adult level of professional development, is passionately involved in more than one domain, and has an insatiable appetite for academic knowledge as well as an extraordinary abstract thinking ability in the mathematical and verbal/linguistic domains. The *prodigy* performs on an above average to an extraordinary level in one domain and is passionately involved in that domain. This is accompanied by abstract thinking ability and may also demonstrate an intense desire to master academic knowledge. The *extraordinarily high IQ child* has unusually high abstract reasoning ability and may have domain-specific gifts in one or more areas. The individual may have difficulty committing to one area, and has a voracious appetite for academic knowledge. The *prodigious savant* has islands of extraordinarily advanced domain-specific gifts in one or more areas with little ability for abstract reasoning.

Silverman (1989) and Gross (1993) have helped to break down the perception that designed curricula and special programs designed for moderately gifted students will also work for the highly gifted. There is a vast range of ability within the gifted population. Silverman and Kearney (1992) and Gross (1993) have begun to investigate two subsets of the highly gifted: children who are exceptional and those who are profoundly gifted. The term *exceptionally gifted* refers to children who score in the IQ range of 160 to 179, whereas *profoundly gifted* refers to those extremely rare individuals who score at or above a 180 IQ. These students require an educational

PERSONAL INTERVIEW
Barry's Story

Barry is a highly gifted young man whose unusual precocity presented many challenges for his mother.

I was not aware of the fact that Barry was different from birth. I had no idea that it was not common for a newborn to be attempting to focus on everything around him. At three months he was duplicating sounds. At this time he became fascinated with children's television programs and appeared to be watching programs such as Electric Company and Sesame Street. He would keep focused and could be attentive for long periods of time. By the time he was a year and a half he was speaking in complete sentences. He wouldn't go to sleep at night unless his bed was full of books that he would "read." I knew he was reading by the age of three, maybe even before because he began reciting excerpts from the Peanuts Comic paperbacks. I had never read these to him. He was mispronouncing words he had apparently tried to sound out. He would walk around the house acting the comic strips out. He had an incredible memory and would remember everything that was said, read, or seen on television.

At age three he was drawing and writing. This is a picture of a snail that I saved from this time period (see Figure 7.1).

Between the ages of two and four he became fascinated by dinosaurs. He learned every fact he could find. He knew every name and type and the basic descriptions. He would quiz all family members (especially grandparents) and would become annoyed when given incorrect responses.

He was an extremely sensitive child—to himself and others. At age four he went into the hospital for a second hernia operation (he was two years old when he had his first). En route to the operating room he was in the elevator with a little girl who was going to have a tonsillectomy. She was very frightened and crying. He comforted her, telling her he'd been through it before. He explained his experience and reassured her she would be fine. By the time they got to the operating room she was totally calm.

Between the ages of three and five, he became mesmerized by classical music. He learned everything he could about all of the composers. By the time he was in first grade he became obsessed with codes and ciphers. He began inventing his own. This was a major focus from first to third grade. His interests and abilities were not appreciated or acknowledged by his first-grade teacher. In the first month of school the students were given a ditto. Barry looked at it, read it from beginning to end, followed the instructions.

Figure 7.1   **Drawing of snail by Barry, age 3**

and completed it. When the teacher found out what he had done, she repri-manded him. I was called in and although I was assured that he had not misbehaved in any way, I was told he was to pay attention only to her and that she would not tolerate him going off and learning on his own.

Fortunately his second-grade teacher confided in me that she had watched him the year before while he would be off by himself in the play-ground usually deep in thought and exploring. She listened while his first-grade teacher complained about how difficult it was to understand why he didn't try to "fit in." The second-grade teacher replied, "I want him next year because I can't wait to find out what's going on in his mind." She did become his second-grade teacher. That year she had found out that the school district planned to start a gifted program and began recommending him for it. She also made sure that he was placed with a third-grade teacher who shared her commitment and enthusiasm.

His sense of humor developed very early. It was never traditional and always slightly "offbeat." Most of his peers did not understand, and seemed uncomfortable with it.

By age six he had expressed anger about death, making me promise to bury his favorite possessions with him were he to die. Within about two years he got over this and began to equate it more with a balance of nature and determined that anything other than cremation was barbaric. This was happening at a time when he was becoming acutely aware of the environment. He was extremely angered when (during the Jaws hysteria) people were killing sharks with a vengeance. He had no patience with people who didn't attempt to understand the value of all life in the greater picture.

In the third grade he was invited to participate in a gifted program in the school district. Group IQ tests were given but other than being told that he qualified for the gifted program, we were never told that Barry's IQ was unusual. In fourth grade he started blinking. Other children were making fun of him and we began to be concerned. We spoke with the school psychologist and interviewed him and met with him on several occasions. We were never told that our child was highly exceptional.

In fifth grade in the gifted program he studied coins and attended university lectures on numismatics. The audience was quite impressed with his presence and knowledge. In middle school he did an exhaustive research study of the brain. The middle school teacher in the gifted program began noticing that Barry might need some guidance and support in high school.

Barry lacked organizational skills. When Barry was involved in a project that he had a passion for, it would receive his total attention until completion. Other assignments would often suffer, would be done unimpressively, and might be late. A middle school teacher seemed to recognize Barry's exceptionality and recommended that we arrange for the psychologist in the high school to meet with Barry to guide him. The school psychologist was notified and informed of Barry's profile and concerns voiced by the teacher.

When he entered high school he became involved in a scientific research program on the brain. He received an almost perfect score on his PSATs. We were told he got only one incorrect response and that this was the highest score anyone in the district had ever received. His program was scheduled so that he didn't have a lunch break. He was taking two languages in addition to all of the other required courses. He never went to see the school psychologist and the psychologist never tried to see Barry.

We didn't realize that Barry had fallen into a state of depression just before his senior year. Barry was applying to colleges and was trying to get to see his guidance counselor. Even though he was in a depressed state when he had taken his SATs, he scored 1470. We knew he was not doing well in all of his subjects. He was experiencing some difficulty in AP chemistry and integrated math, even though he was president of Mathletes and had won several awards. Because his program was so overscheduled he did not get to the guidance counselor's office until the end of the school day. The guidance counselor was coaching the football team. Barry went to see him on the football field. The teacher became enraged. How dare he! He was angry with Barry and wanted to know why he had not participated in sports. He was not impressed with the fact that Barry was involved in Mathletes in the district, was its president, was in the World Cultures Club, and was in a number of other academic clubs. Barry seemed to "crash" at this time and went into therapy three times a week. We were told by the therapist that sometimes "Perfectionism = Procrastination = Paralysis."

Barry applied to five universities. One of them, Colgate, noted something special about Barry's records. They accepted him and told him that when he felt better, there was a place for him. He graduated from Colgate cum laude with High Honors in English. He is now attending the University of Minnesota where he is completing an M.A./Ph.D. program in dramaturgy and critical literature.

An interview with the school psychologist in the elementary school had indicated Barry's exceptionality early on. She believed he was the brightest child she had ever encountered. When tested he "topped out." She recalled how in third grade his writing was brilliant and contained an adult wit that was impressive. She was so impressed with his work that she would bring his stories home. When she discussed his writing with him, he couldn't explain where he got his ideas from. He said he sometimes surprised himself with what he knew and claimed ideas just came to him.

His abilities extended beyond his ability to write. In third grade he became interested in conducting a survey. So he gathered data and analyzed it in ways that were statistically correct without ever being exposed to statistical procedures. There are many individuals who could have helped Barry along the way so that he did not have to suffer emotional trauma.

program that differs significantly in structure, pace, and content from that which might be offered to the moderately gifted student.

Silverman (1993b) suggests using the following definition of giftedness:

Giftedness is Asynchronous Development in which advanced cognitive abilities and heightened intensity combine to create inner experiences and awareness that are qualitatively different from the norm. This asynchrony increases with higher intellectual capacity. The uniqueness of the gifted renders them particularly vulnerable and requires modifications in parenting, teaching and counseling in order for them to develop optimally. (Columbus Group, 1991, p. 36)

CHARACTERISTICS

What do we know about the highly gifted? What are some of the markers that should be noted? How can parents, teachers, and counselors become aware of this type of exceptionality?

Silverman and Kearney (1992) suggest that intellectual characteristics in intellectually gifted children tend to increase in strength in accordance with IQ. They strongly recommend testing, using the Stanford–Binet L-M as a supplemental test to obtain information about highly gifted children. Without the appropriate tools to find these children, they remain doubly at risk. Lovecky (1994a) reports that differences in the cognition of gifted children become more discernable as intellectual capacity increases.

Hollingworth (1975) and Gross (1993) found that among the most striking and visible differences are those in the acquisition of speech, reading, and imagination. Numerous researchers have noticed the early development of speech in highly gifted children, which is also typical in moderately gifted children. Average children can be expected to utter a word at approximately one year; the moderately gifted child begins to speak approximately two months earlier. The median age at which children of 160 IQ begin to speak is eight and a half months, while some of these children utter their first words at four or five months (Gross, 1995). The linking of words into phrases and the formation of short sentences begins earlier in the moderately gifted child and much earlier for the highly gifted. Hollingworth noted that children with an IQ of 180+ began to speak in sentences between the ages of six and nineteen months. The fluent command of language often gives rise to word play.

Highly gifted children usually learn to read earlier than moderately gifted age peers. VanTassel-Baska (1983) reported that 80 percent of a group of 270 highly gifted students started to read by age 5 and 55 percent by age 4.

Lovecky (1994a) reports differences in the cognition of gifted children as intellectual capacity increases. Quantitative and qualitative differences in processing information were observed between children who scored about 170 IQ and their moderately gifted peers. Exceptionally gifted children often have difficulty dealing with material that other gifted children might have no difficulty with. Simple often becomes complex as more is read into a question. Along with the simple being complex, highly gifted children have a great need for precision. They appear to have an inner need for the world to be logical and to correct errors.

Exceptionally gifted children look for underlying patterns, understand concepts, and do not need to practice. The whole is comprehended quickly and thoroughly. They perceive underlying innuendoes, metaphors, and symbols. They are capable of abstract reasoning at an earlier age. They are often analytical thinkers. They are capable of metaphorical thinking at an earlier age. They have a great capacity for empathy, and are able to project identification with others.

Gross (1993) and Lovecky (1994a) report that exceptional memory capacity is often a characteristic of the highly gifted. Exceptionally gifted children often learn in a nonlinear manner. They are capable of taking in and integrating large amounts of information.

IDENTIFICATION

Identification of the exceptionally gifted child is critical. There are many different types of "exceptionality" among the gifted population. The exceptionally gifted child is oftentimes overlooked and misunderstood. Giftedness runs along a continuum of talents and abilities. Sometimes an individual's abilities are so unique that the child does not appear to fit into the school setting. The child may be shunned and viewed as "weird." As a result, social and emotional problems may arise as the child views their exceptionality in a negative light.

Kennedy (1995) reported on the activities and interactions of a highly gifted nine-year-old male in a heterogeneous classroom of twenty-eight students. His asynchronous development created difficulties for him in the school setting. His intellectual ability exceeded his social and emotional development. On a Slosson intelligence test he scored over 200. Joshua's school life demonstrated the asynchronous development typical of the exceptionally gifted child as reported by Silverman (1993b). School modifications did not take into account his affective needs and resulted in limited success in the cognitive area despite considerable efforts on the part of staff. Having Joshua attend a pull-out program with moderately gifted students had a negative impact on Joshua and other students in the group. Students deferred to him. He appeared to develop a condescending attitude. He often engaged in inappropriate behaviors with classmates that left them feeling they had been belittled. Classmates felt intimidated. He would be called on to perform on demand and would otherwise be ignored. What becomes apparent is that with some exceptionally gifted children their social and emotional development and self-esteem suffer, and inappropriate behaviors develop as defense mechanisms.

Gross (1993) stresses the need to identify exceptionally gifted children. She points out that if they are not recognized, they may come to feel that their differences are something to be ashamed of. They are at risk, as much as those whose achievement is below average. It is only by understanding their uniqueness, their special cognitive characteristics, and their special talents that they can reach their potential.

> Many exceptionally gifted children remain invisible in school. Even when special talents are acknowledged. . . . Over time, lack of support for their needs results in social and emotional crisis. (Lovecky, 1994a, p. 120)

The profiles of extremely gifted children show no singular pattern (McGuffog, Feiring, & Lewis, 1987). Extremely gifted children may have emotional problems or they may be well adjusted. They may be gifted in one area or their gifts may cross many areas. They can be highly gifted in one area and delayed in another. They may come from families where achievement is stressed or they may grow up in families where they are allowed to grow at their own pace. Factors that impact underachievement to potential include family environment and personality style.

INTERVENTIONS

If highly gifted students are to find both academic and social success, it seems clear that asynchronous development must receive attention. White and Renzulli (1987) conducted a forty-year follow-up of students who attended the Speyer School for the gifted, an experimental program in New York City established by Leta Hollingworth in 1935. As a result the recommendations shown in Table 7.1 were made for students of exceptional ability.

Assessing areas of giftedness becomes an essential element in planning for exceptionally gifted children. Feldman's (1986) work with prodigies and reports of idiot savants informs us that extreme giftedness can exist in one particular area or more. When working with students in a classroom, the level of giftedness in each content area should be assessed.

Specific concerns that teachers need to address that have plagued gifted students in school (Gailbraith 1983, 1984; Silverman 1993b) include:

- Finding enough hard and interesting work at school; work at school can be boring
- Adjusting to classmates; other students often tease them about being smart
- Being able to play with other children; friends who understand them are few and far between
- Not becoming hermits
- Developing leadership abilities
- Not becoming negativistic toward authority
- Learning to "suffer fools gladly"
- Avoiding the formation of bits of extreme chicanery
- Conforming to rules and expectations; parents, teachers, and friends expect perfection at all times
- Understanding their origin and destiny from an early age
- Dealing with the special problems of being a gifted female.

Depending on the background of the child, and the innate personality characteristics, problems can be nonexistent or become severe. Teachers should become sensitive to the different characteristics that might be present. Teachers in classrooms often do not recognize the uneven development. When exceptional intellectual development is evidenced, it is accompanied by expectations of advanced functioning in all areas. Gifted children often receive "mixed messages" from the environment when they are praised for intellectual performance and expected to perform and behave in other areas that have not reached the same level of development. They are criticized for acts not within their control.

Teachers can address the concerns listed earlier, as discussed in the following paragraphs.

Teachers should group students by ability and assign enough hard work so they do not become bored with schoolwork. Multilevel assignments in the classroom will reduce boredom and assist in the identification process. When students exhibit

Table 7.1 Effects, implications, and recommendations of the Speyer School

Effects	Implications/Recommendations
Peer relationships—being with other students with superior intellectual ability	Students of above average or superior ability could benefit from being placed together during all or part of the school day.
Competition	Students of above average or superior ability should be provided with experiences that challenge their intellectual abilities.
Identified as special	Early identification of students with above average abilities and special talents brings with it certain responsibilities. Because Speyer students were identified as gifted, their parents' expectations changed and many of them applied to more advanced high schools and sought to achieve excellence in later work.
Appreciation for learning/learning by doing	Students should be provided with experiences that encourage discovery and participation.
Exposure to the arts	Students should be provided exposure to art, music, drama, and dance with opportunities to develop these skills and talent areas. Talents cannot be nurtured if students do not know the area exists.
Exposure to modern languages	Exposure to and instruction in languages stimulates interest in the culture of other countries and provides students with above average ability an opportunity to develop appreciation for the skills and techniques of learning a language.
Trips to museums	The value of these exposures to their overall education was pointed out by almost all of the subjects of this study. Students of above average ability can benefit from the opportunity to see products of other creative minds (inventions, art, etc.).
Influenced career choice	Providing exposure to professionals in their own working environment gives students the opportunity to better understand the abilities, interests, and values necessary for successful performance in that job as well as provide role models for students with above average or superior ability.
Opportunity to work independently	Students of above average or superior ability should not only be given the opportunity to work independently but should be expected to do some independent work in school.
Research skills/projects	Students of above average or superior ability should be taught research skills and encouraged to use these skills to develop projects that can be shared with an audience.

Source: Reprinted with permission from White, W. L., & Renzulli, J. S. (1987). A forty-year follow-up of students who attended Leta Hollingworth's school for gifted students. *Roeper Review 10*(2), 89–94. Copyright 1987 *Roeper Review*, P.O. Box 329, Bloomfield Hills, MI 48303.

advanced ability in specific areas, provide opportunities for the student to attend classes at a higher grade or provide mentors.

Teachers can help highly gifted students adjust to their classmates by placing them with other gifted students for part or all of the time depending on levels and domains of giftedness. If children spend part of their time with intellectual peers, the tendency to isolate themselves will become less important. All children need to feel they are members of a group and do not walk alone.

Leadership can be developed in a variety of ways, but for the gifted child, recognition of expertise can be arranged.

> Todd was a slight, sensitive, highly gifted third grader. He would approach his teacher and speak of his depression. He had a younger brother who was his parents' joy. Jimmy was tall, muscular, and athletic. When Todd entered fourth grade he was identified for and participated in a gifted program. The program's focus was independent study and Todd chose electronics. He began designing electrical gadgets at home and school and by the end of the semester he had his entire house wired. His ability was noted at home and school as others came to him to have him share his expertise. In fifth grade he was invited to the middle school to speak. By the time he entered middle school, his demeanor had been transformed. His parents spoke proudly of his accomplishments and his classmates respected his expertise. He ran for officer of the school and won.

With appropriate guidance, counseling, and development of personal skills, gifted students can find positive outlets rather than become negativistic toward authority. Respect by adults should bring respect from students.

Highly gifted students can learn to "suffer fools gladly." Appreciation of the diversity of gifts and talents in an inclusive classroom is a goal for education. Recognizing domain-specific gifts creates an awareness for students that different individuals have different abilities. Simulations, role playing, and bibliotherapy in the area of the personal intelligences help gifted students recognize this diversity and appreciate it.

Teachers need to help gifted students avoid the formation of habits of extreme chicanery by positively engaging them. Gifted children are often not given their due—teachers refuse to call on them, knowing they know the answer. They have much to say and are not given a positive platform with which to express themselves. The need for recognition can sometimes take bizarre forms. When students are positively engaged and challenged, attention-getting behaviors are no longer necessary.

When students are given decision-making power in their own educational plan, the demands for conforming are lessened. Gifted students should be given independent study options and choices as to how they wish to present material covered in the classroom.

Many exceptionally gifted children have a need to understand their origin and destiny from an early age. Gifted children are inquisitive in many areas. Questions and curiosity should be honored and viewed with respect. Adults do not need to know the answers, but should revel in the opportunity to plan journeys to resources with their children.

Female students will need help dealing with the specific problems related to being a gifted female. Helping gifted females reach their potential is covered in greater detail in Chapter 9.

When school districts use IQ tests with students, it is not enough to say they have "topped out." How exceptional is the child? What accommodations need to be made to fit the child rather than making the child fit the accommodations. As a profile emerges, individual educational plans must be developed to provide clear goals and directions for both cognitive and affective areas. Differentiation can take many forms but for the exceptional child it must include appropriate counseling.

Consideration of all content areas should be assessed. A student interested in science should have a curriculum which expands basic skills and comprehension. The tempo, breadth, and depth of assignments should be designed for the individual and such design should include the student's point of view. There should be enough leeway in the plan that a student can add or accelerate in areas of interest as needed.

Classroom teachers, gifted education specialists, the student, parents, and guidance counselors or school psychologists should all be involved in the process. An essential component in programming for exceptionally gifted children involves parents. Parent questionnaires should be elicited when children enter school and kept in the students' files, so the teacher has background information that should be taken into account when diagnosing and planning for a student. The characteristics and behaviors of highly gifted children signal special programming, even before formal tests are given. This information should be used as the basis of diagnosis in the classroom to assess the level of exceptionality. The classroom teacher and the administrator must work together to secure appropriate services for this child.

Contracts or other strategies can provide useful structure; they must be flexible enough to allow for new interests as they develop, and they should consider out-of-school settings such as work with a mentor or participation in after-school or Saturday programs in universities or museums. Radical acceleration can also be considered; as Tomlinson (1994) points out, it is right for some but not all adolescents and preadolescents.

Providing mentors for highly able students can be extremely beneficial. Acceleration in content areas can take many forms. Some other options might include sending the student to another school, high school, or university to study for part of the time. With the advent of distance learning, instruction at an appropriate level can be brought into the classroom or into another room in the building via telecommunications. Intellectual peers and mentors should be sought. In special cases specialty schools and programs should be sought. Parents should be informed of their existence. These would include summer programs, such as the Johns Hopkins program for mathematically or verbally precocious youth. Many university programs offer science research programs. Parents have to be informed of such opportunities. Simon's Rock College and the Advanced Academy of Georgia provide an early transition to college for carefully selected high school juniors and seniors who wish to enroll full time in an enriched residential college program and concurrently complete high school graduation requirements. Parents also need to be advised of weekend programs that will allow their children to pursue interests at a challenging level with intellectual peers. Guidance counselors would do well to become familiar with special opportunities and/or schools for students with exceptional ability. Jarwan and Feldhusen (1993) analyzed admission programs for residential schools of mathematics and science for academically talented youth. These options should be reviewed for students who might do well in such settings. Programming for the exceptionally gifted child involves creative solutions, and parents, teachers, and administrators should work together to pursue the student's best interests.

In her observations of raising a highly gifted child, Mrs. O. summarizes our concerns for the social and emotional development of all of our gifted children:

Having raised a highly gifted child, I can honestly say that they have unique educational and emotional needs. They are often ostracized from the mainstream because of differences in manner (to use the vernacular, nerdy). I found this often extended to the parent as well; in conversations with other parents I frequently felt that I dare not speak about and was resented if I spoke of my gifted child.

The importance of providing a nurturing home base program for a student, whether it is a resource room or a pull-out gifted program, is impossible to measure. The great need is for a place where these children feel accepted, understood, and encouraged; the great need is to be with others who are experiencing the same difficulties and to experience the comfort of knowing they can be themselves without being judged for their abilities.

Gifted children are extremely vulnerable. Their sensitivities extend to their peer group and to authority figures. My gifted child was patterned early on by teachers. He could be easily manipulated into feeling responsible for others, that is, helping with homework, studying, doing projects in excess of the norm. He was never rewarded for his help, but more was simply expected of him.

Unrealistic expectations are often placed on them. The teacher is presuming because of the child's intelligence or physical size or personality that the child can assume responsibilities that the child is not really mature enough to handle or should handle. This kind of pressure can cause the gifted child to be frustrated and doubt his ability. What adults seem to forget is that they are children first, then students with all of the ramifications of being gifted.

An area of concern for gifted children is counseling. Very limited options are presented. The diversity in potentials is never really explored.

Respecting an individual's capabilities is seldom taught or encouraged. I did not find that the school had guidance counselors who could properly match the child's educational needs to the appropriate settings. College list ditto sheets that match up with the child's GPA and SAT scores simply don't cut it. So many colleges have unique programs. Obviously a counselor can't be an expert in all areas, so specializing would seem to be a viable solution.

Chapter 8

Young Gifted Children

Typical questions a classroom teacher might ask include these:

How might I identify the young gifted child?

Do young gifted children develop evenly along the domains?

What special concerns need to be addressed for the young gifted child?

Is it possible to use standardized tests to predict giftedness in young children in the future?

To answer these questions, this chapter does the following:

Describes the uneven development characteristic of the young gifted child.

Provides insights into assessment and evaluation.

Offers alternative performance-based assessment techniques.

Describes programming opportunities.

DEFINITION

Defining giftedness in young children is problematic because they often do not develop evenly. They frequently demonstrate peaks of extraordinary performance in specific domains, rather than in all cognitive areas. A child with exceptional spatial reasoning may not be the one with the highest IQ or may not demonstrate advanced language proficiency. Unique patterns of development may be observed within a group, but uneven development is often evident in individual children. Young gifted children form an extremely heterogeneous group with respect to interests, skill levels, and, in particular, social development and physical abilities (Roedell, 1989).

CHARACTERISTICS

When the school year begins, teachers should note the general characteristics of highly able children (based on characteristics identified in early research by Terman & Oden, 1947, and Treffinger, 1975):

1. Curious, asks many questions.
2. Exhibits long-term memory.
3. Is persistent.
4. Is independent.
5. Is able to sustain interest in more than one area.

PERSONAL INTERVIEW
Adam's Story

Adam's story is told through a personal interview with his mother.

Adam is a very bubbly kindergartner. He exhibits potential in more than one area. He has always been a curious child and has reached all of the developmental milestones on time. When he was three years old his grandfather sent him an astrological chart. This piqued his interest in the solar system. This becomes evident in the work he produces in his journal in school. His interest in the solar system expanded into the realm of geography. He asked to see a globe and asked questions about latitude, longitude, and capitals. He is especially interested in Russia. He enjoys drawing maps of Europe including the boundary of each country. He reads the atlas and writes and knows each of the countries in the world and their ranks by area and population.

Adam enjoys quizzing me. He draws a continent and numbers the countries. He then asks me to name the country noted by each number. He also asks questions such as "Which country has the sixteenth largest population?" He, of course, knows all of the answers.

When he attended nursery school at the age of three and a half, his teacher noted that he was very mathematical. He would do mental addition and subtraction. This was also evidenced on Valentine's Day in his kindergarten room. His teacher had fifty-four chocolate kisses. She asked the students if they each could have one. There were eighteen children in the room. Most thought yes. She then asked if they could have two. Adam responded, "We could each have three because three eighteens equals fifty-four."

In what direction will Adam's interests take him? Is he a potential historian, geographer, or mathematician? How can teachers ensure that he will reach his destiny? Will he be channeled and challenged along the way? These are questions that remain to be answered.

6. Learns easily.
7. Is creative and imaginative.
8. Is self-sufficient.
9. Exhibits originality.
10. Sets high goals.
11. Has special talents.
12. Uses scientific research method.
13. Sees relationships and draws generalities.

14. Creates new ideas.
15. Initiates own activities.
16. Exhibits leadership.
17. Likes to invent and build mechanical devices.
18. Applies learning from one situation to another.
19. Continually questions the status quo.

With preschool-age children precocity in the comprehension and production of oral language has been used as an indicator of high verbal intelligence. This has been used as a predictor of high linguistic performance in school later on. Precocity in reading has been linked to skills in mathematics, music, and computer language (Tannenbaum, 1992). Even though precocity in these areas may be indicators of a gifted child, the absence of precocity does not preclude eminence in the future. Case studies of highly intelligent children and adults who achieved greatness in their respective fields have shown that some were late talkers and readers.

IDENTIFICATION: THE NEED TO BEGIN EARLY

For the classroom teacher, identification of special abilities begins when children enter school. Pringle (1970) makes a plea for the identification and nurturance of the abilities of a young child so as to prevent underachievement. Pringle reports evidence that boredom characterizes an able child's general attitude toward school. Children may lose interest or rebel against what they consider useless activity. This can lead to behavior difficulties and/or underachievement (p. 110). Because of the uneven levels of development (Terrassier, 1979) that can occur within the young gifted individual (often referred to as dyssynchronization), appropriate nurturing is critical. Note, however, that a wide gap between the levels of their intellectual and physical development can occur.

In the Seattle project (Roedell & Robinson, 1977) preschool children were able to read at the fourth-grade level but had difficulty manipulating a pencil. Social and emotional factors come into play as well. Abrams (1982) describes the discrepancies between mental ages of children with their agemates, which can create conflict and disappointment. For example, one bright child kept making appointments with playmates who had no concept of time.

Personality characteristics can also influence teachers (Gordon & Thomas, 1967) . Underestimating a young child's abilities can have a negative impact. Gordon and Thomas grouped students into four categories: *plungers* (children who plunged into new activities quickly and positively); *go-alongers* (children who went along with positive attitudes); *sideliners* (those who watched and waited and gradually became involved); and *nonparticipators* (children who remained negative to situations for months, or even indefinitely). Teachers tended to choose plungers as having above average intelligence. Of the thirty children who were rated as superior, four of the sideliners were missed and six of the plungers were overestimated. Pringle (1970) found that bright children who had been brought to a clinic because of general maladjustment were highly intelligent but suffered from a lack of confidence. When teachers underestimate a child's ability and the academic curriculum provided is not challenging, children may become bored, regress, or begin to exhibit negative behaviors. This was pointed out by Gross (1993), who highlights the danger in not recognizing more able youngsters. Bright children begin norm referencing at an earlier age as opposed to self-referencing. Young children are often proud of their accomplishments based on what they are capable of doing today as opposed to what they were able to do yesterday. Gifted children may become very well aware of their abilities, but in a pejorative sense. When noting that their behaviors are different from their agemates, even though these behaviors indicate advanced abilities, they begin to regress. This was evidenced in the case of one young boy who was writing long stories at the beginning of kindergarten (Figures 8.1 and 8.2). By midyear, to emulate his classmates, he began writing one word that filled the entire page (Figure 8.3). With the appropriate

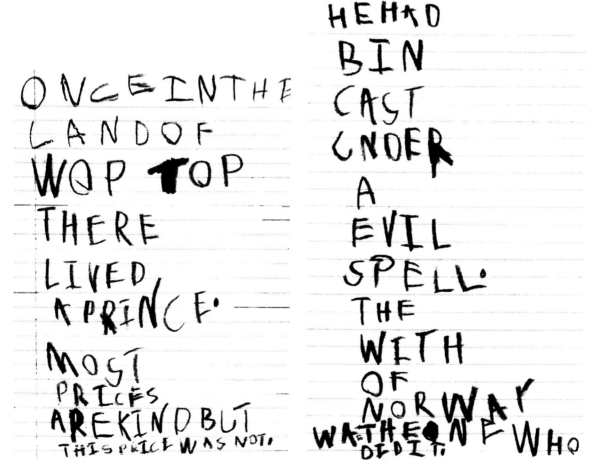

Figure 8.1   **Work produced by a young gifted child at the beginning of kindergarten**

intervention, he began to blossom. By second grade his superior development was evidenced in all areas. He was allotted a small amount of time in the computer room and typed a story in chapters with no assistance.

Without the appropriate intervention a gifted child's first school experience have a negative impact on development. A child may learn to hide or deny his abilities in order to fit in with his classmates and avoid feeling isolated. Uneven development of skills can lead to frustration, and the gap between advanced intellectual skills and emotional and physical development can cause behavior problems. Young gifted children frequently show peaks of extraordinary performance in one cognitive domain that may not be revealed in testing. Whereas it is difficult for the child to develop peer relationships, adults often react to young gifted children with unrealistic expectations, assuming that they are gifted in all areas of development.

THE
WITH
HAD
AN
OGAR.
THE
OGAR
HATED
CHILDREN.
SO HE
DICITED
TO KILL THEM

IT WAS NOT
LONG
BEFORE
HE KILLED
TEN
CHILDREN.

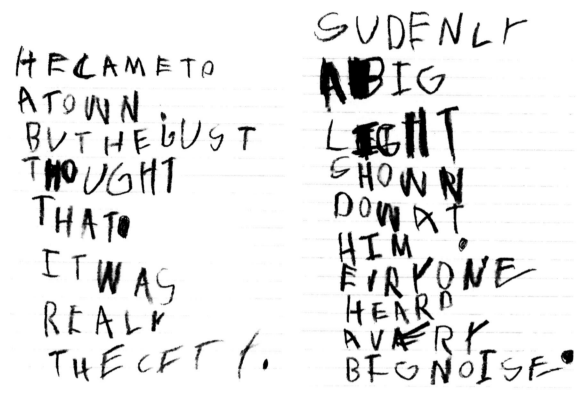

Figure 8.1   *continued*

Use of Standardized Tests to Identify Young Gifted Performers

There is a paucity of research on how to identify the young gifted child. Standardized tests designed to measure individual differences in infant development generally have not been successful in identifying children who will demonstrate intellectual precocity in their later years. However, those who are identified as high-scoring children early on are likely to maintain their precocity in later years if the assessment was motivated by parents' perceptions of the child's behavior (Shapiro et al., 1989). Further, early childhood teachers may have difficulty identifying advanced abilities because young gifted children tend to mask their abilities in order to fit in (ERIC Digest E487). Psychologists disagree about the most appropriate way to assess the general or verbal intelligence of preschool-age children suspected of being intellectually precocious. The most widely used tool is the Woodcock-Johnson Psychoeducational Battery. Giftedness demonstrated during the preschool years will change over time but manifestations will continue throughout development.

There once was a tiger that could roar very, very loudly. He could not get any food because all the animals were afraid of him. But one day the tiger's roaring started to be snoring. So he fell asleep. When he was asleep, the animals came out of their hiding places. Just then, the tiger woke up! But, a mouse came up to him, trembling with fear. He said, "Don't eat me or I'll tell my friends to make a plan." But then the tiger started laughing. "Ha, ha, ha," he roared. "Your friends could never make a plan against me cause I am second king in the jungle, and I really want to see that happen. Ha, ha, ha. They could never do that, I bet. They'd just get eaten by me, you foolish mouse. And you could never do a thing." "Oh, yes I could, you pig-brained tiger." "Now I am NOT pig-brained. I shall eat you 'cause you interrupted by slumber," said the angry tiger. But just then, two hunters came to the jungle. All the animals but the tiger ran away in fear. The tiger wanted to catch his dinner so he rushed toward the animals, but the hunters did not want to run after them. The hunters put a snare in the tiger's lair. And when the tiger came home that night, he didn't know that the snare was in his lair. And he laid in it unaware, and before he knew it, he was trapped, and he couldn't move a muscle. So he started to cry. "Boo hoo hoo," he sobbed. The mouse heard him crying. So she said, "Maybe I should help him 'cause I'm the only one who has sharp enough teeth." So she ran, and ran, and ran to where the tiger was crying. When she arrived, the tiger said, "Do you think you can take this trap off me? I'm that same tiger who terrorized you earlier today. But now I really have to get out of here. I promise I'll help you when you're trapped in a mouse trap if you'll help me." So the mouse said, "It seems complicated," but when she looked down, around, and all over she said, "There's only one thick rope holding you tight. If I could just chew through that rope, tiger, you would be free." So she took up her tiny claws, opened up her tiny jaws, and started nibbling. And finally there was just one thread that was holding the tiger tight. So she opened up her weary mouth and took one last bite. And the rope broke. And the tiger was free. The tiger made up a song about friendship and it went like this—"Me and you together, Me and you forever. We'll be friends 'til the end of time." The end.

Composed in Kindergarten when given the use of a computer.

Figure 8.2   **Work produced on a computer by the same child as in Figure 8.1**

How to Use Existing Screening Instruments

Some districts require that children entering school be screened. These screening programs have been established to detect children with possible giftedness or those at risk for future learning problems. Screening assesses physical, psychomotor, spatial, cognitive, communication, and adaptive abilities. If not already doing so, school districts using such instruments should adapt and modify sections of the instruments by

Figure 8.3   **Work produced by the same child as in Figures 8.1 and 8.2. Note the regression to a one-word-per-page style to emulate his classmates.**

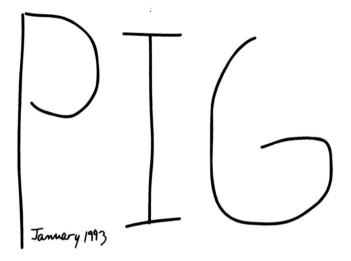

January 1993

raising the ceiling to ensure the inclusion of learners with advanced abilities. Oftentimes examiners are intent on discovering deficits and might not become as aware of special abilities. Here are some examples of activities that might be included:

1. Ability to count beyond twenty.
2. Ability to add.
3. Ability to sequence pictures into a logical story.
4. Ability to read.
5. Evidence of exceptional artistic ability.
6. Ability to see cause-and-effect relationships.
7. Ability to solve problems relating to real-life situations.

In any category being assessed, the tester should provide sufficient advanced material to ensure that the child has reached his or her upper limit. Results should be recorded and parents and teachers notified.

New assessment batteries are being developed. One school district in North Carolina developed a problem-solving assessment tool for identifying young gifted students. Instead of traditional testing models, Gardner's and Sternberg's models were synthesized to identify extraordinary problem solvers. This battery examines linguistic, logical-mathematical, and spatial intelligences through activities that call on creative, analytical, and practical problem-solving abilities (Reid & Romanoff, 1997).

How to Observe Children in a Variety of Settings

It is possible to identify precocity without the use of formalized tests. Classroom teachers, with the assistance of parents, can begin to assess the youngsters in their charge. For example, curriculum-based assessment can be used as students are introduced to challenging curriculum. High abilities will make themselves visible (Ramos-Ford & Gardner, 1997).

Louis, Feiring, and Lewis (1992) have designed a video and teacher's manual in which advanced spatial, verbal, and problem-solving abilities are demonstrated by young children. In each of the settings, three- and five-year-old children are observed. The materials describe and illustrate how the performance of gifted children differs when compared to typical performance for that expected age.

To assess spatial abilities, youngsters are asked to copy a block design and to copy a Tinkertoy model. Checklists are provided with a list of the abilities involved. One can distinguish a good attempt from one that is performed by a gifted child. Children are asked to tell a story based on a picture shown to them. Children are also asked to tell a story about a topic of interest to them. Again, skills involved and checklists are provided. In the problem-solving task, children are required to categorize and classify blocks and beads. The problem has several solutions. Children are asked to plan an event. The youngsters must identify the problem, come up with more than one solution, and evaluate the success of the strategy. The video is very informative in demonstrating how a typical child addresses these situations as opposed to a gifted child.

Block Building

Hirsch (1984) describes how the different stages of block building can be used to assess children's abilities. In the first stage, youngsters carry the blocks with them and do not use them for construction. In the second stage, children begin building with the blocks. Children in stage three begin connecting two blocks with a space to form a bridge. In stage four, blocks are placed so that they enclose spaces. Once facility is acquired, decorative patterns appear. In step five much symmetry can be observed although names are not attached to the buildings. In stage six, naming of structures begins for dramatic play. The names are not necessarily related to functions. In stage seven, buildings are often reproductions of familiar actual structures.

Watching children at play can be very revealing:

> I couldn't have asked for more appropriate demonstration of my belief in the serious value of children's play. Barry was so deeply absorbed . . . he might have been a scientist working out an experiment in a laboratory. . . . With blocks to help him, he was using all his mental powers, reasoning out relationships . . . and drawing conclusions. He was learning to think. (Pratt 1948, pp. 31–32, cited in Hirsch, 1984, p. 4)

Hirsch (1984) points out the potential contributions of blocks to the early childhood curriculum. They can be used in mathematics for comparing and contrasting, symmetry, and measurement; in science to learn about gravity and discovery thinking; in social studies for mapping and grids; in art to determine patterns, symmetry, and balance; in language arts, to plan, name, question, and write stories; in social and emotional development to foster cooperation, respect for others, and autonomy; and in physical development to assist in hand manipulation, eye–hand coordination, visual perception, and cleanup. As children interact with various aspects of the curriculum using blocks, advanced abilities can be observed.

INTERVENTIONS

Young gifted children need to be provided with opportunities to be exposed to and demonstrate gifts in all of the domains. Their performance might demonstrate gifts in one domain or many. Introduction to cognitive processes, which include critical and creative thinking, is essential, especially for children from deprived environments. Ability to make connections in thinking, to problem solve, and to question is an indicator of giftedness and should be noted.

Differentiating the curriculum should take into account the areas of giftedness noted. For example, depending on the domain(s) in which gifts surface, children can be accelerated in mathematics or higher levels of thinking can be incorporated into reading and social studies. They may be guided in the exploration of topics in greater depth or breadth, or children may be permitted to explore their own topics of interest.

Programming for gifted children can take many forms. Opportunities to work with older children can provide young gifted children with the opportunity to be with intellectual peers for part of the time. This can be provided for in the homeroom, or clusters of children with similar levels of ability can be grouped and include children from different grades. Mentors or volunteers should be enlisted when appropriate. Students should be allowed to advance in areas where gifts are demonstrated. Computer programs should be used to allow students to be independent and move ahead at their own speed. Curriculum should be compacted so that students are not involved in repetitive exercises.

Traditionally educators have advanced children or had them "skip" a grade or grades to address educational concerns. The implications of doing so involve the impact on social development as young children are placed in settings with older students as they move through the grades. The child may test well but in actuality may not be "gifted across the board" and may struggle in certain areas.

Chapter 9
Gifted Females

Typical questions a classroom teacher might ask include these:

Are there differences between giftedness in males and females?

Have females had the same opportunities as their male counterparts to exhibit special talents?

Do gifted females have special needs?

How might I be sensitive to the gifted females in my room?

To answer these questions, this chapter does the following:

Describes the barriers to achievement females have experienced over the years.

Describes the special sensitivities of the gifted female.

Provides insight into the ways that classrooms have not provided nurturing environments for females.

Suggests ways to meet the needs of gifted females.

DEFINITION

Giftedness in females exists in each and every one of the domains as described by Gardner. However, women have not had the same opportunities as men to be recognized in specific fields. For instance, in science and math, they have not achieved at the same level as the male members of our society. As giftedness in females is being redefined, rapid changes are occurring in the way females are perceived and how they are guided. Studying the barriers that have prevented them from achieving will allow for appropriate interventions.

Historically women have lacked the opportunity and recognition given to male members of our society. Identification of gifted females has been clouded by society's limited view of female prowess. Sime's biography (1996) of the life of Lise Meitner describes the lack of opportunity, recognition, and credit given to gifted females with scientific orientations who were born in the late 1800s. Meitner completed what was considered to be a normal education for females at the time, which included bookkeeping, handicrafts, and singing. At that time Austrian universities began opening their doors to women. Meitner attended the university and studied physics, when few thought women could be physicists. She finished her doctorate in 1906 in Berlin and began working at Wilhelm University with chemist Otto Hahn. They worked together for thirty-one years, charting families of radioactive elements and mapping the periodic table.

At the age of sixty, because of the political climate, Meitner had to leave Germany. She found a job in a Swedish institute where the director was not supportive

PERSONAL INTERVIEW
Karen's Story

Karen is a highly gifted young lady whose case history demonstrates some of the challenges involved in growing up highly gifted and female in a changing world.

I always did well in school. I always knew I was the smartest. In elementary school I didn't have many friends. They didn't seem to have the same interests as I did. One year stands out in my mind. When I was in fifth grade I became clinically depressed. I became concerned with existential questions. No one in my family understood that these matters concerned me as much as they did. Was there a God? I had a hard time believing. I made an appointment with the priest. I questioned him as to why I was alive and what our purpose was. Why do we live to die? I felt a sense of despair and wondered whether life was worth living. On vacation I went to Bible school. I was told that you had to believe in Jesus or burn in hell. I questioned what would happen to people who believed in other religions. I was told that was just unfortunate.

My fifth-grade elementary teacher was very mean to me. She kept trying to put me down and pitted others against me. She called my mother in and complained that I was disorganized. When I was in fifth grade I wanted to be a priest. I found out I couldn't and would have to become a nun. I began to look at different possible careers. I thought of becoming a doctor, a lawyer, an actress, a newscaster, or a veterinarian. Toward the end of high school I became a part of the popular group. I couldn't bring books home because I would get teased. I kept an extra set at home.

I knew I wanted to go to college. I kept changing my mind until I decided to go into medicine. I decided to become a psychiatrist. I discovered that I was far too empathetic and decided to focus on neurology. I grew up with four brothers and was never told I couldn't become whatever it was I wanted. I was struck by the fact that when I attended a conference on neurosurgery, of the over 100 participants, I was the only female in the room.

I have passed my boards and am a neurologist today. I am married and have a young daughter. My colleagues told me that once I had a baby I wouldn't come back. I did return. We have a nanny and my husband shares in all of our responsibilities. It would have been extremely difficult to have a child during my internship or residency. I received a fellowship and have been doing research putting together drug trials, coordinating between hospitals. I have decisions to make about my future. The message at work is that "one child is the maximum allowed." I would like to stay in academics. I will have to seek my own grants. The government and drug companies have been cutting back so it is very competitive. Once you receive the grant, it gives you a great deal of freedom. At this time, I am not sure which direction I will go in.

Karen's mother continues the story from her viewpoint:

As an infant Karen reached milestones early but not unusually so. She began speaking at about nine months old. By one year old she was speaking in sentences. She began feeding herself at nine months. She always interacted with others and loved animals. I placed her in a playgroup at eighteen months. She was bossy but empathetic. She would observe situations and change her tactics. At one and a half years of age she began to realize that being bossy was not helping her achieve her goals. She learned how to coax the other children by feeding them with new ideas. She enjoyed other children.

She was a rapid learner and was a wizard with puzzles. Between two and a half and three years of age she went to nursery. She got along well and played with the boys as much as girls. She began reading by four and a half years of age. I had her tested and was told her IQ was over 160. She skipped kindergarten and went to a private school in first grade. She began learning French. She didn't like the school. She wanted to go to the public school with her brothers.

Karen was very discriminating. She was concerned about entering bathrooms and wanted to make sure they were clean. She was very aesthetically aware of differences. We moved to the suburbs from an apartment when she was in second grade. The school population was very provincial and different from the one we had lived in. Karen was very independent and stubborn. She was not challenged in school. She was given an advanced workbook and was told to read the directions herself. She was always resourceful and would change her tactics to get what she wanted. I remember one incident when I was talking on the telephone and she wanted more of my attention. She made up a report and graded me. She gave me an excellent on cooking, cleaning, and taking care of children, but gave me a poor on paying attention to children. Her older brother Paul paid more attention to her and would take her to junior high school with him to activities such as the debating club.

In fifth grade she had a difficult time and became quiet and morose. The students started picking on her. Her teacher intimidated her. She was clinically depressed at the time and I didn't recognize it. Animals saved the day. We had four bunnies, a kitten, a pony, and a bird. She had one good friend who was older and gave her riding lessons. She was empathetic, witty, and persuasive.

> *She received a high score on her SAT and was the valedictorian in high school. She had worked for a veterinarian and was accepted into Cornell with the hopes of becoming a veterinarian. In her junior year she met a young man and fell in love. He died accidentally and Karen became clinically depressed again. She studied for her MCATs. She graduated from Cornell with all kinds of awards. She was a presidential scholar. She entered Yale Medical School and suffered from depression once again. With all of this Karen has demonstrated extraordinary leadership qualities. She is still extremely successful in convincing others of her views. She is now sought after as a speaker and is recognized in her field. I realize that her ability to empathize causes her pleasure and pain.*

of women and did not provide her with any experimental equipment. Hahn and Fritz Strassman were continuing their research and wrote to Meitner about their experiments involving firing neutrons at uranium nuclei, and asked her for the explanation. She worked with her nephew Otto Robert Frisch and together they described the physics explanation of "fission." In January 1939, Hahn and Strassman published their chemistry results, and in February Meitner and Frisch published the physics explanation. Hahn took credit for fission and dismissed Meitner's central role in the discovery, winning a Nobel Prize for himself in 1944.

The longitudinal studies of giftedness undertaken by Terman, which began in the early 1900s and are still being followed, reveal that gifted women have not realized their potential. Only 48 percent of gifted women in Terman's study were employed full-time in 1940 and 30.8 percent of that group were working as secretarial and clerical help (Terman & Oden, 1947). Fifteen years later half of the women were still housewives and only 42 percent held full-time jobs. Terman attributes these findings to the lack of desire on the part of gifted females to be nothing more than homemakers, secretaries, teachers, or nurses. This attitude was prevalent at that time.

In a biography of Leta Hollingworth, influential leader in the field of gifted children, her husband described beliefs about females in Leta's day (Hollingworth, 1943):

- Women are actually inferior to men in their abilities.
- Women's talents are just as "good" but in the direction of nurturance, decoration, and the like.
- Women's primary role is based on their reproductive function.
- Women's menstrual cycles interfere with the use of their intellectual abilities.
- Women as a species are less variable than men in psychological characteristics.

These attitudes have provided many stumbling blocks over the years and have prevented females from achieving. Callahan (1979) observed that even though females received higher grades in school, males wrote more books, earned more degrees, produced more works of art, and in general were responsible for making more contributions in all professional fields.

Redefining Giftedness in Females

Gilligan (1982) observed that women have a different view of the world. They view moral concerns in terms of interpersonal relationships and responsibilities to others. They might find it extremely difficult to put their own needs in front of those they care about. Personal attributes might lead women as a group to choose scientific careers less frequently (Lubinski, Benbow, & Sanders, 1993).

Roles of females and definitions of success have to be redefined in light of specific needs and a changing society. According to Lubinski et al. (1993):

> In sum, therefore, mathematically gifted females, in addition to having a more multifaceted interest profile *and* a more complex mixture of value orientations for evaluating their experiences and structuring their life-style, prefer to devote less time to vocational pursuits. They have more to balance, more competing needs at comparable intensities. Mathematically gifted males, however, are more focused on a theoretical/investigative style of life with fewer competing pulls and prefer to devote a greater amount of time to vocational pursuits. (pp. 703–704)

Giftedness is often regarded as the attainment of goals expected of males and occasionally aspired to by females. Subotnik, Arnold, and Noble (1995) address the need to consider gifted women's psychological needs as well as unique dilemmas in their personal and professional lives in assessing giftedness. Reis (1991) suggests redefining the essential components of giftedness to include female perceptions such as aesthetic awareness and sensitivity to societal rather than financial benefits. Giftedness should be viewed as domain specific. In fact, as Kerr (1997) argues: "Gifted girls may possess a wide variety of skills and characteristics that contribute as much to their academic performance as aptitude for particular tasks—for example, leadership skills and creativity. . . . A multidimensional approach will ensure that girls with potential for high performance are identified above and beyond those who score well on objective tests of intellectual aptitude" (p. 490). Redefining giftedness in this way is compatible with Gardner's view of multiple intelligences, which recognizes domains that historically were disregarded. As Kerr reiterates, Gardner's theory has provided us with a new way of understanding and defining how personality and talent interact.

CHARACTERISTICS

Clark's profile (1997) of gifted females indicates that they are often superior physically, have more social knowledge, and are better adjusted than average girls. Gifted girls express their confidence when arguing for their point of view. By the age of ten they communicate their need for self-esteem and pursue school and club achievements to fulfill those needs. Gifted girls fall under the influence of their mothers as opposed to their male counterparts. They have high career goals and are not affected by the occupations of their parents in their career choice. Highly gifted girls demonstrate high academic achievement but are often loners and do not seek recognition. They aspire to careers with moderate status.

Regarding gifted females during adolescence, even though their academics are maintained at a high level, their IQ drops (Clark, 1997). Between the ages of twelve and fourteen there is a noted decline in self-esteem as the gifted adolescent female becomes apprehensive about choices between career and marriage. They take less rigorous courses in high school and become more socially engaged than gifted boys. The highly gifted high school female does very well academically, but receives less recognition and continues on to less prestigious colleges than do gifted males.

Underachievement appears to be a pervading characteristic of gifted females. A discussion of the gifted reveals that characteristically females are compared with their male counterparts yet often lack equitable status. In comparing the characteristics of gifted females to males, Eccles (1985) found the following to be true:

- Gifted females were not achieving as males either educationally or vocationally.
- Gifted females were less likely to seek out advanced educational training.
- Gifted females did not enter the same fields as their male peers.
- Gifted females were overrepresented in the fields of education and literature and underrepresented in science, math, and engineering.
- Gifted females were underrepresented in almost all advanced educational programs.
- Gifted females were underrepresented in the vast majority of high status occupations.
- Gifted females were less likely to have a professional career than their male peers.
- Gifted females tended to select occupations with a lower status.
- Gifted females tended to select occupations that required less education.
- Gifted females were likely to choose occupations that were compatible with family time schedules.

Research supports Eccles's findings in that gifted females tended to deny their special talents and selected traditional female roles in spite of their abilities to pursue other areas of interest. For example, Kerr in her 1985 work *Smart Girls, Gifted Women* followed a group of twenty-three women who had been identified as gifted, ten years after graduation. Most of the women in Kerr's group had chosen the same careers as the women in the Terman group. The group tended to be married, and happy with children. They denied their giftedness, and deemed it irrelevant to their lives. They saw their major obligation as raising their children and supporting the careers chosen by their husbands. In 1992 Kerr conducted a twenty-year follow-up. The women were in much the same circumstances. In 1994 (*Smart Girls Two*) she reported that decisions made in adolescence created clear limits on adult attainment.

In their five-year longitudinal study of gifted women, Fleming and Hollinger (1990) reported that the majority of females were pursuing traditional feminine college majors, that is, education, nursing, the social sciences, and the arts. Piirto (1991) also laments the absence of women in the areas of visual arts, mathematics, and science and stresses the importance of commitment and intensity of interest in a field.

This becomes even more dramatic for the gifted female with a disability. Lang (1994) chronicles studies of gifted scientists with hearing impairments and laments that even though a third of the bachelor's degrees awarded by Gallaudet College went to deaf women between 1922 and 1935, there are no reports of any deaf women scientists.

Underachievement remains a pervasive characteristic for the gifted female. Though gains have been made over the years, gifted females are still not achieving at the same level as their male counterparts. Callahan, Cunningham, and Plucker (1994) report the following:

> Convincing data suggest that gifted female students will face inequities, are still not achieving at the expected levels, and are not choosing career options commensurate with their abilities (see American Association of University Women, 1992; Callahan, 1991; Matyas, 1992). While the incidence of women in various careers such as law, medicine, politics and business increased dramatically in the 1980's, current statistics indicate that gifted women are not achieving preeminence, at least as measured in traditional terms, in the proportion that we would expect given their prevalence in the population. (p. 99)

Over the years researchers have attempted to determine causes of underachievement in females. Lubinski et al. (1993) address issues involved in gender differences. Their review of the literature reported on significant gender differences in mathematical, spatial, and mechanical reasoning, which may explain why there are disparate differences in the proportion of females represented in areas of math and science. Gender differences are only partly responsible. They hypothesize that "satisfactoriness" and "satisfaction" are factors that contribute to individual choices in life. Female achievement depends on the match between innate gifts, background, educational, and professional requirements as well as the support provided by environments.

> Satisfactoriness denotes the degree of correspondence between abilities and the ability requirements of a particular environment (viz., occupation or education curriculum), whereas satisfaction denotes the degree of correspondence between the preferences and the types of reinforcers provided by an occupation or educational track. Collectively, satisfactoriness (how the environment will respond to the individual) and satisfaction (how the individual is likely to respond to the environment) are useful for predicting the length of time individuals are likely to remain in various educational or career tracks. (Lubinski et al., 1993, p. 695)

The factors contributing to achievement by gifted females are quite complex. Barriers to achievement include internal and external factors.

How Internal Barriers Affect Achievement

According to Hollinger and Fleming (1984), internal barriers to achievement include low social self-esteem, fear of success, low achievement motivation, lack of assertiveness, multipotentiality, and perfectionistic expectations. The combination leads to inaccurate self-perceptions and the development of counterproductive female phenomena.

Self-Perceptions   Research indicates that self-perceptions of abilities are more significant in achievement than actual gifts and play a central role in the career development of gifted females (Eccles, 1983; Hollinger & Fleming, 1993; Sternberg & Kolligan, 1990). Perceiving oneself as being self-assertive and competent correlates with achievement as opposed to goals defined by education and career achievement.

> Among the mathematically talented young women, self perceptions of ability were more powerful than actual talent ratings in discriminating those young women aspiring to nontraditional careers in math and science from those aspiring to more traditional careers (Hollinger, 1983b). Furthermore, the nontraditional math career aspirants differed from their traditional counterparts not simply in terms of their self perceptions of high math ability but also in their self perceptions of low artistic ability and friendliness. This profile of self perceptions of ability suggests that the nontraditional math career aspirant may be choosing math "by default," perceiving herself as lacking in abilities except mathematics (Hollinger, 1985b). (Hollinger & Fleming, 1993, p. 159)

Perceptions influence expectations. Santiago and Einarson (1996) report that women enrolled in engineering and physical sciences expect to get lower grades than do men. Students who perceived their gender to be a liability anticipated lower earnings. Even though adolescent females' skills are deemed to be higher than boys in cognitive resources and career planning, females indicated a preference for careers that were lower paying (Kelly & Cobb, 1991).

Arnold and Denny, in their 1985 study of male and female high school valedictorians and salutatorians, reported that even though female valedictorians outperformed men in college, they performed at lower levels in the world of work. According to Arnold (1994), even though males and females received equally high college entrance examination scores and grade point averages, females lowered their estimate of their intelligence over the college years beginning in the senior year of high school and sophomore year in college.

Special Female Phenomena   Much has been written about phenomena that affect the growth and development of all females and have particular relevance for the gifted.

- The *queen bee syndrome* (Staines, Tavis, & Jayaratne, 1974) describes the modern-day superwomen who must perform multiple roles perfectly. "The true Queen Bee has made it in a 'man's world' of work while running a house and family with her left hand" (p. 56).

- The *great impostor syndrome* (Clance, 1985; Machlowitz, 1982; Warschaw, 1985) depicts how successful women believe their accomplishments are attributable to luck—not ability or hard work—and are fearful of being found out. They have an extremely low sense of self and attribute their success to external rather than internal forces. Their success is never truly fulfilling because they are always concerned with not being found out. The impostor phenomenon is caused by mixed messages received from family and society and is rooted in early childhood and family background.
- The *Cinderella complex* (Dowling, 1981) describes females who await a Prince Charming who will come along and take care of everything. Women are crippled by a developed dependency on others, are angry about staying behind, and are too frightened to move ahead.
- The *perfection complex* (Reis, 1987) causes gifted females to establish unrealistic goals for themselves as they try to be the best daughter, the best athlete, the best scholar, the best friend, etc. They strive to be slender, beautiful, and popular.
- The *fear of success syndrome* was first introduced by Horner (1972). Gifted females become fearful of being rejected by peers or appearing undesirable to members of the opposite sex. This fear can negatively impact school performance (Lavach & Lanier, 1975).

How External Barriers Affect Achievement

External barriers that affect the achievement of gifted females include cultural influences, familial influences, role models and mentors, support, and schooling influences.

In terms of cultural and environmental influences, Reis (1985) speaks to the issue of the disadvantaged and expectations that females will care for family members, clean house, and marry young. Women who complete a doctorate are more apt to come from higher socioeconomic homes and have professional or successful executive parents (Groth, 1975). Intervention and counseling strategies are imperative if disadvantaged females are to achieve.

Family attitudes and beliefs greatly impact development. Hildebrand (1991) reports that schools are still failing to draw girls into studies of physical science and technology, both of which areas are considered vital to careers in the twenty-first century. Parents are still telling their daughters that they "look pretty" and are not encouraging them to take courses in physics and calculus. According to Johnson and Lewman (1990), gender stereotypes regarding expectations and achievement are in place before children begin school. Parental expectations influence mathematical self-concept in adolescents (Dickens & Cornell, 1993). Children's beliefs about their own abilities were more strongly influenced by their parents' beliefs than by their past performance (Parsons, Adler, & Kaczala, 1982). Parents usually encouraged gifted females to do well in school, but provided little encouragement to pursue a career after college (Reis, 1995). Parents expected their daughters to marry and have families. Hollinger and Fleming (1993) reported that opportunity emerged as an important factor in career choice. Family values and the choices families make for their daughters play an important part in female development (Fleming & Hollinger, 1990).

Arnold (1993, 1994), in a fifteen-year longitudinal study of male and female valedictorians, reported that, unlike their male counterparts who progressively narrowed their career choices during college, females began planning for contingency careers. The pressure to remain open to marriage and family needs hindered their career planning. Six of the valedictorian women abandoned medical school aspirations, anticipating unrealistic demands of marriage and child rearing. Planning for combining career and family began as early as the sophomore year in college. "The valedictorian story underlines the problematic nature of the transition from school to work for even the best female students and demonstrates the process by which early adult achievements of top female students reflect the influences of values and life role expectations rather than ability and academic performance" (Arnold, 1993, p. 175).

IDENTIFICATION

Identification of the gifted female needs to include the use of multiple criteria and address multiple intelligences. Focusing on special talents or aptitudes may be more productive than simply searching for generally gifted youth (Feldhusen, 1992; Gagne, 1995). IQ tests have not been reliable in measuring giftedness before the ages of nine or ten and have not proven themselves to be predictors of academic performance of gifted women. Even though IQ tests do not always favor the gifted female (Silverman, 1991a), a good intelligence test administered by a qualified professional will identify exceptional verbal skills, which are one of the earliest signs of giftedness in girls. Test bias needs to be addressed in considering the identification of gifted females.

Research has found that gender differences and performances on standardized tests are significant. Fewer females score at higher levels of mathematical reasoning on SAT tests. Kerr and Colangelo (1988) found gender differences on the ACT that favor boys, but found that within tests differences, females scored at a higher level on the English portion and the males scored higher on the mathematics. Tests that include content that is more familiar to males will penalize the female. Sadker and Sadker (1985) argue that the use of test scores that might be sex biased can have a profound negative impact on self-esteem.

Because IQ testing has been more effective in identifying young children with deficits rather than young children with gifts, developmental scales of assessment can provide a better model for identifying young gifted females. Using these scales will allow us to observe advanced skills and provide early education for the students having those skills. An early start will ensure that they receive a level of challenge commensurate with their abilities.

One recommended practice that assists in the identification of the gifted female is to adjust for gender differences in test scores. By accepting a lower cut-off for females, we may in fact be leveling the playing field, thereby offering females an opportunity to excel. A second method involves using Gardner's theory, which is a multidimensional approach. This enables an assessment of a wide range of skills and characteristics that facilitates academic performance such as leadership and creativity. To ensure equitable access to educational services for females with special gifts and talents, the sources of sex bias in the identification and assessment of the gifted female need to be removed.

A Special Concern: Identification of Gifted Female Adolescents

Adolescence appears to be a critical time that negatively affects gifted females. As students progress through school, girls seem to lose ground, or boys get stronger academically and outshine them (O'Tuel & Rawl, 1985). Read (1991) reports a dramatic decline in enrollment of females in gifted programs from grades seven through ten. Data were gathered to explain the decrease, and the factors are listed here in descending order:

- Peer pressure
- Administrator attitudes
- Program content
- Program model
- Parental pressure
- Faculty attitudes
- Counselor attitudes
- Identification process.

Peer pressure was thought to be the greatest factor in discouraging students from participating. Administration, faculty, counselor, and parental attitudes also discouraged females from participating. Gifted females tend to shy away from programs that include math and physics advanced placement examinations. In her work Kerr (1985) suggests that IQ scores for females decline during this period because of their desire not to try.

Self-perceived abilities and confidence for females declined progressively from elementary and primary grades through junior high school, and further declined through senior high school (Kline & Short, 1991). They become less willing to reveal themselves, and they hide their intelligence, sensitivity, and feelings.

Along with their loss of confidence, they begin exhibiting traits of perfectionism. In high school, they feel discouraged, afraid, and worried. This finding suggests that as gifted females mature, they feel pressured to adopt the values, goals, and aspirations compatible with society's preference for traditional male competitiveness and individualism. Establishing relationships becomes a priority. Kerr (1985) denotes that gifted adolescent girls are confronted by social barriers that adversely affect their self-concept. Howard-Hamilton and Robinson (1991) report that gifted females become confused during adolescence when they receive strong social and cultural messages regarding gender. According to Callahan et al. (1994) perceptions of self-concept become a factor in achievement and that gender differences in self-confidence grow larger in high school and college and are not limited to mathematics.

Sands and Howard-Hamilton(1995) address concern for the emotional well-being of the gifted female adolescent. Gifted females feel more worried and frustrated than gifted boys. They become bewildered and overwhelmed by mixed messages from parents, teachers, peers, and society. They feel pulled between choosing achievement or sexual attractiveness. Males tend to prefer compliant, "sweet" females who do not challenge their male egos. Resulting depression is not uncommon. Gifted females should become aware of the harmful effects of our patriarchal society. They should be supported as they explore their inner resources. Career options and lifestyle choices should not be based on gender.

Cantor and Bernay (1992) interviewed twenty-five women in politics who were "at the top," including Pat Schroeder, Dianne Feinstein, and Ann Richards. In their book *Women in Power—The Secrets of Leadership* they reveal that these women received and believed five messages given to them by their parents or other significant figures early in their life:

1. You are loved and special.
2. You can do anything you want to do.
3. You can use and enjoy your creative aggression and still be feminine.
4. You can be courageous and take risks.
5. You are entitled to dream great dreams.

In a 1996 telephone interview by one of the authors with Toni Bernay, she spoke of research currently being undertaken with females who have "reached the top" in the business world. Findings indicate that even though these women have achieved, they are "still shaky inside." While growing up, they received the first two messages, but never received or internalized the last three.

INTERVENTIONS

Importance of Role Models and Mentors for Females

Fox (1977) determined that young girls do better in math with a female teacher. Fox and Richmond (1979) report a lack of suitable career role models. Mentoring can help provide needed role models for gifted females. True mentors can critically impact career aspirations. The importance of appropriate mentoring has been highlighted in a number of studies (Arnold & Subotnik, 1995; Subotnik, 1994a, 1994b).

Subotnik and Steiner (1993) report that mentoring dramatically influences women's involvement in scientific careers. According to Jacobi (1991)and Zuckerman (1983) being invited to work with a powerful mentor is the best predictor of future success in science. Mentoring by college faculty may be related to women's persistence in college (Nora, Cabrera, Hagedorn, & Pascarella, 1996). Subotnik and Steiner (1993) studied ninety-six students who were winners in a Westinghouse Science Talent Search and reported on the importance of the role played by mentors.

Importance of Support

A supportive environment appears to be a prominent factor in the development of gifted females. Parents, peers, counselors, and teachers may discourage girls from pursuing certain careers (Grau, 1985). Nora et al. (1996) report differences between males and females attending college. Females were influenced by encouraging words, support from parents, connections with faculty, and friendships with peers. Encouragement by parents was a key factor in influencing female students enrolled in college to earn a degree. Women, more than men, seek different forms of encouragement, other than their parents, such as faculty members.

Arnold and Denny (1985) found that women who continued to achieve after college had three experiences in common: (1) supportive college environment, (2) significant interaction with both college faculty and professionals in their selected fields, and (3) opportunity to test abilities in a nurturing environment.

Schooling Influences

Sadker and Sadker (1985) found that males received more attention and encouragement than females in fourth-, fifth-, and sixth-grade classes. In all subject areas, boys dominated classroom communication. Reis (1985) and Ellis (1993) purport that classroom dynamics can lead to gifted females doubting their ability, creativity, and importance. Girls have learned verbal and physical self-restraint before attending school, requiring teachers to pay more attention to boys in the classroom. Young boys who call out, debate, argue, and ask questions are labeled bright, whereas females who do so are labeled obnoxious, aggressive, or unfeminine. Boys are freer to develop the self-confidence, adventuresome interests, and independence that are associated with intelligence. Girls learn to appear modest, self-deprecating, passive, and obedient while boys become assertive and self-promoting. The American Association of University Women (1992) conducted an extensive study on the educational experience of females, which had been largely ignored. They reveal that females are not receiving the same quality, or even quantity, of education as males. In *Reviving Ophelia*, Pipher (1994) relates her own experiences:

> Kent, Sam and I were the top students. The teachers praised them for being brilliant and creative, while I was praised for being a hard worker. Kent and Sam were encouraged to go to out-of-state schools to study law or medicine, while I was encouraged to study at the state university to be a teacher. (pp. 237–238)

Nora et al. (1996) report that males receive greater encouragement to attend institutions of higher learning. Female persistence in college was influenced by parental encouragement and academic performance (i.e., grade point average). Males were not discouraged by lower grades whereas earning B's and C's discouraged women from further enrollment. Civian and Schley (1996) report that females who had expressed an initial interest in majoring in math and science, but who later became discouraged, were performing at a lower level in mathematics and science courses at Wellesley. Women attending law school find the large classes and confrontational atmosphere intimidating. There is a question as to whether the Socratic method of teaching negatively impacts females and whether or not male professors take female students seriously.

"There is more laughter when a woman will speak," said Ms. Aste who just finished her first year of law school. "Women's comments aren't taken as seriously as men's. It depends on the professor. Sometimes a professor makes light of a response that comes from a woman." (Bernstein, 1996, p. B10)

Lubinski et al. (1993) purport that inadequate math and science preparation is a factor in curtailing women's career options. Mathematically gifted females take less mathematics (and science) in high school compared to males (Benbow & Minor, 1986; Benbow & Stanley, 1982).

Helping gifted females reach their potential involves a number of factors, including the following (Silverman, 1991a; Subotnik & Arnold, 1993):

- Parent education
- Early identification
- Greater emphasis on demonstrated performance
- Gifted peers
- Early entrance to kindergarten
- Acceleration
- Teacher in-service
- Special programs
- Guidance and career counseling.

PERSONAL INTERVIEW

In a 1996 interview conducted by one of the authors with Dr. Rena Subotnik, researcher in the field, she related some of her own experiences:

My parents spoke French with me at home. When I was tested for admission to a special school for the gifted in kindergarten, it was suggested that I wait because my English was not fluent enough. I was accepted in third grade. Females were encouraged to excel in the school and later I was accepted into a special high school for science. I admired the highly intelligent students in the science high school. I loved the mathematics classes but I wasn't an especially sharp science student.

I considered becoming a math major in college, but my calculus professor was angry with me for correcting his mistakes. He told me that if I promised not to come around the department, he would give me an "A." I ended up studying social sciences and education. After graduation from college, I considered getting a Ph.D., but my major professor in the master's program advised me that this would not be a good idea if I intended to marry. I decided to proceed anyway and eventually fulfilled my dream of becoming a professor.

One of my first big projects as a professor at Hunter College was to conduct a follow-up of graduates of my elementary school. I was struck by how few of my classmates from my special school had become eminent. This realization was instrumental in causing me to reflect about my own desires to make a mark. It was a "kick in the pants" that initiated a more active research and writing agenda. I have come to certain realizations as a result, some of them involving the pressures women experience to conform and marry, and how important it is for females to have a support system. I try to provide that for my students.

In this same 1996 interview, Subotnik outlined some of the prerequisites for female achievement:

- *Elementary, middle, and high schools:*   Early exposure and continued high-quality mathematics and science instruction.
- *Middle and high schools:*   Supportive counseling. If females qualify for special programs, except in rare cases (deep commitment to another field, for example), they should not be given choices but should be placed in them.
- *College:*   Women entering college programs should assess available support systems. If a support system is not existent, they need to establish one.
- *After graduation:*   Continued networking to establish support for career goals.

Our society is in a state of transformation with regard to career roles. Fitting family needs into career trajectories is difficult and challenging in most professional fields. To keep women on the path leading to significant creative contributions, solutions for dealing with sharing responsibilities at work and at home will have to be found.

With equal opportunity, gifted females can achieve at the same levels as their male counterparts. This is apparent when we look at the number of women of eminence who have graduated from single-sex institutions of higher learning. Until there is equal access in the public school setting within the coeducational setting, single-sex schooling may be a viable option.

In answer to one of the concerns affecting female achievement, introduction to all of the domains to determine domain-specific talents is essential. Gifted women need to be identified in domain-specific areas (Reis, 1991). Quality science and mathematics instruction should be offered early. As areas of gifts are noted, differentiation should be planned and gifted females appropriately placed. Differentiating the curriculum and maintaining a level of challenge in areas of gifts should be planned on an individual basis and include a variety of options. Programming should include appropriate grouping as gifts are identified. Grouping may take place in the classroom, but, when necessary, should be extended. Some options would include an honors or accelerated class.

Role models should be provided whenever possible and should include mentors and internships. Programming for the gifted female should emphasize counseling. Gifted females often suffer from multipotentiality and may need help in establishing direction. Teachers and counselors should be sensitive to the supportive environment necessary for female achievement. Parents should be counseled as well.

FOR FURTHER READING

American Association of University Women. (1992). *How schools shortchange girls—A study of major findings on girls and education.* Annapolis Junction, MD: American Association of University Women.

Cantor, D. W., & Bernay, T. (1992). *Women in Power—The Secrets of Leadership.* Boston: Houghton Mifflin.

Freeman, J. (1993). Parents and families in nurturing giftedness and talent. In K. Heller, F. Monks, & A. H. Passow (Eds.), *International Handbook of Research and Development of Giftedness and Talent* (pp. 669–683). Oxford: Pergamon Press.

Gilligan, C. (1982). *In a different voice.* Cambridge, MA: Harvard University Press.

Kerr, B. (1985). *Smart girls, gifted women.* Columbus, OH: Ohio Psychology Press.

Kerr, B. (1994). *Smart girls two.* Columbus, OH: Ohio Psychology Press.

Pipher, M. (1994). *Reviving Ophelia.* New York: Ballantine Books.

Reis, S. M., & Dobyns, S. M. (1991, April). An annotated bibliography of non-fictional books and curricular materials to encourage gifted females. *Roeper Review 13*(3), 129–134.

Section 4

Issues and Concerns

Addressing the Needs of Students with Exceptional Abilities in the Twenty-First Century

Chapter 10 : **Social and Emotional Concerns and Underachievement**

Chapter 11 : **Reconceptualizing Gifted Education: Creating an Inclusive Community of All Learners**

Chapter 10 presents different views regarding the social and emotional development of the gifted. Different factors that affect the social and emotional development of gifted children are discussed, and the concept of overexcitabilities are reviewed. Emotional and moral development is discussed as are special concerns regarding gifted children at risk and those who underachieve. Suggestions are made as to how to address these concerns.

Chapter 11 addresses the need for school restructuring to include a new paradigm in education. In the past, teachers have been prepared to work with one particular type of student: "regular," "special," or "gifted." With the move toward more inclusive school settings, teacher preparation must be reconceptualized to address the diverse nature of the classroom population today. Teachers are responsible for all students and must be properly prepared to meet their needs.

We must begin to examine ways in which students with gifts can be provided with programs that extend and eliminate the barriers to appropriate educational opportunities. The application of multiple intelligence philosophy provides future teachers with positive ways in which students can be viewed so that giftedness is observed.

Chapter 10

Social and Emotional Concerns and Underachievement

Typical questions a classroom teacher might ask include these:

Do gifted students have special social and emotional needs?

What are some of the causes of underachievement in the gifted?

Are there measures I can take to assist gifted children so that they can reach their potential?

To address these questions, this chapter does the following:

Discusses different views of social and emotional sensitivity in the gifted.

Outlines causes of underachievement.

Suggests ways in which teachers can gain insight into the social and emotional needs of children who are gifted.

Suggests programming alternatives to avoid underachievement.

ON BEING GIFTED: CONCERNS, RAMIFICATIONS, AND INTERVENTIONS

Specific areas that can cause concern for the gifted population include social and emotional issues, unusual sensitivities, and underachievement.

Social and Emotional Development of Gifted Children

Specialists in the field hold different views as to the social/emotional needs of gifted children. In his review of the literature Webb (1993) reported the following: Altman (1983), Delisle (1986), Hayes and Sloat (1989), Kaiser and Berndt (1985), Kaplan (1983), and Silverman (1991b) view gifted children as having special sensitivities and being prone to problems that need special counseling and/or interventions. Colangelo and Brower (1987) and Scholwinski and Reynolds (1985) see gifted children as being able to fare quite well on their own, and Dirkes (1983), Janos and Robinson (1985), and Shore, Cornell, Robinson, and Ward (1991) believe gifted children with problems requiring special interventions are in the minority. Webb (1993) postulates that even though the various views of these specialists appear to be divergent, they do not contradict one another because gifted children who are faring well are those involved in academic programs specifically designed for them. When students are not placed in appropriate settings behaviors result that can be a cause for concern. Even though gifted children do not suffer severe maladjustment because of their giftedness, the combination of sensitivities and high intellectual functioning can cause problems that should be addressed in school.

The literature reveals that little has been written about gifted children who also have emotional disturbances. The gifted experience the same percentage of severe social and emotional difficulties as the general population (Terman & Oden, 1959). In his longitudinal studies of the gifted, Terman found that 7 to 10 percent of his subjects tended toward maladjustment. Maladjustment among women, but not among men, increased with IQ. Maker (1977) postulates that if intelligence is interpreted, in its broad sense, as the ability to function successfully in some area of human endeavor rather than as a score on an IQ test, it is doubtful that severely and profoundly disturbed children, even with successful treatment, would be able to function at such a high level. However, with appropriate intervention children who are emotionally disturbed and achieving at grade level or slightly above, could be achieving at four or more grade levels above. Psychological treatment should be advised to see if children's performance can be brought up to potential. According to McKnight-Taylor (1997), inclusion in the regular classroom would depend on the severity of the problem. Highly aggressive or disruptive students should not be included.

Social and Emotional Development and Self-Esteem

Characteristics of the gifted make them more vulnerable to low self-esteem and underachievement, which may be the precursors of problematic social and emotional development. Factors that critically affect the social and emotional development of gifted students include premature or dyssynchronous development, innate personality characteristics, and pressures from home and school.

Premature or Dyssynchronous Development   Gifted children often exhibit uneven development, causing dyssynchrony (Terrasier, 1979). When uneven development is not recognized and accepted, healthy social and emotional development is thwarted. Areas of development might include developmental delays (e.g., motor skills, particularly fine motor skills, often lag behind intellectual development). The disparity between a child's language skills and handwriting skills can be very frustrating. A child with advanced intellectual functioning may find it difficult for his hands to keep pace with his cognitive abilities. Social immaturity manifests itself in the child's inability to deal with interpersonal concepts. Lack of coping skills can often cause conflicting drives and internal dyssynchrony. Situations occur that cause reactions or feelings that they do not have the ability to express.

Innate Personality Characteristics   Innate personality characteristics affect a number of areas for gifted children. Webb, Meckstroth, and Tolan (1982) and Whitmore (1980) have estimated that many highly able children may be significantly hindered by perfectionism at some point in their academic careers. Hamachek (1978) describes two types of perfectionism: normal and neurotic. The normal perfectionist derives pleasure from painstaking efforts to seek excellence, which is observed in the work of eminent individuals. The neurotic perfectionistic never takes pleasure in his or her accomplishments or assesses any effort as good enough. Perfectionists strive toward impossible goals and measure their worth in terms of

their accomplishments. Striving for impossible goals can cause psychological problems. Parker and Adkins (1995) postulate that healthy and unhealthy perfectionism
should be viewed differently, noting healthy and unhealthy consequences. When perfectionists become overly concerned about mistakes and doubt their performance,
suicidal ideation may result. Kline and Short (1991) report that for gifted females
perfectionism becomes more accentuated in high school. They want to achieve and
establish high standards for themselves which they feel they fall short of. They
become afraid, worried, and feel less appreciated than in grade school. "The pattern
takes on alarming proportions when girls feel despair or loss of meaning to the point
of not wanting to live. Simply put, gifted girls are more vulnerable to the stressors of
depression, worry, and fear as they grow older" (p. 120).

Gifted children may have difficulty relating to their chronological peers. Ten-
sions result when gifted children try to impose their way of thinking on their peers.

Some gifted students avoid involvement in any endeavors in which they are not
assured of success. This failure to "take a chance" limits the child's scope and can lead
to underachievement. Their abilities to see possibilities and alternatives cause them to
have unrealistic expectations for themselves. The gifted child who has advanced capabilities in more than one area may have difficulty choosing one career path, and this
hesitation may cause anxiety and depression. Gifted children may suffer from existential depression and spend inordinate amounts of time searching for meaning in life.

Family relationships are quite complex and can involve power struggles and
problematic sibling relationships. Children have to be accepted for who they are and
should not be judged only by their achievements.

Expectations of others affect the gifted because parents and educators sometimes forget that they are children first and gifted second. Problems also emerge for
gifted children who are nonconforming. Gifted children sometimes feel a sense of
gloom and doom and a feeling of impotence in their desire to effect change. Gallagher (1978) addressed the sensitivities of gifted children with regard to the world
around them. As gifted children read newspapers, evidence of gloom and doom sur-
rounds them. They do not always have the ability to put the news in proper perspective Pipher (1994) describes an interview with a young gifted women who was worried
about oil spills and rain forests. She could not forget about Somalia or Bosnia and felt
like the world was falling apart.

> I see these problems in other highly gifted girls. Often because they are so
> bright, adults expect them to be mature emotionally. And they aren't. They react
> to global tragedies with the emotional intensity of adolescents. Though bright
> girls are perceptive enough to see through the empty values and shallow behavior
> of their peers, they have the social needs of adolescents. They feel utterly alone
> in their suffering. They have the intellectual abilities of adults in some areas and
> can understand world problems, and yet have the political power of children.
> (Pipher, 1994, p. 162)

Gailbraith (1983, 1984) and Silverman (1993b) note the specific concerns that
have plagued gifted students in school, including the lack of challenge and the need

for intellectual peers rather than agemates, which often results in these students becoming hermits.

Teachers in classrooms often do not recognize the uneven development. When exceptional intellectual development is evidenced, it is often accompanied by expectations of advanced functioning in all areas. Gifted children receive "mixed messages" from the environment when they are praised for intellectual performance and expected to perform and behave in other areas that have not reached the same level of development. They are criticized for acts not within their control.

SPECIAL SENSITIVITIES: LOOKING AT THE GIFTED THROUGH A DIFFERENT LENS

Personality Characteristics: Dabrowski's Theory of Overexcitabilities

There are certain personality characteristics of the gifted that intelligence tests do not measure (Piechowski, 1986). Piechowski proposes a model of endowment for giftedness and creativity derived from Dabrowski's (1964) theory of positive disintegration.

Dabrowski developed his concept of developmental potential from extensive clinical and biographic studies of gifted, creative, and eminent individuals (Dabrowski, 1937, 1967, 1972). He proposed five levels of development: At the integrated primary level, the individual is concerned with survival and self-protection; at the secondary level, the personality ideal is attained; and then there are three transitional states that represent phases of disintegration. Disintegration allows instinctive modes of functioning to deteriorate, enabling higher-order value systems to develop.

Developmental potential is defined as the original endowment that determines what level of development a person may reach given optimal conditions. In his observations of gifted children and adolescents, patients, artists, writers, and members of religious orders, Dabrowski (1964) noted differences in behaviors that he termed *overexcitabilities*, characterized as a consistent overreaction to external and internal stimuli that appeared limited to certain areas of expression (Piechowski, 1975). This term describes intensification of mental activities and responses that would be considered to be above and beyond what can be considered common. Dabrowski's concept of developmental potential included talents and abilities, plus five primary components: psychomotor, sensual, intellectual, imaginational, and emotional (Piechowski, 1986). These dimensions can be thought of as channels of information flow and as modes of experiencing (Piechowski, 1979) and can be broad, narrow, or almost nonexistent. Piechowski organized the forms and expressions of psychic overexcitability in an attempt to convey the characteristics and variations within each form (Figure 10.1). He cautions that these categories are not complete or final and are not exclusive of each other.

Sensitivity, perfectionism, intensity, and introversion are all aspects of emotional excitability. The extremely sensitive, empathic individual would prefer to withdraw rather than retaliate. Comparative studies conducted by Silverman and

PSYCHOMOTOR

Surplus of energy

rapid speech, marked enthusiasm, fast games and sports, pressure for action, e.g., organizing, marked competitiveness

Psychomotor expression of emotional tension

compulsive talking and chattering, impulsive actions, delinquent behavior, workaholism, nervous habits (tics, nail-biting), acting out

SENSUAL

Enhanced sensory and aesthetic pleasure

seeing, smelling, tasting, touching, hearing, and sex; delight in beautiful objects, sounds of words, music, form, color, balance

Sensual expression of emotional tension

overeating, sexual overindulgence, buying sprees, wanting to be in the limelight

INTELLECTUAL

Intensified activity of the mind

curiosity, concentration, capacity for sustained intellectual effort, avid reading; keen observation, detailed visual recall, detailed planning

Penchant for probing questions and problem solving

search for truth and understanding; forming new concepts; tenacity in problem solving

Reflective thought

thinking about thinking, love of theory and analysis, preoccupation with logic, moral thinking, introspection (but without self-judgment), conceptual and intuitive integration; independence of thought (sometimes very critical)

IMAGINATIONAL

Free play of the imagination

frequent use of image and metaphor, facility for invention and fantasy, facility for detailed visualization, poetic and dramatic perception, animistic and magical thinking

Capacity for living in a world of fantasy

predilection for magic and fairy tales, creation of private worlds, imaginary companions; dramatization

Spontaneous imagery as an expression of emotional tension

animistic imagery, mixing of truth and fiction, elaborate dreams, illusions

Low tolerance for boredom

Figure 10.1   Forms and expressions of overexcitability

Source: Reprinted with permission from Piechowski, M. M. (1997). Emotional giftedness: The measure of intrapersonal intelligence. In N. Colangelo & G. A. Davis (Eds.), *Handbook of gifted education*. Boston: Allyn & Bacon.

EMOTIONAL

Feelings and emotions intensified
positive feelings, negative feelings, extremes of emotion, complex emotions and feelings, identification with others' feelings, awareness of a whole range of feelings

Strong somatic expressions
tense stomach, sinking heart, blushing, flushing, pounding heart, sweaty palms

Strong affective expressions
inhibition (timidity, shyness); enthusiasm, ecstasy, euphoria, pride; strong affective memory; shame; feelings of unreality, fears and anxieties, feelings of guilt, concern with death, depressive and suicidal moods

Capacity for strong attachments, deep relationships
strong emotional ties and attachments to persons, living things, places; attachments to animals; difficulty adjusting to new environments; compassion, responsiveness to others, sensitivity in relationships; loneliness

Well-differentiated feelings toward self
inner dialogue and self-judgment

Figure 10.1   *continued*

Ellsworth (1981) of overexcitability profiles of intellectually gifted adults and a heterogeneous sample of graduate students revealed that the gifted group showed higher scores on sensual, intellectual, imaginational, and emotional overexcitabilities. Piechowski (1979) has developed an overexcitability questionnaire that Ackerman (1996) suggests using as an additional measure to assist in identifying the gifted. Posing some of the questions in the classroom can assist teachers in identifying special sensitivities. There are twenty-one items in the Overexcitability Questionnaire that includes some of the following:

What has been your experience of the most intense pleasure?

What kinds of things get your mind going?

When do you feel the most energy and what do you do with it?

How do you act when you get excited?

What do you like to concentrate on the most?

What kind of physical activity (or inactivity) gives you the most satisfaction?

Do you ever think about your own thinking? Describe.

When do you feel the greatest urge to do something?

Does it ever appear to you that the things around you may have a life of their own, and that plants, animals, and things in nature have their own feelings? Give examples.

If you come across a difficult idea or concept, how does it become clear to you? Describe what goes on in your head in this case.

In her research using the Overexcitability Questionnaire, Ackerman (1996) reported:

> There are four main points that can be made based on the results of this study. Of primary importance is that the gifted subjects were differentiated from their nonidentified peers based on their higher psychomotor, intellectual, and emotional overexcitability scores. While this is an unexpected finding, it clearly illustrates that scores on the OEQ can differentiate between gifted and nongifted students. Because of the central part psychomotor overexcitability played in the analysis, which has not been noted in previous studies, it is important that further research be conducted to verify these findings. (p. 15)

Application   Ackerman (1996) reported that even though the Overexcitability Questionnaire was not a tenable instrument in its present form (because of the length of administration time, the level of writing skills and expressive language, and the cost of scoring or training to become a rater), Dabrowski's concept provides another lens through which to view students in the classroom. If a child is not attending, what might be the reasons? Individuals may have any combination of overexcitabilities. Noting behaviors and questioning motivations can promote tolerance and understanding of individual differences. Some of the questions from the questionnaire can be incorporated into lessons during the year to gain greater insight into student profiles:

1. What activities make you think?
2. What activities do you find the most satisfying?
3. What do you like to concentrate on the most?

Or as Dr. Jane Piirto of Ohio State University recommends to students in her program, use one question at a time for purposes of starting discussions in fifth grade. Children can pass if they wish. Information gleaned can be used in designing curriculum for individual students.

MORAL DEVELOPMENT AND THE GIFTED

In Chapter 2, the need to address moral education as a component in the education of the gifted was stressed. Being gifted or creative imposes a special moral responsibility on an individual (Gruber, 1985).

Dabrowski (1964, 1967, 1972) postulated that overexcitability patterns provided the foundation for the development of higher-order values in adult life. Silverman (1995) reported on Dabrowski's five stages of emotional development:

Level I: Self-serving; little concern for others (no introspection, absence of inner conflict, externalize all conflict and blame others)

Level II: Group domination; motivated by desire for approval and fear of punishment (ambivalence and ambitendencies, no inner core of values, easily swayed)

Level III: Self-examination; transition into advanced development (development of an inherent set of values, experience their own inadequacies intensely, troubled by gap between "what is" and "what ought to be")

Level IV: Self-actualization; gap narrows as individual learns to live with ideals ("What ought to be will be" becomes the metaphor for the self-actualizing life)

Level V: Attainment of the personality ideal; attainment of authenticity, harmony, altruism, and empathy for all living creatures.

Piechowski (1986) addresses the need to acknowledge self-actualization and advanced moral development for the gifted, rather than merely to address productivity in adult life. Andreani and Pagnin (1993) report on the lack of relationship between morality and intelligence. The relationship between moral development and giftedness can be described from two perspectives (Narvaez, 1991): (1) Giftedness is dependent on intellectual giftedness, and (2) giftedness is not a general factor but is highly specific, since particular skills are fairly autonomous.

Kohlberg (1976), who developed a cognitive-developmental theory of moralization involving six stages, also reported that moral stage is related to cognitive advance and to moral behavior, but identification of the moral stage was based on moral reasoning alone. Kohlberg's stages include these:

Level I: Preconventional
   Stage 1: Heteronomous morality; doesn't consider interests of others
   Stage 2: Individualism, instrumental purpose, and exchange; aware that everyone has his or her own interests to pursue
Level II: Conventional
   Stage 3: Mutual interpersonal expectations, relationships, and interpersonal conformity; aware of shared feelings, puts himself in the other person's shoes
   Stage 4: Social system and conscience; believes in rules and authority
Level III: Postconventional
   Stage 5: Social contract or utility and individual rights; considers moral and legal points, looking for decisions based on the greatest good for the greatest numbers
   Stage 6: Universal ethical principles; development of universal moral principles with a commitment to them.

In spite of this, Andreani and Pagnin (1993) report that

> . . . there are many signs of potentially positive moral development in the gifted, based on social competence or abilities. . . . It can therefore be concluded that the gifted have the potential for a high level morality development, which would give them the opportunity to become real leaders, making a positive contribution to their community and to humanity. However, this potential will not be realized in a simple and automatic way in the absence of educational support and favorable intervention. There is the danger that the bright picture of gifted personalities, potentially ready to restructure ways of thinking and social situations with

creative inventions, is obscured and deformed in the "gifted syndrome," which emphasizes inner life and intellectual traits, leading to excessive abstraction (and perhaps even autistic thinking), to impulsive reactivity, anxiety, and rebelliousness. (pp. 546–547)

In appreciating intellectual superiority, personal success should not take precedence over social goals. Values education and moral development should become part of the curriculum. Kohlberg's (1976) cognitive-developmental approach emphasizes rational justification of values (discussed in Chapter 1). Moral dilemmas should be discussed and decisions justified using his model. Students should be exposed to value clarification exercises and be taught decision-making strategies that highlight the consequences of actions taken. According to Rest and Thoma (1986), moral education programs that emphasize dilemma discussion and personality development produce positive results.

SPECIAL CONCERNS

The Gifted Child at Risk: Suicide Prevention

Delisle (1986) acknowledges the special sensitivities of gifted children as well as similarities to other children the same age. All children need acceptance, companionship and self-understanding. He suggests that suicide prevention programs be included in the health curriculum for all students and suggests the following:

- Do not wait until a suicide or suicide attempt occurs to implement a suicide prevention program.
- Include a unit on suicide prevention as part of the mental health curriculum beginning in middle school.
- Provide in-service training on suicide prevention to school personnel and parents.
- Appreciate the crucial role that students play in recognizing other adolescents who are suicidal.
- Provide resources on suicide prevention to teachers.
- Be prepared to act specifically should a suicide, or a suicide attempt, occur in your school.

Social and Emotional Development and Underachievement

Concerns about the social and emotional development of the gifted should be addressed early to avoid experiencing difficulties later. The sensitivities of gifted children often make them vulnerable, preventing them from achieving their potential. Much has been written about the social and emotional development of the gifted and underachievement. The two are often inextricably linked. Based on a review of the literature, implementation of special programs will assist in helping gifted students to develop a healthy self-concept and preventing underachievement.

As one observes the traits of underachievers as reported by Whitmore (1980), it becomes apparent that underachievement is the result of not recognizing the special needs of gifted children. Whitmore suggests that if a student exhibits ten of the following characteristics, consideration should be given to further evaluation so that a determination can be made as to whether children are underachieving:

1. Daily work frequently poorly done and incomplete
2. Large gap between oral and written work
3. Superior understanding and retention of concepts when interested
4. Excellent general knowledge
5. Highly imaginative and creative
6. Poor test performance, achieving at or below grade level expectations in one or all of the basic skills
7. Persistent dissatisfaction with work accomplished
8. Avoiding new activities to prevent imperfect performance
9. Evidences self-criticism and perfectionism
10. Shows initiative in pursuing self-selected assignments at home
11. Has a wide range of interests and special expertise
12. Low self-esteem and tendencies to withdraw or aggressive behavior in the classroom
13. Shows sensitivity in perceptions of others and life in general
14. Tends to set unrealistic self-expectations
15. Dislikes practice work, drill, or memorization
16. Easily distracted
17. Unable to focus concentration and efforts on tasks
18. Has poor attitudes toward school
19. Resists teacher efforts to motivate or discipline behavior
20. Has difficulty in peer relationships.

Other Factors Contributing to Underachievement

Janos and Robinson (1985) contend that underachievement may be the result of a variety of factors, including unsupportive backgrounds, conflicts in family and other relationships, poor personal adjustment, and inadequate educational provisions. Krouse and Krouse (1981) believe that weak academic skills and poor self-control are contributing factors. Risk factors for underachievement of the gifted as identified by Butler-Por (1993) include the following:

1. *Unwanted children:* The socialization pattern of unwanted children does not provide them with the psychological conditions necessary to develop self-confidence. "Unwanted" children are often insecure and may withdraw.
2. *Rejected children:* Rejection of children may be conscious or unconscious. Children who do not receive the appropriate nurturing do not acquire appropriate coping skills. They may withdraw or become aggressive.

3. *Children of divorced parents:*   Divorce may not always affect gifted children negatively. If both parents provide support and enthusiasm for children's interests, children should be able to overcome the initial trauma.
4. *Highly creative children:*   Highly creative children are often reluctant to conform and as a result are brought into conflict with parents and teachers. Creative or divergent thinking styles may not be recognized. The failure of the environment to provide the freedom of choice necessary for the creative child to work at optimum levels may cause underachievement.
5. *Gifted females:*   The dilemmas facing gifted females was covered in Chapter 9.
6. *Culturally different gifted students:*   Culturally different students are underrepresented in gifted programs and are at risk of becoming underachievers. They often do not receive the exposure, stimulation, and challenge that fosters intellectual development.
7. *Children with learning disabilities:*   Learning disabilities and attention deficit disorder were covered in earlier chapters. Reasons for underachievement can be related to schools (Butler-Por, 1987; Gallagher, 1975; Pringle, 1970; Raph, Goldberg, & Passow; 1966; Rimm, 1986; Whitmore, 1980): curriculum and teaching methods, attitudinal factors, and teacher variables.

Bricklin and Bricklin (1967) and Fine (1967) found that poor teaching was a major cause of underachievement in gifted students. Evans (1965) identified specific teaching behaviors that contribute to underachievement. These include teachers' need to maintain superiority in the field of knowledge. They impose unrealistic goals and standards or use threats to ridicule students.

Some teachers expect gifted students to conform, thus alienating them. For the gifted underachiever, special abilities have often gone unrecognized because teachers have not provided the educational experiences and reinforcement necessary to assist them in developing their potential.

Gifted students need to be challenged. They become bored with routine tasks. Whitmore (1980) and Butler-Por (1987) reported that lack of challenge in traditional classroom settings is responsible for much of the underachievement in gifted students. According to the U.S. Department of Education (1993), gifted students come to school knowing 35 percent of what is to be taught. Boredom leads to lack of motivation and underachievement. Inflexibility and rigidity of expectations of performance, curriculum choices, deadlines, sequence of time periods, and lack of opportunity to pursue individual interests were factors reported by underachievers as contributing to their negative behaviors (Davis & Rimm, 1989; Whitmore, 1980). The curriculum was not individualized and little attention was given to abilities of students.

Underachievers generally express negative attitudes toward school (Frankel, 1960; Raph et al., 1966; Rimm, 1986). When parents do not feel schools are meeting children's needs, they develop negative attitudes along with their children. Gifted children sometimes see academic success as a handicap (Tannenbaum, 1983). Hildreth (1966) reported that high school underachievers rebelled against authority and were fearful of peer ridicule or alienation. According to Ziv (1977), gifted underachievers invested more effort in nonschool activities. For example, involvement in athletic activities provides peer acceptance, whereas the school's atmosphere is often anti-intellectual.

SUMMARY

What becomes evident is that the following areas need to be addressed:

- Children need to be identified as gifted in domain-specific areas.
- Emphasis should be placed on inter- and intrapersonal skill development.
- Values education should be integrated into the curriculum.
- Guidance and counseling specialists for the gifted should be provided.

Maslow (1959) in his hierarchy of human needs noted the individual's need to belong. All members of our society should feel they have a place and are appreciated for what they can do. Recognizing and emphasizing individual gifts is essential for the development of human potential. As a society we should help one another to develop the sensitivities required to accomplish this task.

As Webb, Meckstroth, and Tolan (1982) state: "In summary, more important than being gifted is feeling good about oneself, feeling that what one does is important, and that one fits with the world" (p. 30).

Values education should be incorporated into the curriculum. Providing students with the opportunity to pursue areas of interest in all of the domains will assist in identifying gifts so that they can be recognized and nurtured. This in turn will assist in the prevention of underachievement. Providing a level of challenge will help prevent boredom and underachievement. According to Hollingworth (1942), gifted children with IQs of 140 waste half their time in school and children with IQs over 170 waste all of their time in school. Domains of giftedness and level of ability should be the determining factors for programming for gifted children. Acceleration should not be limited by one year or to one subject.

Personal skill development is important to the development of a healthy self-concept. Curriculum for the gifted should include awareness, understanding, and acceptance of self and others as well as communication skills. The environment should be nurturing and introduce students to creative thinking, relaxation, and imagery. The problems associated with being gifted should be addressed. Programming alternatives should include a variety of options to meet individual needs. Parents need to be included every step of the way.

FOR FURTHER READING

Bireley, M., & Genschaft, J. (Eds.). (1991). *Understanding the gifted adolescent: Educational, developmental, and multicultural issues.* New York: Teachers College Press.

Colangelo, N., & Zaffran, R. T. (1970). *New voices in counseling the gifted.* Dubuque, IA: Kendall, Hunt.

Delisle, J. R. (1992). *Guiding the social and emotional development of gifted young: A practical guide for educators and counselors.* New York: Longman.

Gailbraith, J. (1983, 1984). *The gifted kids survival guides, I & II.* Minneapolis: Free Spirit.

Gailbraith, R. E., & Jones, T. M. (1976). *Moral reasoning: A teaching handbook for adapting Kohlberg to the classroom.* Minneapolis: Greenhaven Press.

Kerr, B. A. (1991). *A handbook for counseling the gifted and talented.* Alexandria, VA: American Counseling Association.

Rimm, S. B. (1986). *Underachievement syndrome: Causes and cures.* Watertown, WI: Apple Publishing.

Schmitz, C., & Gailbraith, J. (1985). *Managing the social and emotional needs of the gifted: A teacher's survival guide.* Minneapolis: Free Spirit.

Silverman, L. K. (Ed.). (1992). *Counseling the gifted and talented.* Denver, CO: Love Publishing Company.

Simon, S. B., Howe, L. W., & Kirschenbaum, H. (1972). *Values clarification: A handbook of practical strategies for teachers and students.* New York: Hart Publishing.

VanTassel-Baska, J. (Ed.). (1990). *A practical guide to counseling the gifted in a school setting.* Reston, VA: Council for Exceptional Children.

Webb, J., Meckstroth, E. A., & Tolan, S. S. (1982). *Guiding the gifted child: A practical source for parents and teachers.* Columbus, OH: Ohio Psychology Press.

Whitmore, J. R. (1980). *Giftedness, conflict and underachievement.* Boston: Allyn & Bacon.

Chapter 11

Reconceptualizing Gifted Education

Creating an Inclusive Community of All Learners

Typical questions a classroom teacher might ask include these:

How can we rethink the way we provide instruction to students in an inclusive classroom setting?

Is it possible for one teacher to meet the needs of all children?

Do I need to have special training to meet the needs of all children?

To answer these questions, this chapter does the following:

Addresses the need to reconceptualize how we view students going from a deficit to a growth paradigm.

Presents the need for teachers to be properly prepared and supported.

Suggests ways that services can be delivered in an inclusive classroom.

CHANGING THE PARADIGM

Gifted children exist in all segments of the population. Barriers to identification and nurturance need to be eliminated. The masks that have been created that have hidden these gifts must be lifted, and each and every child must be viewed in terms of his or her strengths. In an attempt to help students with special needs to succeed in school, the history of the special education movement in the United States reveals a tendency to use a deficit paradigm—focusing on what students can't do, as opposed to what they can do.

Viewing children using a multiple intelligence lens helps educators to focus on a wide spectrum of abilities. With multiple intelligence philosophy as a backdrop, children with special needs can be viewed as individuals who possess strengths in many intelligence areas. In the past, attention to deficits has overshadowed the ore that must be mined from within. Using a multiple intelligence lens provides educators with ways in which students' talents and abilities can be identified and nurtured. This is especially critical for students from diverse populations who may have specific impairments that mask their potential.

As Armstrong (1994) points out: "We do not have to regard children with special needs primarily in terms of deficit, disorder, and disease. We can instead begin to work within the parameters of a growth paradigm."

Table 11.1   **The deficit paradigm versus the growth paradigm in special education**

Deficit Paradigm	Growth Paradigm
Labels the individual in terms of specific impairment(s) (e.g., ED, BD, EMR, LD).	Avoids labels; views the individual as an intact person who happens to have a special need.
Diagnoses the specific impairment(s) using a battery of standardized tests; focuses on errors, low scores, and weaknesses in general.	Assesses the needs of an individual using authentic assessment approaches within a naturalistic context; focuses on strengths.
Remediates the impairment(s) using a number of specialized treatment strategies often removed from any real-life context.	Assists the person in learning through a rich and varied set of interactions with real-life activities and events.
Separates the individual from the mainstream for specialized treatment in a segregated class, group, or program.	Maintains the individual's connections with peers in pursuing as normal a life pattern as possible.
Uses an esoteric collection of terms, tests, programs, kits, materials, and workbooks that are different from those found in a regular classroom.	Uses materials, strategies, and activities that are good for *all* kids.
Segments the individual's life into specific behavioral/educational objectives that are regularly monitored, measured, and modified.	Maintains the individual's integrity as a whole human being when assessing progress toward goals.
Creates special education programs that run on a track parallel with regular education programs; teachers from the two tracks rarely meet except in IEP meetings.	Establishes collaborative models that enable specialists and regular classroom teachers to work hand in hand.

Source: Reprinted with permission from Armstrong (1994). Copyright 1994 Association for Supervision and Curriculum Development.

As we move from a deficit-driven perspective to a growth model (Table 11.1), we must recognize the fact that that all children can learn and should celebrate individual differences. Gardner (1998) claims that no two people have exactly the same intelligence profile: "It is what makes life interesting" and "It's the great challenge for schools." He argues that we can fashion education to reach each individual child rather than teach all children the same way. He recommends that we find out as much as possible about each child and create schools that are centered on the individual student. With the help of current technology we can more easily accomplish these goals.

TEACHER PREPARATION FOR INCLUSIVE CLASSROOMS

Teacher preparation becomes an integral part of this new vision. The move to inclusion has forced institutions of higher learning in education to rethink their mission and reconstruct their programs. The need for merged competencies so that teachers can work with children with diverse learning profiles becomes evident as we examine recommendations set forth by various educational associations. For example, the

National Association for Gifted Children (NAGC) in its 1994 position paper stresses the need for teachers to provide better learning experiences for gifted and talented students. Some of the competencies cited include a knowledge and understanding of the cognitive, social, and emotional characteristics; needs and potential problems experienced by gifted and talented students from all cultural groups; an ability to develop a differentiated curriculum appropriate for meeting the unique intellectual and emotional needs and interests of gifted and talented students; and an ability to create an environment in which gifted and talented students can feel challenged and safe to explore and express their uniqueness.

The NAGC (1994) also recommends that teachers model openness, curiosity, and enthusiasm. Clearly these competencies cited are necessary skills for all teachers in all classrooms so that gifts and talents can be recognized and nurtured as diversity is honored.

Teacher preparation is driven by endorsements and/or certification criteria established by state departments of education. This has been problematic because while federal mandates for teaching students with disabilities exist, there are no national standards for teacher preparation. With the reauthorization of IDEA (1997), general educators are now required to participate as members of a Special Education Team, including the IEP (Individualized Education Program) process for students with disabilities. These same educators may or may not have any background knowledge because there are no national standards. These problems also exist for teachers when working with children who are potentially gifted. There are no national standards, and required competencies vary from state to state (Passow & Rudnitski, 1993). Karnes and Whorton (1996) also report on the inconsistencies from state to state in teacher education programs in gifted education. Their investigation into teacher certification revealed that twenty-seven states have a standard, of which twenty-four require certification and three provide an option.

The same inconsistencies exist in the preparation of elementary teachers who must work with students with disabilities. Only thirty-seven states (Patton & Braithwaite, 1990) require preparation in special education. Inconsistencies exist within states as well. For example, although New York State does not require preservice training in special education for elementary education certification, New York City requires all new teachers to complete six semester hours in special education for licensure. Because certification requirements do not always address teacher preparation for inclusive classroom settings, programs in higher education have begun to offer degrees leading to multiple certifications.

In New York State, for example, a systems change movement seeking to integrate regular and special education is under way. Schools across New York State are developing inclusive classroom models. The 1997 Report of the New York State Higher Education Task Force on Quality Inclusive Schooling discusses various combined programs that are currently emerging in teacher preparation programs. Ryan, Callahan, Krajewski, and Flaherty (1997), for example, have developed a program at Providence College leading to dual certification in elementary and special education.

In addition to merging elementary and secondary education with special education, teachers need to be trained to recognize gifts and talents in all children in all domains. Therefore, gifted education needs to be included as part of teacher preparation programs. Hansen and Feldhusen (1994) describe the results of their study, which demonstrates that teachers who have had specialized training in meeting the needs of gifted students are more effective than teachers who have had no such training. The need to provide training has been highlighted by Tomlinson et al. (1994). If we are to begin to prepare teachers to create classrooms that will meet the needs of "academic outliers," such as gifted, special education, or remedial learners, we must make instruction for academically diverse learners a priority in our teacher education institutions. If we do not make this a priority, preservice training for teachers

> rather than being a time of internship or residency during which special diagnostic and prescriptive skills will be developed for addressing needs of academically diverse learners, preservice teachers will gain tacit permission to dispense learning as though all students need the same prescription or treatment. (Tomlinson et al., 1994, p. 113)

Regardless of the inclusiveness of the individual teacher's preservice training, we must also recognize that no one teacher can be expected to have complete expertise in meeting the needs of every type of learner. Teachers must have support systems available to them that can provide assistance and collaboration with other professionals and enable them to problem solve cooperatively with their colleagues. Scheduling time for conferencing and planning teams are important tools for building collaborative models of education (Council for Exceptional Children, 1994; National Center on Educational Restructuring and Inclusion, 1994, 1995; Roach, 1995).

AN INCLUSIVE COMMUNITY OF LEARNERS

The personal stories of John and Barbara underscore the need to move away from segregated models of education and stereotypical notions of child development. Classroom environments need to be created in which children are exposed to all of the intelligences and where children can stimulate and talk with one another. As teachers observe students interacting with a differentiated curriculum, strategies can be integrated into classroom instruction that recognize and celebrate specific gifts and ensure a level of challenge. Classroom teachers need to provide opportunities for flexible grouping and, when indicated, extend opportunities for students beyond the classroom. Concentrating on deficits rather than strengths does a great disservice to our society.

The *Salamanca Statement Framework for Action for Special Needs Education* (UNESCO, 1994) has been adopted by ninety-two governments and twenty-five international organizations. Lipsky and Gartner (1996) state:

> Inclusion and participation are essential to human dignity and to the enjoyment and exercise of human rights. Within the field of education, this is reflected in the development of strategies that seek to bring about a genuine equalization of opportunity. (p. 762)

As educators, we have a responsibility to teach children to live together and to respect each other's abilities and potential contributions. The application of multiple intelligence approaches and the various strategies described in each of the preceding chapters will facilitate effective instruction in inclusive classrooms.

Every child is entitled to an educational setting that allows potential to surface in every one of the domains. Once potential is noted, it needs to be nurtured. This can be provided as classroom teachers work collaboratively with specialists on both ends of the spectrum. Experts in gifted education and special education need to be part of the team that designs environments that are appropriate for those who are highly able. This means that glass ceilings need to removed so that students are challenged in areas of potential gifts as they progress.

Providing for diverse populations in classrooms today is not an easy task. If we are to implement inclusive practices in classrooms, factors that need to be considered include these:

- Establishing a vision
- Articulating the vision
- Enlisting support of staff and community
- Planning for necessary resources
- Providing for teacher training and staff development
- Monitoring and evaluating progress
- Instituting changes as needed
- Providing ongoing support.

All members of the educational community need to join forces and share information as to the special needs of the diverse populations in our classrooms. If the needs of all of our students are to be met within classrooms, school staffing should include specialists in special education, gifted education, health services, social workers, guidance counselors, and multicultural education.

Each school district needs to assess carefully the populations currently being served in the regular classroom; populations that need to be included; resources available; and support needed. As populations are considered, staff capable of teaching those populations successfully need to be prepared and supported. Ongoing evaluation should take place to ensure success.

The information offered in this text provides the values, knowledge, and skills needed to create such an inclusive environment.

How many Flowers fail in Wood–
Or perish from the Hill–
Without the privilege to know
That they are Beautiful–

Emily Dickinson

References

Abbott, J. A. (1983). *The gifted attitudes inventory for Navajos: Directions for administering and scoring the GAIN & technical supplement.* Unpublished manuscript. Farmington, NM: The Dine Bi'olta Research Institute.

Abroms, K. (1982). Classroom interaction of gifted preschoolers. *Teaching Exceptional Children, 14,* 223–225.

Ackerman, C. M. (1996, April). *Personality characteristics: A new approach for identifying gifted adolescents.* Paper presented at the annual meeting of the American Educational Research Association, New York.

Ackerman, D., & Perkins, D. N. (1989). Integrating thinking and learning skills across the curriculum. In H. Hayes-Jacobs (Ed.), *Interdisciplinary curriculum: Design and implementation* (pp. 77–99). Alexandria, VA: Association for Supervision and Curriculum Development.

AEGIS (1998, Winter). Policy 2510: Testing out for credit. *Newsletter of the WVAGT.* Romney, WV: West Virginia Association for the Gifted and Talented.

Akamatsu, C. T. (1996) *Language for thought and language for literacy: The necessary and sufficient for school-based learning.* Paper presented at the annual meeting of the American Educational Research Association, New York.

Alexander, P., & Muia, J. (1982) *Gifted education, a comprehensive roadway.* Rockville, MD: Aspen Publications.

Allman, W. F. (1996, May 20). The dawn of creativity. *U.S. News & World Report, 120*(20), 52–58.

Altman, R. (1983). Social–emotional development of gifted children and adolescents: A research model. *Roeper Review, 6*(2), 65–68.

American Association of University Women (1992). *How schools shortchange girls—Study of major findings on girls and education.* Annapolis Junction, MD: American Association of University Women.

American Psychiatric Association. (1994). *Diagnostic and statistical manual of mental disorders* (4th ed.). Washington, DC: Author.

Andreani, O. D., & Pagnin, A. (1993). Nurturing the moral development of the gifted. In K. Heller, F. Monks, & A. H. Passow (Eds.), *International handbook of research and development of giftedness and talent* (pp. 539–552). Oxford: Pergamon Press.

American Teacher. (1995, May/June). Attention deficit: Attacking the myths. *American Teacher, 79*(8), 1.

Angier, N. (1995, May 14). Why science loses women in the ranks. *New York Times,* p. D5.

Archambault, F., Westberg, F., Brown, S., Hallmark, B., Zhang, W., & Emmons, C. (1993). Classroom practices used with gifted third and fourth grade students. *Journal for the Education of the Gifted, 16,* 103–119.

Archambault, F. X., Jr., Westberg, K. L., Brown, S. W., Hallmark, B. W., Emmons, C. L., & Zhang, W. (1993). *Regular classroom practices with gifted students: Results of a national survey of classroom teachers.* Storrs, CT: The National Research Center on the Gifted and Talented.

Armstrong, T. (1994). *Multiple intelligences in the classroom.* Alexandria, VA: Association for Supervision and Curriculum Development.

Arnold, K. D. (1993). Undergraduate aspirations and career outcomes of academically talented women: A discriminant analysis. *Roeper Review 15*(3), 169–175.

Arnold, K. D. (1994). The Illinois Valedictorian Project: Early adult careers of academically talented male high school students. In R. F. Subotnik & K. D. Arnold (Eds.), *Beyond Terman: Contemporary longitudinal studies of giftedness and talent* (pp. 24–51). Norwood, NJ: Ablex.

Arnold, K., & Denny, T. (1985). *The career aspirations of male and female valedictorians and salutatorians.* Paper presented at the annual meeting of the American Educational Research Association, Chicago, IL.

Arnold, K. D., & Subotnik, R. F. (1995). Mentoring the gifted: A differentiated model. *Roeper Review, 73*(3), 118–123.

Association for Children and Adults with Learning Disabilities (1985, Winter). ACLD-proposed definition and rationale. *LD Forum.*

Baldwin, A. Y. (1985). Programs for the gifted and talented: Issues concerning minority populations. In F. D. Horowitz & M. O'Brien (Eds.), *The gifted and talented: Developmental perspectives.* Washington, DC: American Psychological Association.

Baldwin, A., & Wooster, J. (1977). *Baldwin identification matrix inservice kit for the identification of gifted and talented students.* Buffalo, NY: D.O.K.

Baldwin, L. J., & Garguilo, D. A. (1983). A model program for elementary-age learning-disabled gifted youngsters. In L. H. Fox, L. Brody, & D. Tobin (Eds.), *Learning-disabled/gifted children—identification and programming* (pp. 207–221). Baltimore, MD: University Park Press.

Banks, J. A. (Ed.) (1995). *Handbook of research on multicultural education.* New York: Macmillan.

Barraga, N. C., & Erin, J. N. (1992). *Visual handicaps and learning.* Austin, TX: PRO-ED.

Barron, J. (1990, January 15). Laurence J. Peter is dead at 70; his "Principle" satirized business. *New York Times*, p. D9.

Barton, J. M., & Starnes, W. T. (1989). Identifying distinguishing characteristics of gifted and talented/learning disabled students. *Roeper Review, 12*(1), 23–29.

Batshaw, M. L., & Perret, Y. (1993). *Children with disabilities.* Baltimore: Paul H. Brookes.

Baum, S. (1984). Meeting the needs of gifted learning disabled students. *Roeper Review, 7*(1), 16–19.

Baum, S. M. (1988). An enrichment program for gifted learning disabled students. *Gifted Child Quarterly, 32*(1), 226–230.

Baum, S. M., & Dixon, J. (1985). *Program for handicapped students who are gifted or talented. Funded project.* Cheshire, CT: Connecticut State Education Department.

Baum, S. M., & Owen, S. (1988). High ability learning disabled students: How are they different? *Gifted Child Quarterly, 32*(3), 321–326.

Baum, S. M., Owen, S. V., & Dixon, J. (1991). *To be gifted & learning disabled.* Mansfield Center, CT: Creative Learning Press.

Bemberger, J. (1986). Cognitive issues in the development of musically gifted children. In R. J. Sternberg & J. E. Davidson (Eds.), *Conceptions of giftedness* (pp. 388–416). New York: Cambridge University Press.

Benbow, C. P., & Minor, L. L. (1986). Mathematically talented males and females and achievement in high school sciences. *American Educational Research Journal, 23,* 425–436.

Benbow, C. P., & Stanley, J. C. (1982). Consequences in high school and college of sex differences in mathematical reasoning ability: A longitudinal perspective. *American Educational Research Journal, 19,* 598–622.

Bereiter, C. (1984). How to keep thinking skills from going the way of all frills. *Educational Leadership, 42*(1), 75–80.

Bereiter, C., & Englemann, S. (1966). *Teaching disadvantaged children in the preschool.* Upper Saddle River, NJ: Prentice Hall.

Bernstein, E. M. (1996, June 5). Law school women question the teaching. *New York Times,* p. B10.

Bess, F. H., & McConnell, F. E. (1981). *Audiology education and the hearing impaired child.* St. Louis, MO: C. V. Mosby.

Bireley, M., & Genschaft, J. (Eds.). (1991). *Understanding the gifted adolescent: Educational, developmental, and multicultural issues.* New York: Teachers College Press.

Blakeslee, S. (1990, November 20). Perfect pitch: The key may lie in the genes. *New York Times,* p. C1.

Blakeslee, S. (1995, February 3). Scientists find place on left side of the brain where perfect pitch is heard. *New York Times,* p. A16.

Bloom, B. S. (Ed.). (1956). *Taxonomy of educational objectives: Cognitive and affective domains.* New York: David McKay.

Bloom, B. S. (Ed.). (1985). *Developing talent in young people.* New York: Ballantine Books.

Board of Education of the Hendrick Hudson Central School District, Westchester County, et al., Petitioners v. Amy Rowley, by her parents and natural guardians, Clifford and Nancy Rowley, etc. No. 80-1002 Supreme Court of the United States, argued March 23, 1982, decided June 28, 1982. (Cite as 458 U.S. 176, 102 S.Ct. 3034.)

Bricklin, B., & Bricklin, P. (1967). *Bright child—poor grades: The psychology of underachievement.* New York: Delacorte.

Burks, B. S., Jensen, D. W., & Terman, L. M. (1930). *Genetic studies of genius* (Vol. III), *The promise of youth.* Stanford, CA: Stanford University Press.

Burns, D. (1985, March, April). Land of opportunity. *G/C/T* (pp. 14–15).

Burt, C. (1949). The structure of the mind: A review of the results of factor analysis. *British Journal of Educational Psychology, 19,* 100–111, 176–19.

Butler-Por, N. (1987). *Underachievers in school: Issues and intervention.* New York: Wiley.

Butler-Por, N. (1993). Underachieving gifted students. In K. Heller, F. Monks, & A. H. Passow (Eds.), *International handbook of research and development of giftedness and talent* (pp. 649–668). Oxford: Pergamon Press.

Callahan, C. M. (1979). The gifted and talented women. In A. H. Passow (Ed.), *The gifted and talented* (pp. 401–423). Chicago: National Society for the Study of Education.

Callahan, C. M. (1991). An update on gifted females. *Journal for the Education of the Gifted, 14*, 284–311.

Callahan, C. M. (1997). *When a bull's-eye is not in the middle: The challenge of learning to respond to academic and cultural diversity in heterogeneous settings.* Paper presented at the annual meeting of the American Educational Research Association, Chicago, IL.

Callahan, C. M., Cunningham, C. J., & Plucker, J. A. (1994). Foundations for the future: The socio-emotional development of gifted, adolescent women. *Roeper Review, 17*(2), 99–105.

Cantor, D. W., & Bernay, T. (1992). *Women in power—The secrets of leadership.* Boston: Houghton Mifflin.

Cattell, R. B. (1971). *Abilities: Their structure, growth, and action.* New York: Houghton Mifflin.

Cattell, R. B. (1987). *Intelligence: Its structure, growth and action.* New York: North Holland.

Chall, J. S., & Conrad, S. S. (1991). *Should textbooks challenge students?: The case for easier or harder textbooks.* New York: Teachers College Press.

Chan, S. (1986). Curriculum development for limited-English-proficient exceptional Chinese children. In M. K. Kitano & P. C. Chinn (Eds.), *Exceptional Asian children and youth* (pp. 61–68). Reston, VA: Council for Exceptional Children.

Civian, J., & Schley, S. (1996, April). *Pathways for women in the sciences II: Retention in math and science at the college level.* Paper presented at the annual meeting of the American Educational Research Association, New York.

Clance, P. R. (1985). The imposter phenomenon. *New Woman, 15*(7), 40–43.

Clark, B. (1997). *Growing Up Gifted.* Upper Saddle River, NJ: Merrill/Prentice Hall.

Cline, S. (1984). *Teaching for talent.* New York: D.O.K. Publishers.

Cline, S. (1986). *The independent learner.* New York: D.O.K. Publishers.

Cline, S. (1989). *What would happen if I said yes?: A guide to creativity for parents and teachers.* New York: D.O.K. Publishers.

Cohen, A. (1995, December). *Identifying the ADHD child.* Lecture given at the Denton Avenue School, New Hyde Park, NY.

Colangelo, N., & Brower, P. (1987). Labeling gifted youngsters: Long-term impact on families. *Gifted Child Quarterly, 31*(2), 75–78.

Colangelo, N., & Zaffran, R. T. (1970). *New voices in counseling the gifted.* Dubuque, IA: Kendall, Hunt.

Coleman, L. (1994). Portfolio assessment: A key to identifying hidden talents and empowering teachers of young children. *Gifted Child Quarterly, 38*(2), 65–69.

Columbus Group (1991, July). Unpublished transcript of the meeting of the Columbus Group. Columbus, OH: Author.

Corn, A. L. (1986, Summer). Gifted students who have a visual handicap: Can we meet their educational needs? *Education of the Visually Handicapped,* XVIII, 2.

Corn, A. L., Hatlen, P., Huebner, K. M., Ryan, F., & Siller, M. A. (1995). *The national agenda for the education of children and youths with visual impairments, including those with multiple disabilities.* New York: National Foundation for the Blind.

Corn, A., & Ryser, G. (1989). Access to print for students with low vision. *Journal of Visual Impairment and Blindness, 83*(7), 340–349.

Council for Exceptional Children. (1994). *Creating schools for all of our students: What 12 schools have to say.* Reston, VA: Author.

Council of State Directors of Programs for the Gifted. (1991). *The 1990 state of the states gifted and talented education report.* Results of survey conducted by the Council of State Directors of Programs for the Gifted.

Council of State Directors of Programs for the Gifted. (1994). *The 1994 state of the states gifted and talented education report.* Results of survey conducted by the Council of State Directors of Programs for the Gifted.

Council of State Directors of Programs for the Gifted. (1996). *The 1996 state of the states gifted and talented education report.* Results of survey conducted by the Council of State Directors of Programs for the Gifted.

Cox, C. M., et al. (1926). *Genetic studies of genius* (Vol. II), *The early mental traits of three hundred geniuses.* Stanford, CA: Stanford University Press.

Csikszentmihalyi, M. (1990). *Flow: The psychology of optimal experience.* New York: Harper & Row.

Csikszentmihalyi, M., Rathunde, K., & Whalen, S. (1997). *Talented teenagers. The roots of success & failure.* United Kingdom: Cambridge University Press.

Dabrowski, K. (1937). Psychological bases of self-mutilation. *Genetic Psychology Monographs, 19,* 1–104.

Dabrowski, K. (1964). *Positive disintegration.* Boston: Little Brown.

Dabrowski, K. (1967). *Personality-shaping through positive disintegration.* Boston: Little Brown.

Dabrowski, K. (1972). *Psychoneurosis is not an illness.* London: Gryf.

Davis, G., & Rimm, S. (1989). *Education of the gifted and talented.* Upper Saddle River, NJ: Prentice Hall.

Davis, H., & Silverman, S. R. (Eds.). (1960). *Hearing and deafness.* New York: Holt, Rinehart and Winston.

Dehaene, S. (1998). *The number sense.* New York: Oxford Press.

Delisle, J. R. (1986). Death with honors: Suicide among gifted adolescents. *Journal of Counseling and Development, 64,* 558–560.

Delisle, J. R. (1992). *Guiding the social and emotional development of gifted young: A practical guide for educators and counselors.* New York: Longman.

Deno, E. (1970). Special education as developmental capital. *Exceptional Children, 37,* 123–130.

Department of Education. (1990). *Education of exceptional children.* INAR/NACIE Joint Issues Sessions presented at 22nd National Indian Education Association annual conference, San Diego, CA. (ERIC Document Reproduction Service No. ED 341 533)

Diaz, E. I. (1996). *Creating a culture of achievement: Case studies of talented minority students in an urban setting.* Paper presented at the annual meeting of the American Educational Research Association, New York.

Dickens, M. N., & Cornell, D. G. (1993). Parent influences on the mathematics self-concept of high ability adolescent girls. *Journal for the Education of the Gifted, 17*(1), 1993, 53–73.

Dirkes, M. A. (1983). Anxiety in the gifted: Pluses and minuses. *Roeper Review, 6*(2), 68–70.

Dixon, J., & Baum, S. (1986). *Focus on talent: An enrichment program for gifted/LD students* (state funded grant, Project Rescue). Litchfield, CT: Connecticut Department of Education.

Dowling, C. (1981). *The Cinderella complex.* New York: Summit Books.

Draze, D. (1987). *Winners' circle: A guide for achievement.* San Luis Obispo, CA: Dandy Lion Publications.

Eberle, B. (1982). Visual thinking. New York: D.O.K. Publishers.

Eccles, J. (1983). Expectances, values and academic behaviors. In J. T. Spence (Ed.), *Achievement and achievement motives.* San Francisco: W. H. Freeman.

Eccles, J. S. (1985). Why doesn't Jane run? Sex differences in education and occupational patterns. In F. D. Horowitz & M. O'Brien (Eds.), *The gifted and talented: Developmental perspectives* (pp. 251–295). Washington, DC: American Psychological Association.

Education for All Handicapped Children Act, P.L. 94-142 (1975). S. 6, 94th Congress [613(a)(4), 1st session, June]. Report No. 94-168.

Ellis, J. (1993). Supporting giftedness in girls in the classroom. In *Nurturing potential, proceedings of the Society for the Advancement of Gifted Education annual conference.* (ERIC Document Reproduction Service No. ED 371 555)

Evans, E. (1965). Pupil underachievement. Are we responsible? *Instructor, 75,* 25–42.

Everhart, V., Stinson, M., McKee, B., & Giles, P. (1996). *Evaluation of a speech-to-print transcription system as a resource for mainstreamed deaf students.* Paper presented at the annual meeting of the American Educational Research Association, New York.

Ewing, N. J., & Lan Yong, F. (1992). A comparative study of the learning style preferences among gifted African-American, Mexican-American, and American-born Chinese middle grade students. *Roeper Review, 14*(3), 120–123.

Falk, R. F., & Piechowski, M. M. (1991). *Criteria for rating levels of intensity of overexcitabilities.* Unpublished manuscript. Akron, OH: University of Akron.

Falk, R. F., Piechowski, M. M., & Lind, S. (1997). Criteria for rating the intensity of overexcitabilities. In N. Colangelo and G. A. S. Davis (Eds.), *Handbook of gifted education.* Boston: Allyn & Bacon.

Falvey, M. A., Givner, C. C., & Kimm, C. (1995). What is an inclusive school? In R. A. Villa & J. S. Thousand (Eds.), *Creating an inclusive school.* Alexandria, VA: Association for Supervision and Curriculum Development.

Feldhusen, J. F. (1992). *TIDE: Talent identification and development in education.* Sarasota, FL: Center for Creative Learning.

Feldhusen, J. F. (1994). Leadership curriculum. In J. VanTassel-Baska (Ed.), *Comprehensive curriculum for gifted learners* (pp. 347–398). Boston: Allyn & Bacon.

Feldhusen, J. F. (1997). *Talent identification and development in education; The basic tenets.* Paper presented at The First Annual Summer Institute—Integrating Gifted Education into the Fabric of the School, Garden City, NY.

Feldman, D. H. (1986). *Nature's gambit: Child prodigies and the development of human potential.* New York: Basic Books.

Fine, B. (1967). *Underachievers—How they can be helped.* New York: E. P. Dutton.

Fleming, E. S., & Hollinger, C. L. (1990). *Project CHOICE: Gifted young women ten years later.* Paper presented at the National Association for Gifted Children Convention, Little Rock, AR.

Ford, D. (1994). *The recruitment and retention of African-American students in gifted education programs: Implications and recommendations*. Storrs, CT: National Research Center on the Gifted and Talented.

Ford, D. Y. (1992). Determinants of underachievement as perceived by gifted, above average, and average black students. *Roeper Review, 14*(3), 130–136.

Ford, D. Y. (1994). *The recruitment and retention of African-American students in gifted education programs: Implications and recommendations*. Storrs, CT: National Research Center on the Gifted and Talented.

Fox, L. H. (1977). Sex differences: Implications for program planning for the academically gifted. In J. C. Stanley, W. C. George, & C. H. Solano (Eds.), *The gifted and the creative: A fifty year perspective* (pp. 113–138). Baltimore: Johns Hopkins University Press.

Fox, L. H., & Richmond, L. J. (1979). Gifted females: Are we meeting their counseling needs? *Personnel and Guidance Journal, 57*(4), 256–260.

Frankel, E. A. (1960). A comparative study of achieving and underachieving high school boys of high intellectual ability. *Journal of Educational Research, 53*, 172–180.

Frasier, M. (1992, March). Ethnic/minority children: Reflections and directions. In *Challenges in gifted education: Developing potential and investing in knowledge for the 21st century*. (ERIC Document Reproduction Service No. ED 344 407, EC 301 136)

Frasier, M., Garcia, J., & Passow, A.H. (1995). *A review of assessment issues in gifted education and their implications for identifying gifted minority students*. Storrs, CT: National Research Center on the Gifted and Talented.

Freeman, J. (1993). Parents and families in nurturing giftedness and talent. In K. Heller, F. Monks, & A. H. Passow (Eds.), *International handbook of research and development of giftedness and talent* (pp. 669–683). Oxford: Pergamon Press.

Frierson, H. T. (1996, April). *Comparing science and non-science minority students' perceptions and satisfaction with a short-term research and mentoring program*. Paper presented at the American Educational Research Association Meeting, New York.

Furth, H. (1966). *Thinking without language: Psychological implications of deafness*. New York: Free Press.

Furth, H. (1973). *Deafness and learning*. Belmont, CA: Wadsworth.

Gage, N. L. (1976, Spring). A factorially designed experiment on teacher structuring, solicity, and reacting. *Journal of Teacher Education, 27*(1), 35–38.

Gagne, F. (1995). From giftedness to talent: A developmental model and its impact on the language of the field. *Roeper Review, 18*(2), 103–111.

Gailbraith, J. (1983, 1984). *The gifted kids survival guides, I & II*. Minneapolis: Free Spirit.

Gailbraith, R. E., & Jones, T. M. (1976). *Moral reasoning: A teaching handbook for adapting Kohlberg to the classroom*. Minneapolis: Greenhaven Press.

Gallagher, J. J. (1975). *Teaching the gifted child*. Boston: Allyn & Bacon.

Gallagher, J. J. (1978). *Guiding the gifted child*. Presentation at the Graduate Leadership Training Institute, Columbia University, New York.

Gallagher, J. J. (1987). Notes from the editor's desk. *Journal for the Education of the Gifted, 10*(3), 353–360.

Gallagher, J., Herradine, C. C., & Coleman, M. R. (1997). Challenge or boredom? Gifted students' view on their schooling. *Roeper Review, 19*(3), 132–136.

Gallagher, J. J., Oglesby, K., Stern, A., Caplow, D., Courtright, R., Fulton, L., Guiton, G., & Langenbach, J. (1982). *Leadership unit: The use of teacher–scholar teams to develop units for the gifted.* New York: Trillium.

Gamble, H. W. (1985). A national survey of programs for intellectually and academically gifted hearing-impaired students. *American Annals of the Deaf, 130*(6), 508–518.

Gardner, H. (1975). *The shattered mind.* New York: Knopf.

Gardner, H. (1983). *Frames of mind: The theory of multiple intelligences.* New York: Basic Books.

Gardner, H. (1987). Beyond the IQ: Education and human development. *Harvard Educational Review, 57*(2), 187–195.

Gardner, H. (1988). Creative lives and creative works: A synthetic scientific approach. In R. Sternberg (Ed.), *The nature of creativity* (pp. 298–324). New York: Cambridge University Press.

Gardner, H. (1989). *To open minds: Chinese clues to the dilemma of contemporary education.* New York: Basic Books.

Gardner, H. (1993). *Multiple intelligences: The theory in practice.* New York: Basic Books.

Gardner, H. (1994, June 2). *Multiple intelligences: The ideas and the promise.* Paper presented at the Multiple Intelligence Symposium, Columbia University, New York.

Gardner, H. (1997). More ways to be smart. *Education Update, 39*(3), 1.

Gardner, H. (1998, April 24). Keynote address. Presented at the Fourth International Teaching for Intelligence Conference, New York.

Gardner, H., & Boix-Mansilla, V. (1994). Teaching for understanding in the disciplines and beyond. *Teachers College Record, 96*(2), 198–218.

Gardner, H., & Hatch, T. (1989). Multiple intelligences go to school: Educational implications of the theory of multiple intelligences. *Educational Researcher, 18*(8), 4–10.

Gearheart, B. R., Weishahn, M. W., & Gearheart, C. J. (1992). *The exceptional child in the regular classroom* (5th ed.). Upper Saddle River, NJ: Merrill/Prentice Hall.

Gilligan, C. (1982). *In a different voice.* Cambridge, MA: Harvard University Press.

Goleman, D. (1995). *Emotional intelligence.* New York: Bantam Books.

Gordon, E. M., & Thomas, A. (1967). Children's behavioral style and the teacher's appraisal of their intelligence. *Journal of School Psychology, 5,* 292–300.

Grau, P. N. (1985, May/June). Counseling the gifted girl. *Gifted Child Today,* pp. 8–11.

Gross, M. (1993). *Exceptionally gifted children.* New York: Routledge.

Gross, M. (1995, Winter). Highly gifted/highly talented: Seeing the difference and making the difference for highly gifted students. *Tempo, XV*(1), 1, 11–14.

Groth, N. J. (1975). Success and creativity in male and female professors. *Gifted Child Quarterly, 19*(4), 328–335.

Gruber, H. E. (1985). Giftedness and moral responsibility: Creative thinking and human survival. In F. D. Horowitz & M. O'Brien (Eds.), *The gifted and talented: Developmental perspectives.* Washington, DC: American Psychological Association.

Guilford, J. P. (1967). *The nature of human intelligence.* New York: McGraw-Hill.

Hacker, A. (1995). *Two nations: Black and white, separate, hostile, unequal.* New York: Ballantine Books.

Hacker, A. (1997). *Money*. New York: Simon & Schuster.

Hahn, H. (1989). The politics of special education. In D. K. Lipsky & A. Gartner (Eds.), *Beyond separate education: Quality education for all* (pp. 225–241). Baltimore: Paul H. Brookes.

Hahn, H. (1994). *New trends in disability studies: Implications for educational policy.* Paper prepared for the National Center on Educational Restructuring and Inclusion Invitational Conference on Inclusive Education. Racine, WI: Wingspread Conference Center.

Hallahan, D. P., & Kauffman, J. M. (1997). *Exceptional children*. Boston: Allyn & Bacon.

Hamachek, D. E. (1978). Psychodynamics of normal and neurotic perfectionism. *Psychology, 15,* 27–33.

Hansen, J. B., & Feldhusen, J. F. (1994). Comparison of trained and untrained teachers of gifted students. *Gifted Child Quarterly, 38*(3), pp. 115–121.

Harris, C. R. (1993). *Identifying and serving recent immigrant children who are gifted.* (ERIC Document Reproduction Service No. ED 358676)

Hasegawa, C., Gallagher, R., Kitano, M., & Tanaka, K. (1989). Asian-Americans—The problem of defining Asian-Americans. In C. J. Maker and S. W. Schiever (Eds.), *Critical issues in gifted education—Defensible programs for cultural and ethnic minorities.* Austin, TX: PRO-ED.

Hatlen, P. (1996). The core curriculum for blind and visually impaired students, including those with additional disabilities. *RE:view, 28*(1), 25–32.

Hayes, M. L., & Sloat, R. S. (1989). Gifted students at risk for suicide. *Roeper Review, 12*(2), 102–107.

Hegeman, K. (1997, August). *The moral development of young gifted children.* Paper presented at the 12th world conference of the World Council for Gifted and Talented Children, Seattle, WA.

Heller, K. A., Monks, F. J., & Passow, A. H. (Eds.). (1993). *International handbook of research and development of giftedness and talent.* Oxford: Pergamon Press.

Hess, R. D., and Shipman, V. C. (1968). Maternal influences upon early learning; the cognitive environments of urban pre-school children. In R. D. Hess & R. M. Bear (Eds.), *Early education.* Chicago: Aldine.

Hildebrand, J. (1991, January 15). Girls still avoid physics class. *Newsday,* pp. 21, 24.

Hildreth, G. H. (1966). *Introduction to the gifted.* New York: McGraw Hill.

Hilliard, A. (1976). *Alternative to IQ testing; An approach to the identification of the gifted in minority children* (Report No. 75175). San Francisco State University.

Hirsch, E. S. (1984). *The block book.* Washington, DC: National Association for the Education of Young Children.

Hollinger, C. L. (1983). Multidimensional determinants of traditional and nontraditional career aspirations of mathematically talented female adolescents. *Journal for the Education of the Gifted, 6,* 245–265.

Hollinger, C. L. (1985). Self perceptions of ability of mathematically talented female adolescents. *Psychology of Women Quarterly, 9*(3), 323–336.

Hollinger, C. L., & Fleming, E. S. (1984). Internal barriers to the realization of potential correlates and interrelationships among gifted and talented female adolescents. *Gifted Child Quarterly, 28,* 135–139.

Hollinger C. L., & Fleming, E. S. (1993). Project CHOICE: The emerging roles and careers of gifted women. *Roeper Review, 15*(3), 156–160.

Hollingworth, H. L. (1943) *Leta Hollingworth: A biography*. Lincoln, NE: University of Nebraska Press.

Hollingworth, L. S. (1926). *Gifted children: Their nature and nurture*. New York: Macmillan.

Hollingworth, L. S. (1938). An enrichment curriculum for rapid learners at Public School 500: Speyer School. *Teachers College Record, 39*, 296–306.

Hollingworth, L. S. (1942). *Children above 180 I.Q.: Origin and development*. Yonkers-on-Hudson, NY: World Book Company.

Hollingworth, L. S. (1975). *Children above 180 I.Q., Stanford–Binet*. New York: Arno Press. (Original work published 1942)

Hoover, S. M., Sayler, M., & Feldhusen, J. F. (1993). Cluster grouping of gifted students at the elementary level. *Roeper Review, 16*(1), 13–15.

Horner, M. S. (1972). Toward an understanding of achievement related conflicts in women. *Journal of Social Issues, 28*, 157–175.

Howard-Hamilton, M., & Robinson, T. (1991, July/August). Sex role characteristics of female governor's school students. *Gifted Child Today, 14*(4), 32–35.

Hughes, C. E. (1995, November). *Language arts instruction for gifted/LD students*. Paper presented at the National Association for Gifted Children Conference, Tampa, FL.

Hughes, H. (1969). The enhancement of creativity. *Journal of Creative Behavior, 3*, 73–83.

Hunt, M. (1986). *The universe within*. New York: Simon & Schuster.

Hyatt, C., & Gottlieb, L. (1987). *When smart people fail*. New York: Simon & Schuster.

Jackson, N. E., & Klein, E. J. (1991). Gifted performance in young children. In N. Colangelo & G. A. Davis (Eds.), *Handbook of gifted education* (pp. 460–474). Boston: Allyn & Bacon.

Jackson, R. M. (1986, May). Thumbs up for the direct teaching of thinking skills. *Educational Leadership, 43*(8), 32–36.

Jacobi, J. (1991). Mentoring and undergraduate academic success: A literature review. *Review of Educational Research, 61*(4), 505–532.

Janos, P. M., & Robinson, N. M. (1985). Psychosocial development in intellectually gifted children. In F. D. Horowitz & M. O'Brien (Eds.), *The gifted and talented: Developmental perspectives* (pp. 149–196). Washington, DC: American Psychological Association.

Jarwan, F. A., & Feldusen, J. F. (1993). *Residential schools of mathematics and science for academically talented youth: An analysis of admission programs*. Storrs, CT: The National Resource Center on the Gifted and Talented.

Johnsen, S. K., & Corn, A. L. (1989). The past, present, and future of education for gifted children with sensory and/or physical disabilities. *Roeper Review, 12*(1) 13–23.

Johnson, D. J., & Myklebust, H. R. (1964). *Learning disabilities—educational principles and practices*. New York: Grune & Stratton.

Johnson, J. (1997). Math curriculum extensions: Using the web. *Systems Newsletter—Center for Gifted Education—The College of William and Mary, 5*(2), 5.

Johnson, L. J., & Lewman, B. S. (1990). Parent perceptions of the talents of young gifted boys and girls. *Journal for the Education of the Gifted, 13*, 176–188.

John-Steiner, V. (1985). *Notebooks of the mind*. New York: Harper & Row.

Kaiser, C. F., & Berndt, D. J. (1985). Predictors of loneliness in the gifted adolescent. *Gifted Child Quarterly, 29*(2), 74–77.

Kaplan, L. (1983). Mistakes gifted young people too often make. *Roeper Review, 6*(2), 73–77.

Karnes, F. A., & Whorton, J. E. (1996). Teacher certification and endorsement in gifted education: A critical need. *Roeper Review, 19*(1), 54–56.

Karnes, M. B. (Ed.). (1983). *The underserved gifted child: Our young gifted children*. Reston, VA: Council for Exceptional Children.

Kearney, K., & LeBlanc, J. (1992). Forgotten pioneers in the study of gifted African-Americans. *Roeper Review, 15*(4), 192–199.

Kelly, K. R., & Cobb, S. J. (1991). A profile of the career development characteristics of young gifted adolescents: Examining gender and multicultural differences. *Roeper Review, 13*(4), 202–206.

Kennedy, K. (1995). Glimpses of a highly gifted child in a heterogeneous classroom. *Roeper Review, 17*(3),164–168.

Kerr, B. A. (1985). *Smart girls, gifted women*. Columbus, OH: Ohio Psychology Press.

Kerr, B. A. (1991). *A handbook for counseling the gifted and talented*. Alexandria, VA: American Counseling Association.

Kerr, B. A. (1992). A twenty-year follow-up of gifted women. In N. Colangelo, S. C. Assouline, & D. L. Ambroson (Eds.), *Talent development: Proceedings from the 1991 Henry B. and Jocelyn Wallace National Research Symposium on Talent Development* (pp. 240–247). New York: Trillium Press.

Kerr, B. A. (1994). *Smart girls two*. Columbus, OH: Ohio Psychology Press.

Kerr, B. A. (1997). Developing talents in girls and young children. In N. Colangelo & G. A. Davis (Eds.), *Handbook of gifted education* (pp. 483–497). Boston: Allyn & Bacon.

Kerr, B. A., & Colangelo, N. (1988). The college plans of academically talented students. *Journal of Counseling and Development, 67,* 42–49.

Klaus, R. A., & Gray, S. W. (1968). The early training project for disadvantaged children: A report after five years. *Monographs of the Society for Research in Child Development, 33,* 4.

Kleinfeld, J. S. (1973). Intellectual strengths in culturally different groups: An Eskimo illustration. *Review of Educational Research, 43*(3), 341–359.

Kleinman, G., Humphrey, M., & Lindsay, P. H. (1981). *Microcomputers and hyperactive children*. Comput 7.

Kline, B. E., & Short, E. B. (1991). Changes in emotional resilience: Gifted adolescent females. *Roeper Review, 13*(3), 118–121.

Knutson, K. A., & McCarthy-Tucker, S. N. (1993, April 15). *Gifted education of Native American students: A state of affairs*. Roundtable presentation at the meeting of the American Education Research Association, Atlanta, GA. (ERIC Document Reproduction Service No. ED 362 372)

Kohlberg, L. (1976). Moral stages and moralization: The cognitive-developmental approach. In T. Lickona (Ed.), *Moral development and behavior: Theory, research, and social issues*. New York: Holt, Rinehart & Winston.

Krashen, S. (1988). *On course: Bilingual education's success in California*. The California Association of Bilingual Education.

Krathwohl, D. R., Bloom, B. S., & Masia, B. B. (1956). Taxonomy of educational objectives. The classification of educational goals. Handbook II: Affective domain. In B. Bloom (Ed.), *Taxonomy of educational objectives.* New York: David McKay.

Krouse, J., & Krouse, H. (1981). Toward a multimodal theory of academic underachievement. *Educational Psychologist, 16*(3), 151–164.

Kurtz, B. E. (1990). Cultural influences on children's cognitive and metacognitive development. In W. Schneider & F. E. Weinert (Eds.), *Interactions among aptitudes, strategies and knowledge in cognitive performance* (pp. 177–199). New York: Springer.

Lang, H. G. (1994). *Silence of the spheres—The deaf experience in the history of science.* Westport, CT: Greenwood.

Lavach, J. F., & Lanier, H. B. (1975). The motive to avoid success in 7th, 8th, 9th, and 10th grade high-achieving girls. *The Journal of Educational Research, 68,* 216–218.

Lewin, T. (1996, February 29). Study of welfare families warns of problem for schoolchildren. *New York Times,* p. A14.

Lindsay, B. (1988, October). A lamp for Diogenes: Leadership giftedness and moral education. *Roeper Review, XI*(l) 8–11.

Lipsky, D. K., & Gartner, A. (1996, Winter). Inclusion, school restructuring, and the remaking of American society. *Harvard Educational Review, 66*(4).

Lipsky, D. K., & Gartner, A. (Eds.). (1989). *Beyond separate education: Quality education for all* (pp. 225–241). Baltimore: Paul H. Brookes.

Louis, B., Feiring, C., & Lewis, M. (1992). *Identifying gifted preschoolers* (Teachers Manual and Video). Institute for the Study of Child Development. New Brunswick, NJ: Robert Wood Johnson Medical School.

Lovecky, D. V. (1994a). Exceptionally gifted children: Different minds. *Roeper Review, 17*(2), 116–120.

Lovecky, D. V. (1994b). Gifted children with attention deficit disorder. *Understanding Our Gifted, 6*(5), 1, 7–9.

Lubinski, D., Benbow, D. P., & Sanders, C. E. (1993). Reconceptualizing gender differences in achievement among the gifted. In K. A. Heller, F. J. Monks, & A. H. Passow (Eds.), *International handbook of research and development of giftedness and talent.* Oxford: Pergamon Press.

Machlowitz, M. (1982). The great impostors. *Working Women, 7,* 97–98.

Mager, G. M., & Bernazzani, J. (1998). *Report on the activities of the higher education task force on quality inclusive schooling for 1996–1997.* Syracuse, NY: School of Education, Syracuse University.

Maker, C. J. (1977). *Providing programs for the gifted handicapped.* Reston, VA: Council for Exceptional Children.

Marland, S. P., Jr. (1972). *Education of the gifted and talented* (2 vols.). Washington, DC: U.S. Government Printing Office.

Maslow, A. (1959). Creativity in self: Actualizing people. In H. H. Anderson (Ed.), *Creativity and its cultivation.* New York: Harper & Row.

Matyas, M. L. (1992). Overview: The status of women in science and engineering. In M. L. Matyas & L. S. Dix (Eds.), *Science and engineering programs: On target for women?* (pp. 27–39). Washington, DC: National Academy Press.

McClelland, D. C. (1973). Testing for competence rather than intelligence. *American Psychologist, 28,* 1–14.

McDonald, E. J. (1976, Spring). Report on phase II of the beginning teacher evaluation study. *Journal of Teacher Education, 27*(1), 39–42.

McGuffog, C., Feiring, C., & Lewis, M. (1987, December). The diverse profile of the extremely gifted child. *Roeper Review, 10*(2) 82–89.

McKnight-Taylor, M. (1997). Making education special for all young adolescents. *Childhood Education, 73*(5), 260–261.

Mercer, J. R., & Lewis, J. F. (1978). Using the system of multicultural pluralistic assessment (SOMPA) to identify the gifted minority child. In A. Y. Baldwin, G. H. Gear, & L. J. Lucity (Eds.), *Educational planning for the gifted* (pp. 7–14). Reston, VA: Council for Exceptional Children.

Michigan State Board of Education (1987). *A report on Indian-American education in Michigan.* Lansing, MI: Michigan State Board of Education. (ERIC Document Reproduction Service No. ED 345 892)

Miller-Jones, D. (1981). *Future follow through documentation and research; the assessment of academic/cognitive abilities of black children.* Washington, DC: National Institute of Education.

Montague, M. (1991). Gifted and learning-disabled gifted students' knowledge and use of mathematical problem-solving strategies. *Journal for the Education of the Gifted, 14*(4), 393–411.

Moores, D. F. (1987). *Educating the deaf: Psychology, principles, and practices.* Boston: Houghton Mifflin.

Morelock, M. J., & Feldman, D. H. (1997). In N. Colangelo & G. A. Davis (Eds.), *Handbook of gifted education* (pp. 439–455). Boston: Allyn & Bacon.

Muscott, H. S. (1991). *Teachers' standards, students' behavior, and the cascade of services model for youth with emotional disturbances: A differential analysis of classroom ecologies.* Doctoral dissertation, Teachers College, Columbia University.

Myklebust, H. R. (1964). *The psychology of deafness: Sensory deprivation, learning and adjustment.* New York: Grune & Stratton.

Narvaez, D. (1991). *Studies of moral judgement in gifted students.* Paper presented at IXth World Conference on Gifted and Talented Children, The Hague, The Netherlands.

National Association for Gifted Children. (1994). *Competencies needed by teachers of gifted and talented students.* Washington, DC: Author.

National Center on Educational Restructuring and Inclusion. (1994). *National study of inclusive education.* New York: Author, City University of New York, Graduate School and University Center.

National Center on Educational Restructuring and Inclusion. (1995). *National study of inclusive education.* New York: Author, City University of New York, Graduate School and University Center.

Newby, H. A. (1964). *Audiology.* New York: Appleton-Century-Crofts.

Nora, A., Cabrera, A., Hagedorn, L. S.. & Pascarella, E. T. (1996, April). *Gender differences in underlying structural patterns among behavioral, cognitive, attitudinal, and outcome factors among four-year college students.* Paper presented at the annual meeting of the American Educational Research Association, New York.

O'Tuel, F. S., & Rawl. (1985, November). *Sex differences in school variables for gifted students.* Paper presented at the annual meeting of the National Association for Gifted Children, Denver.

Parker, W. D., & Adkins, K. K. (1995). Perfectionism and the gifted. *Roeper Review, 17,* 173–176.

Parsons, J., Adler, T., & Kaczala, C. (1982). Socialization of achievement attitudes and beliefs. Parental influences. *Child Development, 53,* 310–321.

Passow, A. H. (Ed.). (1979). *The gifted and the talented: Their education and development. The 78th yearbook of the National Society for the Study of Education.* Chicago: University of Chicago Press.

Passow, A. H. (1982a, March). *Differentiated curricula for the gifted/talented: A point of view.* In *Curricula for the Gifted.* Selected Proceedings of the First National Conference for the Gifted/Talented, National State Leadership Training Institute, Ventura, CA.

Passow, A. H. (1982b). The gifted disadvantaged: Some reflections. In *Identifying and educating the disadvantaged gifted and talented.* Selected proceedings from the Fifth National Conference on disadvantaged gifted and talented, Los Angeles, CA.

Passow, A. H. (1986). Reflections on three decades of education of the gifted. *Gifted Child Quarterly, 8*(4), 223–226.

Passow, A. H., & Rudnitski, R. A. (1993). *State policies regarding education of the gifted as reflected in legislation and regulation.* Storrs, CT: National Research Center for the Gifted and Talented.

Patton, J. M. (1994, April 7). *African American students with gifts and talents in an inclusive classroom.* Paper presented at the 72nd Annual International Convention of the Council for Exceptional Children, Denver, CO. (ERIC Document Reproduction Service No. ED 371 497)

Patton, J. M., & Braithwaite, R. (1990). Special education certification/recertification for regular educators. *Journal of Special Education, 24*(1), 117–124.

Peterson, I. (1995, September 26). For black recruits, prep school, now in peril, is path to West Point. *New York Times,* p. A1, B5.

Phenix, P. H. (1964). *Realms of meaning: A philosophy of the curriculum for general education.* New York: McGraw-Hill.

Piechowski, M. M. (1970). Developmental potential. In N. Colangelo & R. T. Zaffrann (Eds.), *New voices in counseling the gifted* (pp. 25–27). Dubuque, IA: Kendall/Hunt.

Piechowski, M. M. (1975). A theoretical and empirical approach to the study of development. *Genetic Psychology Monographs, 92,* 231–275.

Piechowski, M. M. (1979). Developmental potential. In N. Colangelo & R. T. Zaffran (Eds.), *New voices in counseling the gifted.* Dubuque, IA: Kendall/Hunt.

Piechowski, M. M. (1986). The concept of developmental potential. *Roeper Review, 8*(3), 190–197.

Piechowski, M. M. (1997). Emotional giftedness: The measure of intrapersonal intelligence. In N. Colangelo & G. Davis (Eds.), *Handbook of gifted education.* Boston: Allyn & Bacon.

Piechowski, M. M., & Cunningham, K. (1985). Patterns of overexcitability in a group of artists. *Journal of Creative Behavior, 19*(3), 153–174.

Piirto, J. (1991). Why are there so few? (Creative women: Mathematicians, visual artists, musicians). *Roeper Review, 13*(3), 142–147.

Pipher, M. (1994). *Reviving Ophelia.* New York: Ballantine Books.

Plummer, E. E. (1996, April). Founder and director of the Wadleigh Scholarship Program, 215 East 114th Street, New York, New York 10026. (Telephone interview)

Polsky, C. (1996, April 16). Silence surrounded by sound. *Newsday,* p. B4.

Pratt, C. (1948). *I learn from children.* New York: Simon & Schuster.

Pringle, M. L. K. (1970). *Able misfits.* London: Longman Group.

Ramos-Ford, V., & Gardner, H. (1997). Giftedness from a multiple intelligences perspective. In N. Colangelo & G. Davis (Eds.), *Handbook of gifted education* (pp. 54–66). Boston: Allyn & Bacon.

Raph, J. B., Goldberg, M. L., & Passow, A. H. (1966). *Bright underachievers.* New York: Columbia University Teachers College Bureau of Publications.

Raths, L., Harmin, M., & Simon, S. (1966). *Values and teaching.* Columbus, OH: Merrill.

Raths, L. E., Jonas, A., Rothstein, A., & Wassermann, S. (1967). *Teaching for thinking, theory and application.* Columbus, OH: Merrill.

Raven, J. (1956). *Progressive matrices.* London: H. K. Lewis & Co.

Read, C. R. (1991). Achievement and career choices: Comparisons of males and females: Gender distribution in programs for the gifted. *Roeper Review, 13*(4), 188–193.

Reid, C., & Romanoff, B. (1997). Using multiple intelligence theory to identify gifted children. *Educational Leadership 55*(1), 71–74.

Reis, S. M. (1985, November). *We can't change what we don't recognize: Understanding the special needs of gifted females.* Paper presented at the annual meeting of the National Association for Gifted Children, Denver, CO.

Reis, S. M. (1987). We can't change what we don't recognize: Understanding the special needs of gifted families. *Gifted Child Quarterly, 31*(2) 83–89.

Reis, S. M. (1991). The need for clarification and research designed to examine gender differences in achievement and accomplishment. *Roeper Review, 13*(4), 193–198.

Reis, S. M. (1995). Older women's reflection on eminence: Obstacles and opportunities. *Roeper Review, 18*(1), 66–72.

Reis, S. M., Burns, D. E., & Renzulli, J. Z. (1991). *Curriculum compacting: The complete guide to modifying the regular curriculum for high ability students.* Mansfield Center, CT: Creative Learning Press.

Reis, S. M., & Dobyns, S. M. (1991, April). An annotated bibliography of non-fictional books and curricular materials to encourage gifted females. *Roeper Review 13*(3), 129–134.

Reis, S. M., & Gavin, M. K. (1997). *Why Jane can do math: How teachers can encourage talented girls in mathematics.* Paper presented at the annual conference of AGATE (Advocacy for Gifted and Talented Education), New York.

Renzulli, J. S. (1977). *The enrichment triad.* Wethersfield, CT: Creative Learning Press.

Renzulli, J. S., & Reis, S. (1986). The enrichment triad/revolving door model: A schoolwide plan for the development of creative productivity. In J. S. Renzulli (Ed.), *Systems and models for developing programs for the gifted and talented* (pp. 216–305). Mansfield Center, CT: Creative Learning Press.

Renzulli, J. S., Reis, S., & Smith, L. (1981). *The revolving door identification model.* Mansfield Center, CT: Creative Learning Press.

Renzulli, J. S., & Smith, L. H. (1978). *The learning styles inventory: A measure of student preference for instructional techniques.* Mansfield Center, CT: Creative Learning Press.

Renzulli, J. S., Smith, L. H., White, A. J., Callahan, C. M., & Hartman, R. K. (1977). *Scales for rating the behavioral characteristics of superior students.* Mansfield Center, CT: Creative Learning Press.

Rest, J., & Thoma, S. J. (1986). Educational programs and interventions. In J. R. Rest (Ed.), *Moral development: Advances in research and theory* (pp. 59–88). New York: Praeger.

Reynolds, M. C. (1962). A framework for considering some issues in special education. *Exceptional Children, 28,* 367–379.

Rhodes, L. (1992). Focusing attention on the individual in identification of gifted black students. *Roeper Review, 14*(3), 108–110.

Rigney, J. W. (1980). Cognitive learning strategies and qualities in information processing. In R. Snow and P. Federco (Eds.), *Aptitudes, learning, and instruction* (Vol. I). Hillsdale, NJ: Erlbaum.

Rimm, S. B. (1986). *Underachievement syndrome: Causes and cures.* Watertown, WI: Apple Publishing.

Roach, V. (1995). *Winning ways: Creating inclusive schools, classrooms and communities.* Alexandria, VA: National Association of State Boards of Education.

Roedell, W. C. (1989). Early development of gifted children. In J. VanTassel-Baska & P. Olszewski-Kubilius (Eds.), *Patterns of influence on young gifted learners: The home, the self, and the school* (pp. 13–28). New York: Teachers College Press.

Roedell, W. C., Jackson, N. E., & Robinson, H. B. (1980). *Gifted young children.* New York: Teachers College Press.

Roedell, W. C., & Robinson, H. B. (1977). *Programming for intellectually advanced children: A program development guide.* Seattle, WA: University of Washington, Child Development Research Group. (ERIC Document Reproduction Service No. ED 151 094)

Rosenshine, B., & Furst, N. (1971). Current and future research on teacher performance criteria. In B. O. Smith (Ed.), *Research on teacher education, A symposium.* Upper Saddle River, NJ: Prentice Hall.

Ross, P. O. (1994). Introduction to descriptions of Javits grant projects. *Gifted Child Quarterly, 38*(2), 64.

Ryan, L., Callahan, J., Krajewski, J., & Flaherty, T. (1997). A merged elementary/special education program in a 4-year liberal arts college: Providence College. In L. Blanton, C. Griffin, J. Winn, & M. Puch (Eds.), *Teacher Education in transition: Collaborative programs to prepare general and special educators.* Denver, CO: Love Publishing.

Sadker, M., & Sadker, D. (1985, October). Sexism in the classroom. *Vocational Education Journal, 60*(7), 30–32.

Sands, T., & Howard-Hamilton, M. (1995). Understanding depression among gifted adolescent females: Feminist therapy strategies. *Roeper Review, 17*(3), 192–195.

Santiago, A. M., & Einarson, M. K. (1996, April). *The graduate experience in engineering and the physical sciences: Gender and ethnic differences in initial expectations and departmental incorporation.* Paper presented at the annual meeting of the American Educational Research Association, New York.

Sattler, J. M. (1974). *Assessment of children's intelligence.* Philadelphia: W. B. Saunders.

Sattler, J. M. (1992). *Assessment of children* (rev. ed.). San Diego: Jerome M. Sattler Publisher, Inc.

Schmitz, C., & Gailbraith, J. (1985). *Managing the social and emotional needs of the gifted: A teachers survival guide.* Minneapolis: Free Spirit.

Scholwinski, E., & Reynolds, C. (1985). Dimensions of anxiety among high IQ children. *Gifted Child Quarterly, 29*(3), 125–130.

Shapiro, B. K., Palmer, F. B., Antell, S. E., Bilker, S., Ross, A., & Capute, A. J. (1989). Giftedness: Can it be predicted in infancy? *Clinical Pediatrics, 28,* 205–209.

Shore, B. M., Cornell, D. G., Robinson, A., & Ward, V. S. (1991). *Recommended practices in gifted education.* New York: Teachers College Press.

Silverman, L. K. (1989). Invisible gifts, invisible handicaps. *Roeper Review, 12*(1), 37–42.

Silverman, L. K. (1991a). Helping gifted girls reach their potential. *Roeper Review, 13*(3), 122–123.

Silverman, L. K. (1991b). Family counseling. In N. Colangelo & G. Davis (Eds.), *Handbook of gifted education* (pp. 307–320). Boston: Allyn & Bacon.

Silverman, L. K. (Ed.). (1992). *Counseling the gifted and talented.* Denver, CO: Love Publishing.

Silverman, L. K. (1993a). The gifted individual. In L. K. Silverman (Ed.), *Counseling the gifted and talented* (pp. 51–78). Denver, CO: Love Publishing.

Silverman, L. K. (1993b). Counseling needs and programs for the gifted. In K. A. Heller, F. J. Monks, & A. H. Passow (Eds.), *International handbook of research and development of giftedness and talent* (pp. 631–648). Oxford: Pergamon Press.

Silverman, L. K. (1995, October). *The emotional development of the gifted through the lifespan.* Paper presented at the annual meeting of AGATE (Advocacy for Gifted and Talented Education), New York.

Silverman, L. K., & Ellsworth, B. (1981). The theory of positive disintegration and its implications for giftedness. In N. Duda (Ed.), *Theory of positive disintegration: Proceedings of the third international conference on the theory of positive disintegration* (pp. 179–194). Miami, FL: University of Miami School of Medicine.

Silverman, L. K., & Kearney, K. (1992). The case for the Stanford–Binet L–M as a supplemental test. *Roeper Review, 15*(1), 34–37.

Sime, R. L. (1996). *Lise Meitner—A life in physics.* Berkeley: University of California Press.

Simon, H. A., & Chase, W. G. (1973). Skill in chess. *American Scientist, 61,* 394–403.

Simon, S. B., Howe, L. W., & Kirschenbaum, H. (1972). *Values clarification: A handbook of practical strategies for teachers and students.* New York: Hart Publishing.

Sisk, D. A., & Shallcross, D. J. (1986). *Leadership—Making things happen.* New York: Bearly Limited.

Staines, G., Tavris, C., & Jayaratne, C. (1974). The queen bee syndrome. *Psychology Today, 7,* 55–60.

Sternberg, R. J. (1988). *The triarchic mind: A new theory of human intelligence.* New York: Viking Press.

Sternberg, R. J., & Davison, J. E. (Eds.). (1986). *Conceptions of giftedness.* New York: Cambridge University Press.

Sternberg, R. J., & Kolligan, J., Jr. (Eds.). (1990). *Competence considered.* New Haven, CT: Yale University Press.

Stevens, K. C. (1980). The effect of topic interest on the reading comprehension of high ability students. *Journal of Educational Research, 7*(3), 365–368.

Subotnik, R. F. (1994a). Conversations with masters of the arts and sciences. *Journal for the Education of the Gifted, 17*(3), 306–322.

Subotnik, R. F. (1994b). Talent developed: Conversations with masters of the arts and sciences. Jeffrey Borer: Research cardiologist. *Journal for the Education of the Gifted, 17*(2), 198–211.

Subotnik, R., & Arnold, K. (Eds.). (1993a). *Beyond Terman: Contemporary longitudinal studies of giftedness and talent.* Norwood, NJ: Ablex.

Subotnik, R. F., & Arnold, K. D. (1993b). Time for a change. *Roeper Review, 15*(3), 118–120.

Subotnik, R. F., & Arnold, K. D. (1995). Passing through the gates: Career establishment of talented women in science. *Roeper Review, 18*(1), 55–61.

Subotnik, R. F., Arnold, K. D., & Noble, K. D. (1995). Gifted is as gifted does, but what does gifted do? *Roeper Review, 18*(1), 4–5.

Subotnik, R. F., & Steiner, C. L. (1993). Adult manifestations of adolescent talent in science. *Roeper Review, 15*(3), 164–169.

Swisher, K., & Deyhle, D. (1989). The styles of learning are different, but the teaching is just the same: Suggestions for teachers of American Indian youth. *Journal of American Indian Education, Special Issue,* 1–14.

Talan, J. (1996, July 16). Attention deficit linked to brain. *Newsday,* p. A19.

Tannenbaum, A. J. (1979). Pre-Sputnik to post-Watergate: Concern about the gifted. In A. H. Passow (Ed.), *The gifted and the talented: Their education and development. The 78th yearbook of the National Society for the Study of Education* (pp. 5–27). Chicago: University of Chicago Press.

Tannenbaum, A. J. (1983). *Gifted children: Psychological and educational perspectives.* New York: Macmillan.

Tannenbaum, A. J. (1986). Giftedness: A psychosocial approach. In R. J. Sternberg & J. E. Davidson (Eds.), *Conceptions of giftedness* (pp. 21–52). New York: Cambridge University Press.

Tannenbaum, A. J. (1992). Early signs of giftedness. In P. Klein & A. J. Tannenbaum (Eds.), *To be young and gifted* (pp. 3–32). Norwood, NJ: Ablex.

Tannenbaum, A. J. (1993). History of giftedness and "gifted education" in world perspective. In K. Heller, F. Monks, & A. H. Passow (Eds.), *International handbook of research and development of giftedness and talent* (pp. 3–28). Oxford: Pergamon Press.

Tannenbaum, A. J., & Baldwin, L. J. (1983). Giftedness and learning disability: A paradoxical combination. In L. H. Fox, L. Brody, & D. Tobin (Eds.), *Learning-disabled gifted children—identification and programming* (pp. 11–36). Baltimore: University Park Press.

Taylor, S. J., & Searl, S. J., Jr. (1987). The disabled in America: History, policy and trends. In P. Knoblock (Ed.), *Understanding exceptional children and youth* (pp. 5–64). Boston: Little Brown.

Terman, L. M. (1925). *Genetic studies of genius* (Vol. I), *Mental and physical traits of a thousand gifted children* (2nd ed.). Stanford, CA: Stanford University Press.

Terman, L. M., & Oden, M. H. (1947). *Genetic studies of genius* (Vol. IV), *The gifted child grows up: Twenty-five years' follow-up of a superior group.* Stanford, CA: Stanford University Press.

Terman, L. M., & Oden, M. H. (1959). *Genetic studies of genius* (Vol. V), *The gifted group at midlife: Thirty-five year's follow up of the superior child.* Stanford, CA: Stanford University Press.

Terrassier, J. (1979). Gifted children and psychopathology: The syndrome of dyssynchrony. In J. J. Gallagher (Ed.), *Gifted children: Reaching their potential. Proceedings of the Third International Conference on Gifted Children* (pp. 434–440). Jerusalem, Israel: Kollek & Sons, Ltd.

Thurstone, L. L. (1947). *Multiple-factor analysis: A development and expansion of "the vectors of the mind."* Chicago: University of Chicago Press.

Tillman, L. C. (1996, April). *Mentoring minority undergraduates: The Summer Research Opportunity Program.* Paper presented at the annual meeting of the American Educational Research Association, New York.

Tobin, K. G., & Schiffman, G. B. (1983). Computer technology for learning-disabled/gifted students. In L. H. Fox, L. Brody, & D. Tobin (Eds.), *Learning-disabled/gifted children—identification and programming* (pp. 195–206). Baltimore: University Park Press.

Tomlinson, C. (1994). Middle school and acceleration: Guidance from research and the kids. *The Journal of Secondary Gifted Education, V*(4), 42–51.

Tomlinson, C. (1995a). Deciding to differentiate instruction in middle school: One school's journey. *Gifted Child Quarterly, 39*(2), 77–87.

Tomlinson, C. A. (1995b). *How to differentiate instruction in mixed ability classrooms.* Alexandria, VA: Association for Supervision and Curriculum Development.

Tomlinson, C. A., Tomchin, E. M., Callahan, C. M., Adams, C. M., Pizzat-Tinnin, P, Cunningham, C. M., Moore, B., Lutz, L., Roberson, C., Eiss, N., Lundram, M., Hunsaker, S., & Imbeau, M. (1994). Practices of preservice teachers related to gifted and other academically diverse learners. *Gifted Child Quarterly, 38*(3), 106–114.

Tonemah, S. A. (1990, October 13). *American Indian teacher training program.* Paper presented at the 22nd Annual Conference of the National Indian Education Association, San Diego, CA. Norman, OK: American Indian Research & Development, Inc. (ERIC Document Reproduction Service No. ED 331 656)

Tonemah, S. (1991). *Gifted and talented American Indian and Alaska Native students.* Washington, DC: Department of Education. (ERIC Document Reproduction Service No. ED 343 769)

Tonemah, S. A. (1992). *American Indian teacher training program: The next to last piece of the puzzle.* Norman, OK: American Indian Research & Development, Inc.

Tonemah, S., & Brittan, M. (1985). *American Indian gifted and talented assessment model (AIGTAM).* Norman, OK: American Indian Research & Development, Inc.

Torrance, E. P. (1977). *Discovery and nurturance of giftedness in the culturally different.* Reston, VA: Council for Exceptional Children.

Torrance, E. P. (1988). *Style of learning and thinking.* Bensenville, IL: Scholastic Testing Service.

Treffinger, D. J. (1975). Teaching for self-directed learning: A priority for the gifted and talented. *Gifted Child Quarterly, 19*(1), 46–59.

Turnbull, A. P., Turnbull, H. R., Shank, M., & Leal, D. (1995). *Exceptional Lives.* Upper Saddle River, NJ: Merrill/Prentice Hall.

Turnbull, H. R. (1986). Appropriate education and Rowley. *Exceptional Children, 52*(4), 347–352.

Udall, A. J., and Maker, C. J. (1983). A pilot program for elementary-age learning-disabled/gifted students. In L. H. Fox, L. Brody, & D. Tobin (Eds.), *Learning-disabled gifted children—identification and programming* (pp. 223–242). Baltimore: University Park Press.

UNESCO. (1994). *The Salamanca statement and framework for action on special needs education: World conference on special needs education. Access and equality.* New York: Author.

U.S. Department of Education, Office of Educational Research and Improvement. (1993). *National excellence: A case for developing America's talent.* Washington, DC: U.S. Government Printing Office.

U.S. Office of Education. (1977). Education of handicapped children. *Federal Register, 42,* 65082–85.

VanTassel-Baska, J. (1983). Profiles of precocity—The 1982 Midwest talent search finalists. *Gifted Child Quarterly, 27*(3), 139–144.

VanTassel-Baska, J. (1988). *Comprehensive curriculum for gifted learners.* Boston: Allyn & Bacon.

Vernon, M., and LaFalce-Landers, E. (1993, December). A longitudinal study of intellectually gifted deaf and hard of hearing people—Educational, psychological and career outcomes. *American Annals of the Deaf, 138*(5), 427–434.

Vernon, P. E. (1950). *The structure of human abilities.* New York: John Wiley & Sons.

Vernon, P. E. (1979). *The structure of human abilities* (2nd ed.). Westport, CT: Greenwood Press.

Villa, R. A., Van der Klift, E., Udis, J., Thousand, J. S., Nevin, A. I., Kunc, N., & Chapple, J. W. (1995). Questions, concerns, beliefs, and practical advice about inclusive education. In R. A. Villa and J. S. Thousand (Eds.), *Creating an inclusive school* (pp. 136–161). Alexandria, VA: Association for Supervision and Curriculum Development.

Vygotsky, L. S. (1978). *Mind in society: The development of higher psychological processes* (Eds. M. Cole, V. John-Steiner, S. Scribner, & E. Souberman). Cambridge: Harvard University Press.

Walberg, H. J. (1988). Creativity and talent as learning. In R. Sternberg (Ed.), *The nature of creativity* (pp. 340–361). New York: Cambridge University Press.

Walker, B. J., Dodd, J., & Bigelow, R. (1989). Learning preferences of capable American Indians of two tribes. *Journal of American Indian Education, Special Issue,* 63–71.

Wallas, G. (1926). *The art of thought.* New York: Harcourt Brace.

Walsh, D. (1985, Summer). Socrates in the classroom—Strategies for enhancing critical thinking skills. *American Educator,* pp. 20–25.

Warschaw, T. (1985). The "I-don't-deserve-it" syndrome. *New Woman, 15,* 135–137.

Webb, J. T. (1993). Nurturing social–emotional development of gifted children. In K. Heller, F. Monks, & A. H. Passow (Eds.), *International handbook of research and development of giftedness and talent* (pp. 525–538). Oxford: Pergamon Press.

Webb, J. T., & Latimer, D. (1993, July). *ADHD and children who are gifted*. Reston, VA: Council for Exceptional Children. (ERIC Document Reproduction Service No. ED 358 673)

Webb, J., Meckstroth, E. A., & Tolan, S. S. (1982). *Guiding the gifted child: A practical source for parents and teacher.* Columbus, OH: Ohio Psychology Press.

Weill, D., (1993). Towards a critical multicultural literacy: Advancing an education for liberation. *Roeper Review, 15*(4), 211–217.

Wernick, S. (1992, July 8). Interest renewed in grade skipping as an inexpensive way to aid the gifted. *New York Times*, p. A17.

Westberg, K., Archambault, F., Dobyns, S., & Slavin, T. (1993). The classroom practices observational study. *Journal for the Education of the Gifted, 16*, 120–146.

Westgard, L. (1996). Personal interview.

Whimbey, A., & Whimbey, L. S. (1975). Intelligence can be taught. New York: E. P. Dutton.

White, W. L., & Renzulli, J. S. (1987). A forty year follow-up of students who attended Leta Hollingworth's school for gifted students. *Roeper Review, 10*(2), 89–94.

Whitmore, J. (1980). *Giftedness, conflict and underachievement.* Boston: Allyn & Bacon.

Whitmore, J. R. (1981). Gifted children with handicapping conditions. A new frontier. *Exceptional Children, 48*(2), 106–114.

Whitmore, J. (1987). Conceptualizing the issue of underserved populations of gifted students. *Journal for the Education of the Gifted, 10*(3), 141–153.

Whitmore, J. R., & Maker, C. J. (1985). *Intellectual giftedness in disabled persons.* Rockville, MD: Aspen Systems Corporation.

Willard-Holt, C. (1994, September). *Recognizing talent: Cross-case study of two high potential students with cerebral palsy.* Storrs, CT: National Research Center on the Gifted and Talented, University of Connecticut.

Williams, L., & DeGaetano, Y. (1985). *ALERTA: A multicultural, bilingual approach to teaching young children.* Menlo Park, CA: Addison Wesley.

Winebrenner, S. (1992). *Teaching gifted kids in the regular classroom.* Minneapolis: Free Spirit.

Wolfle, J. A., & French, M. P. (1990, October). *Surviving gifted attention deficit disorder children in the classroom.* Paper presented at the annual conference of the National Association of Gifted Children, Little Rock, AR.

Woodcock, R. W., & Johnson, M. B. (1989). *Woodcock-Johnson psychoeducational battery–revised.* Allen, TX: DLM Teaching Resources.

Wright, L., & Borland, J. H. (1992, March). A special friend: Adolescent mentors for young economically disadvantaged, potentially gifted students. *Roeper Review, 14*(3), 124–129.

Wright, L., & Borland, J. (1993). Using early childhood developmental portfolios in the identification of young economically disadvantaged, potentially gifted students. *Roeper Review, 15*(4), 205–210.

Yewchuk, C. R., & Bibby, M. A. (1989, September). Identification of giftedness in severely and profoundly hearing impaired students. *Roeper Review, 12*(1), 42–48.

Zametkin, A. J. (1995). Attention deficit disorder: Born to be hyperactive? *Journal of American Medical Association, 273*(23), 1871–1874.

Ziv, A. (1977). Parental perceptions and self-concept of gifted and average ability underachievers. *Perceptual and Motor Skills, 44,* 560–568.

Zorman, R. (1993). Mentoring and role modeling programs for the gifted. In K. Heller, F. Monks, & A. H. Passow (Eds.). *International handbook of research and development of giftedness and talent* (pp. 727–742). Oxford: Pergamon Press.

Zuckerman, H. (1983). The scientific elite: Nobel laureates' mutual influences. In R. S. Albert (Ed.), *Genius and eminence* (pp. 241–252). Washington, DC: National Academy Press.

Index